Pragmatics of Vietnamese as Native and Target Language

Pragmatics & Interaction

Editor
Gabriele Kasper

PRAGMATICS & INTERACTION, a refereed series sponsored by the University of Hawai'i National Foreign Language Resource Center, publishes research on topics in pragmatics and discourse as social interaction from a wide variety of theoretical and methodological perspectives. P&I particularly welcomes studies on languages spoken in the Asia-Pacific region.

L2 Learning as social practice: Conversation-analytic perspectives
Gabriele Pallotti & Johannes Wagner (Eds.), (2011)
ISBN 978–0-9800459–7-0

Talk-in-interaction: Multilingual perspectives
Hanh thi Nguyen & Gabriele Kasper (Eds.), (2009)
ISBN 978–0–09800459–1–8

ordering information at nflrc.hawaii.edu

Pragmatics of Vietnamese as Native and Target Language

edited by
Carsten Roever
& Hạnh thị Nguyễn

NATIONAL FOREIGN LANGUAGE RESOURCE CENTER
University of Hawai'i at Mānoa

Manufactured in the United States of America.

The contents of this publication were developed in part under a grant from the U.S. Department of Education (CFDA 84.229, P229A100001). However, the contents do not necessarily represent the policy of the Department of Education, and one should not assume endorsement by the Federal Government.

ISBN: 978–0–9800459–7–0
Library of Congress Control Number: 2012952501

distributed by
National Foreign Language Resource Center
University of Hawai'i
1859 East-West Road #106
Honolulu HI 96822–2322
nflrc.hawaii.edu

About the National Foreign Language Resource Center

The National Foreign Language Resource Center, located in the College of Languages, Linguistics, & Literature at the University of Hawai'i at Mānoa, has conducted research, developed materials, and trained language professionals since 1990 under a series of grants from the U.S. Department of Education (Language Resource Centers Program). A national advisory board sets the general direction of the resource center. With the goal of improving foreign language instruction in the United States, the center publishes research reports and teaching materials that focus primarily on the languages of Asia and the Pacific. The center also sponsors summer intensive teacher training institutes and other professional development opportunities. For additional information about center programs, contact us.

J.D. Brown, Director
National Foreign Language Resource Center
University of Hawai'i at Mānoa
1859 East-West Road #106
Honolulu, HI 96822–2322
email: nflrc@hawaii.edu
website: nflrc.hawaii.edu

Contents

About the Authors

Helen Basturkmen is a senior lecturer in the Department of Applied Language Studies and Linguistics at the University of Auckland where she teaches courses in languages for specific purposes, discourse analysis, and research methodology. She has published two books on teaching languages for specific purposes (Erlbaum, 2006; Palgrave Macmillan, 2010) and articles in various international journals on topics including teaching pragmatics and description of specialist discourses. Email: h.basturkmen@auckland.ac.nz

Hà Thị Thanh Đỗ (Ha Do) is currently a lecturer in the Department of Linguistics and Cultures of English Speaking Countries, ULIS, Vietnam National University. Hà has recently finished her PhD at the University of Melbourne, Australia. Her PhD thesis is on pragmatic acquisition in natural settings. Email: hadtt@vnu.edu.vn

Lê Gia Anh Hồ teaches Vietnamese at the National University of Singapore. Her areas of research include the use of blogging and social media in pedagogy, Vietnamese pragmatics, second language acquisition, and the characteristics of advanced language learners. Email: clshgal@nus.edu.sg

Hạnh thị Nguyễn is an associate professor at Hawai'i Pacific University. Her recent publications include *Developing interactional competence: A conversation analytic study of patient consultations in pharmacy* (Palgrave-MacMillan, 2012), *Pragmatics & Language Learning Vol. 12* (NFLRC, 2010, co-edited), *Talk-in-interaction: Multilingual perspectives* (NFLRC, 2009, co-edited), and various articles on the development of interactional competence, classroom interaction, learners' identity, and Vietnamese applied linguistics. Email: hnguyen@hpu.edu

Minh thị Thủy Nguyễn is an assistant professor at the National Institute of Education, Nanyang Technological University, Singapore. Her research interests are in pragmatics and language pedagogy. Her recent publications include *Learning to give and respond to peer-feedback in the L2: The case of EFL criticisms and responses to criticisms* (Lincom Europa, 2007), and various articles and book chapters on the development of pragmatic competence in a second language and second language pragmatic instruction. Email: thuyminhnguyen@gmail.com, thithuyminh.nguyen@nie.edu.sg

Quynh Thi Ngoc Nguyen is the Vice-Dean of the Faculty of English Language Teacher Education at Vietnam National University, Hanoi, where she lectures in English and Applied Linguistics. She finished her PhD in Applied Linguistics at the University of Melbourne in 2011. Her research interests include the acquisition of English and Vietnamese as a second language, bilingual education, cognitive linguistics, and discourse analysis. Email: ngquynh@gmail.com

Carsten Roever is a senior lecturer in Applied Linguistics at the University of Melbourne. He holds a PhD in Second Language Acquisition from the University of Hawai'i at Mānoa. His research interests include language testing and interlanguage pragmatics, especially the development of interactional competence in a second language. He is coauthor of *Language testing: The social dimension* with Tim McNamara (Blackwell, 2006). Email: carsten@unimelb.edu.au

Vân Thị Thanh Trần is currently working towards her PhD in Applied Linguistics at the University of Melbourne, Australia. She is also a lecturer at Vietnam National University. Her research interests include second language acquisition, interlanguage pragmatics, and Vietnamese applied linguistics. Email: vantranthanh@yahoo.com

Acknowledgments

We would like to thank the following external reviewers for their input during the blind review process.

Machiko Achiba, *Tokyo Women's Christian University*
Saad Al-Gahtani, *King Saud University*
Mahmoud Al-Khatib, *University of Science and Technology, Irbid*
Margaret A. Dufon, *California State University, Chico*
César Félix-Brasdefer, *Indiana University at Bloomington*
Carmen Garcia-Fernandez, *Arizona State University*
Rod Gardner, *Griffith University*
Timothy Hassall, *Australian National University*
Trine Heinemann, *University of Southern Denmark*
Matthew Heinz, *Royal Roads University*
Mai Kuha, *Ball State University*
Emi Morita, *National University of Singapore*
Ken Rose, *City University of Hong Kong*
Anna Trosborg, *Aarhus University*
Amy Von Canon, *University of Colorado, Denver*

Notes on Vietnamese particles and function words in the transcripts and examples

(based on Hoàng, 1994)

AffM (affirmative marker) *có*	(used before adjectives or verbs) particle to affirm the state or happening of something
AffM (affirmative marker) *cứ*	particle to affirm an activity or state despite all conditions
AffM (affirmative marker) *đó/đấy*	(sentence-final) particle to express affirmation of the definite and exact nature of what was said
AlignM (alignment marker) *nhé* (Northern Vietnamese) *nghe* (Southern Vietnamese)	(sentence-final) particle to express agreement (falling intonation) or to seek agreement (rising intonation)
AlignM (alignment marker) *đi*	(sentence-final) particle to express an order, suggestion, or to urge someone in a friendly way to do something
AlignM (alignment marker) *cái/với*	(sentence-final) particle to add friendliness and strength to a request to someone to do something for oneself or someone close to oneself
Class.	classifier (preceding nouns; e.g., *cái, chiếc, con)*
chẳng	emphasized form of negation (cf. the plain negative *không*)
CondM (conditional marker) mà	function word to mark the next idea as a conditional statement
EmM (emphasis marker) *ấy/ ý*	(sentence-final) particle to express emphasis in the reference to an object or event that is known to the hearer
EmM (emphasis marker) *cơ/ kia*	(sentence-final) particle expressing emphasis, implying that the speaker means exactly what she or he is saying and not otherwise
EmM (emphasis marker) *cũng*	function word to mean that a situation is the same as other situations, even though the mentioned situation is unusual; often used to add assertiveness to a statement

EmM (emphasis marker) *là*	(used before adjectives or adverbs) particle to emphasize the degree of the adjective or adverb with which it is being used
EmM (emphasis marker) *nào*	(utterance-final) function word to emphasize what is being said, usually to convince the recipient
EmM (emphasis marker) *nào là*	function word to emphasize the concentration of many things or events in the same place or time, often used before nouns/verbs as part of a list
EmM (emphasis marker) *thì*	(sentence-initial) function word expressing emphasis in the upcoming statement, often in contrast to a previous statement; this is not to be confused with the other functions of *thì* (see below)
DisM (discourse marker) *thôi*	(utterance-initial) used to initiate the closure or upshot of a decision-making process or discussion, followed by a solution; often presented as something acceptable because there is no other solution (may occur in alternative form as *thôi thì*)
Past	past tense marker
Perf.	perfect aspect
PluM	plural marker (e.g., *những, các)*
PolM (politeness marker) *ạ*	(utterance-final) particle to mark politeness and respect
PolM (politeness marker) *dạ*	(utterance-initial) particle to mark politeness and respect, always utterance-initial
PosM (positive marker) được	function word to mark events as positive (good); this is in contrast to the negative marker (*bị*)
Prog.	progressive aspect
QuesM (question marker) *há/ hả/ á/ à*	particle placed after an affirmative statement to seek confirmation from the recipient
StaM (stance marker) *ấy mà*	(sentence-final) particle to mark the statement as something that should be of obvious knowledge, to affirm, persuade, or explain, with the

	implication that the recipient should be able to arrive at this knowledge on his or her own
StaM (stance marker) *chứ*	(in questions, sentence-final) particle to affirm what is being questioned, marking the question as only seeking extra verification from the listener (in statements, sentence-final) particle to assert the opposite to what the recipient has just said or implied
StaM (stance marker) *đâu*	(in statements, sentence-final) particle to emphasize a negation, in order to persuade or reject the recipient's explicit or implicit idea
StaM (stance marker) *mà*	(utterance-final) particle to express affirmation in order to persuade or explain, with the allusion that the recipient will infer the implication of what is being said on his or her own
StaM (stance marker) *lại*	(before a verb) adverb to indicate that the action or event being referred to is contrary to what is normally expected
thì (translated as "then")	time adverb to mark sequence of events, with the event introduced by thì being the later one
thì (translated as "so")	conjunction to show that the proposition to be mentioned is a certain or likely consequence of the proposition just mentioned
TopM (topical marker) *thì, là*	function word used after the topic in a topicalization construction

Reference

Hoàng Phê, Bùi Khắc Việt, Chu Bích Thu, Đào Thản, Hoàng Tuệ, Hoàng Văn Hành, Lê Kim Chi,...Vương Lộc. (1994). *Từ điển tiếng Việt [Vietnamese dictionary]* (3rd ed.). Hà Nội: Nhà Xuất Bản Khoa Học Xã Hội–Trung Tâm Từ Điển Học.

Introduction: Pragmatics Research and Vietnamese

Carsten Roever
The University of Melbourne

Hạnh thị Nguyễn
Hawai'i Pacific University

This is the first book-length volume to investigate the pragmatics of Vietnamese as a native and target language. Although Vietnamese is spoken as a native language by 86% of Vietnam's 90.5 million people and by expat Vietnamese around the world, it is still clearly a Less Commonly Taught Language (LCTL). And although grammatical descriptions of Vietnamese exist, the literature on Vietnamese pragmatics is very scarce. With this volume, we hope to contribute to filling this gap and to the wider teaching of Vietnamese around the world.

Pragmatics research

Work in pragmatics has virtually exploded in the last 25 years in Applied Linguistics, and is now a well-established area of research. It empirically investigates, in Crystal's (1997) classic definition, "language from the point of view of users, especially the choices they make, the constraints they encounter in using language in social interaction and the effects their use of language has on other participants in the act of communication" (p. 301). Pragmatics research in Applied Linguistics concerns itself with two large fields: cross-cultural pragmatics and interlanguage

Pragmatics of Vietnamese as a native and target language, pp. 1–12
Carsten Roever & Hạnh thị Nguyễn (Eds.), 2013
Honolulu, HI: University of Hawai'i, National Foreign Language Resource Center

pragmatics. The former compares pragmatic norms and discursive practices of language users with different native languages, whereas the latter focuses on the learning of these pragmatic norms and discursive practices by second language users.

Following from Austin's (1962) early conceptualization of pragmatics as the study of how individual utterances can constitute real-world acts and Searle's (1969) subsequent taxonomy of these speech acts, pragmatics research has had a strong orientation towards atomistic, individual instances of language use, such as requests, apologies, refusals, complaints, suggestions, advice, compliments and their responses, expressions of gratitude, and others. Inspired by Brown and Levinson's (1987) anthropological work, pragmatics research also frequently integrates considerations of politeness, and traditionally endeavors to elucidate what features of the discourse-external context affect the implementation of speech acts and their politeness, how cultures differ in their politeness norms, and how learners develop the ability to speak at the appropriate level of politeness in another language (see Martínez-Flor & Usó-Juan, 2010, for a recent collection of speech-act-based studies).

Methodologically, speech-act research is primarily associated with the discourse completion task (DCT), which elicits target speech acts through situational prompts, although other instruments such as questionnaires or role plays are also used (see Kasper, 2008, for an overview). DCT prompts can implement different degrees of the social context factors power, distance, and degree of imposition identified by Brown and Levinson (1987). While instrument development can require a significant time commitment, DCTs allow rapid data collection. Also, they facilitate purposive sampling of respondents along the lines of native language or target language proficiency or exposure to the target language community. Data obtained from DCTs is commonly coded following a scheme like the one developed in the Cross-Cultural Speech Act Realization Project (CCSARP; Blum-Kulka, House, & Kasper, 1989) and is taken to allow insight into differences in pragmatic competence between groups. The majority of the papers in the present volume follow a speech-act orientation, with three employing DCTs (Hạnh thị Nguyễn on inviting, Hà Thanh Đỗ on complaints, and Vân thị Thanh Trần on address terms) and two employing role plays (Lê Gia Anh Hồ on apology, and Minh thị Thủy Nguyễn & Helen Basturkmen on requests).

Although a speech-act framework as a view of linguistic action is still dominant in pragmatics research, it is not the only theoretical orientation. Dissatisfaction with its deterministic conceptualization of context and its inability to account for larger stretches of discourse and their sequential organization as well as doubts about the validity of conclusions drawn from DCT data (Golato, 2003) have led to calls for a discursive reorientation of pragmatics research, commonly along the lines of Conversation Analysis (CA; Kasper, 2006, 2009). CA was originally designed for investigating how social structure is instantiated at the microlevel of interaction (Hutchby & Wooffitt, 2008; ten Have, 2009) but its strong focus on sequential organization of interaction and large research base makes it an attractive approach for pragmatics research. It does, however, contrast starkly with the speech-act approach in employing a data-driven, bottom-up approach, whereas speech-act pragmatics takes a taxonomic, top-down approach. Also, and problematically for Applied Linguistics research, CA does not elicit data but relies on natural data. This makes it difficult to sample purposively and investigate variables of interest (such as native language or proficiency level), but some recent studies have shown ways to employ CA for acquisitional pragmatics research (Al-Gahtani & Roever, 2012; Hellermann, 2008; Ishida, 2009, 2011; Kim, 2009; Pekarek Doehler & Pochon-Berger, 2011). One study in the present volume uses CA (Quỳnh Nguyễn on listener responses) but stays within Vietnamese as a native language.

While the CA approach to pragmatics is gaining momentum in Applied Linguistics, there is no "single best" way to do pragmatics research. A speech-act framework may be problematic in not being able to investigate the sequential organization of extended discourse and may use data different from natural interaction, eliciting what respondents think they would say, not what they actually do say. However, research has shown a reasonable degree of empirical fit between DCT responses and natural data (Beebe & Cummings, 1996; Hartford & Bardovi-Harlig, 1992), and DCTs are suitable for eliciting respondents' knowledge of the strategies and semantic formulae available. This description of the pragmatic inventory of a language is particularly useful at the early stages of pragmatics research into that language, as is the case for Vietnamese. As a first step in a long-term research program, this volume aims to cast the net wide and examine what linguistic forms L1 speakers use to implement different speech acts in relation to a range of social parameters. It is also helpful to see what L2 speakers of Vietnamese know about pragmalinguistic resources and their sociopragmatic meanings, both in relation to L1 speakers and across different levels of overall proficiency in Vietnamese. These fundamentally comparative goals require controlled methods of data generation. To this end, the chapters in this volume predominantly draw on such well-established methods as discourse completion tasks, role plays, and elicited conversation.

Vietnamese pragmatics

Research on the pragmatics of Vietnamese as a native or target language is still a small field, and published studies in this area have only appeared in recent years. The scarcity of research on Vietnamese pragmatics is made more acute by the fact that only a few are published in English. The journal of the Vietnamese Institute of Linguistics, *Ngôn Ngữ [Language]*, has published several studies on pragmatics over the last two decades; however, these studies are only available in Vietnamese and unfortunately, most of them rely heavily on literary works or observational notes as data sources and do not report fully on their methodologies, making their results valuable only as preliminary findings. In this introduction, we survey both English and Vietnamese sources[1] in order to sketch an overview of the Vietnamese pragmatics landscape.[2]

We found that a number of studies on Vietnamese pragmatics touch on the meanings of lexical items and discourse and stance markers in context. Most of these studies tend to have a linguistic starting point, and pragmatics is used as an added layer to understand the targeted lexical items. Several other studies describe speech acts in Vietnamese, either in their own right or in contrast to another language. Only a few studies have begun to examine the sequential organization of certain types of social interaction and how social identities and ideologies are expressed and constructed via language. We will review each of these areas in more detail below.

Research that relates to the contextual meanings of lexical items so far has mainly concentrated on person references and personal pronouns, the topicalizer *thì,* classifiers, and some stance markers or discourse markers. The complex Vietnamese system of person references is covered most comprehensively by H. V. Lương (1990), who described the use of person references (kinship terms, proper nouns, and personal pronouns) as discursive choices influenced by context, social relationship, and sociocultural values. Adding to research in this area, Bùi (1990) observed how married couples use different address terms toward each other in different emotional contexts, including peaceful and conflict situations. Rosen (1996) turned our attention to a particular phenomenon of reference in Vietnamese, the use of empty pronouns, and discovered that although the retrieval of the intended referent depends on several syntactic factors, speakers and listeners can infer the referent by identifying similarities in context. This pragmatic inferability may explain why empty pronouns in Vietnamese occur not only in topic chains, but also in cases of changing referents. Another important area in research on word meanings in context examines the commonly used topicalizer *thì.* Clark (1991, 1992) conceptualized *thì* as participating in the following discourse pattern: background state of affairs – new focus in contrast to background – *thì* – information about new focus. In other words, *thì* as a topicalizer "implies some degree of contrast or comparison, usually with an actual or implied antecedent" (1992, p. 93). Also highlighting the role of context in shaping words' meanings, Daley (1998) investigated the use of classifiers in discourse. She examined written folktales and observed that classifiers function as markers of initial mentioning, individualization (vs. generic mentioning), and salience from the perspective of the speaker. As such, classifiers are found to co-occur more frequently with topic discontinuation than topic continuation, and more frequently with main topics or important characters than peripheral topics or unimportant characters. Being perhaps the only study so far to examine classifiers from a pragmatic perspective, Daley's study could be strengthened by more transparent interpretations of saliency and more accurate identification of classifiers. Finally, several studies explored the contextual meanings of discourse markers and stance markers. For example, Michaelis (1994) examined the stance marker *cũng* and found that this lexical item signals that what is being said is in opposition to what is expected based on the given discourse context or general world knowledge. Chew Chye Lay (2005) investigated the strategic and polite functions of *được* in business communication in Vietnamese and demonstrated that *được* expresses an explorative stance by setting the starting point for further discussion to reach a more definite outcome, at which point speakers may use the stronger expression *chắc chắn được* [certainly can/OK]. *Được* thus functions as a "non-committal 'conflict-avoidance device' and 'face–saver'" (p. 229). Some other authors looked at the contextual meanings and usage constraints of common discourse markers in the language, such as *thôi* [no more] (P. K. Trần, 2011) and *kẻo* [unless] (Lâm, 2010). Although research in this area has offered valuable information about how meanings are obtained in context, most researchers have taken a top-down approach to describe an inventory of the phenomena under study. Further research is needed to examine how speakers and listeners negotiate language choices in ongoing discourse (see further discussion below).

Although research on speech acts in Vietnamese has only appeared in more recent years, politeness strategies in speech acts have attracted much attention. Sophana (2004) observed how Vietnamese speakers convey politeness through linguistic expressions in the speech acts of greeting, leave-taking, thanking, requesting, refusing, complaining, complimenting, criticizing, and disagreeing. P. N. Đào (2004) focused on politeness strategies in requests and observed that politeness is achieved by (a) the use of address terms in the speech act itself, (b) the use of honorifics, (c) probing strategies, and (d) postrequest strategies. Postrequest strategies include (a) if the request is granted, the requester may give thanks or make promises, while the request grantor may give advice or supportive remarks; or (b) if the request is not granted, the requester may apologize or make statements of some optimistic projections, and the person who refused the request may make promises, give advice, or produce consoling remarks. Also focusing on politeness, Vũ (2008) listed the types of hedges that speakers may use to express politeness in some key speech acts. These hedges include (a) formulaic polite expressions before a request; (b) preannouncements to prepare the listener for an upcoming complaint, negative assessment, refusal, or threatening question; (c) compensating, self-effacing, or anticipating the listener's response before a negative assessment; (d) flattering the hearer before a request; and (e) honorifics. Finally, Y. V. M. Trần (2010) analyzed recorded conversations among young female speakers and found that the women expressed politeness through the use of the address term pairs *bà*

– *tôi* [madam – I], *mình – mình* [self – self], and *chị–em* [older sister – younger sibling], as well as smiling at particular points in the conversations.

In addition to research of politeness strategies, there have also been a number of studies on the realizations of specific speech acts in Vietnamese. Examining a common speech act, request, Đ. V. Nguyễn (2004) reported that it may take on four structures in Vietnamese: (a) imperatives; (b) interrogatives; (c) declaratives expressing needs, wants, or obligations (either as hints or statements); and (d) elliptical constructions without verbs, without objects, or without both verbs and objects. He concluded that requests in Vietnamese are quite similar to those in English, with only minor differences in the use of hints. On the speech act of compliment response, G. Q. Trần (2010) showed that in role plays, Vietnamese speakers tend to respond to a compliment with disagreement, downgrade, or explanation, and they rarely use strategies common in English such as agreement or appreciation (see also T. Đ. Nguyễn, 2005). Some other speech acts in Vietnamese that have also been described in detail include introductions (L. T. Nguyễn, 2010), refusals (Lưu & T. T. P. Trần, 2008), invitations (Chu, 1995; L. T. Đào, 2011), thanks (H. Lương, 2010; L. T. Nguyễn, 2010), price negotiations at the market (V. T. Trần, 2011), and peddlers' cries (T. Q. Nguyễn, 1990). Overall, research on speech acts in Vietnamese has provided important understandings about their structures and factors that may influence their realizations. Although there have been some studies that used role plays and DCTs in addition to those that are limited to literary texts or observational notes, more research is needed to test the validity of findings based on elicited data and to provide further information about how speech acts are used sequentially in actual social interactions.

Focusing on how social interaction is organized, a few studies have reported on interactional phenomena and the sequential structure of particular interactional practices in Vietnamese. Thanh Hương (1990) took observational notes of opening sequences in doctor-patient medical encounters at an occupational medicine clinic and a general clinic. She noted that greetings are often absent and doctors usually initiate the interaction by asking an opening question. At the occupational medicine clinic, the doctor's opening question is about the patient's occupation or place of work, which serves to gather information to assist the diagnosis. The patients tend to respond briefly to these questions with no elaboration; however, some patients take this opportunity to describe details about their work conditions that may be related to their sickness. At the general medicine clinic, the doctor's opening question is about the patient's health condition. Similar to the occupational setting, most patients here also respond briefly about their complaint. The author noted that when some patients respond to the doctor's opening questions with details about their conditions, including main symptoms, diagnoses, and sometimes even a direct request for a specific form of treatment, the doctors seem to treat these extended responses as violations of roles by not taking up the patients' description, interrupting the patients, or not acknowledging what the patients have said. In another study, Đỗ (2008) analyzed topic shifts in audio-recorded ordinary conversations in dormitories and reported that participants may shift topics by selecting an aspect of the current topic and developing it into a new focus or by producing a second pair part in an adjacency pair that does not align with the first pair part (e.g., an assessment in response to a list or an explanation may shift the conversation to more assessments). In another study, H. t. Nguyễn (2009) recorded a family conversation and described how the father gives recommendations to his adult son. She found that while the father has the authority to issue the recommendation sequences, the son, who is away from the father on business, has knowledge about his own situation, thus creating an asymmetry of power. Her conversation analysis shows how the father, the son, and the eldest daughter (who acts as a neutral party) construct and negotiate their positions and finally resolve the conflict in harmony. By focusing on the sequentially unfolding processes of social interaction, research in this area has provided a more thorough understanding about how language is used in context. Given the scant number of studies in this area, more research is definitely needed.

Finally, only a few studies have begun to examine how social identities and ideologies are constructed via language in Vietnamese. Kleifgan (2001) analyzed social positioning during a troubleshooting episode among Vietnamese immigrant workers in a circuit-board manufacturing plant in the United States (the talk is mainly in Vietnamese). She discovered that during the high-pressure moments of problem solving when the workers disagree with each other, they perform symmetrical positioning by avoiding the Vietnamese kinship and status terms and using English expressions of solidarity. When the solution begins to emerge, the supervisor positions himself as having authority by utilizing directives, vocatives, and an authoritative announcement tone. In a follow-up study, Kleifgan and Lê (2007) showed video excerpts of their data to Vietnamese living in Hanoi, Vietnam, and asked them to role-play a similar situation in Vietnamese. They noted that in this mock interaction, the Vietnamese speakers still maintain the kinship and status terms to position themselves as supervisor and subordinates, although they are (supposedly) operating under the same situational pressure of the situation as the Vietnamese immigrants in the United States. These two studies show how speakers may select among an array of linguistic choices available to them to index their social relationships and identities given the situation and their linguistic repertoire. Taking a critical perspective to examine how ideology may be expressed in language, V. T. H. Trần and Thompson (2008) analyzed an article about the Iraq war published in the newspaper of the Vietnamese communist party. Focusing on attitude and engagement, they identified specific expressions used by the reporter to express a negative attitude toward the United States government while engaging the readers in the support of his viewpoint.

Adding to this growing body of research on Vietnamese pragmatics, this volume introduces six empirical studies, covering the speech acts of requesting (Minh thị Thủy Nguyễn), apologizing (Lê Gia Anh Hồ), inviting (Hạnh thị Nguyễn), and complaining (Hà Thanh Đỗ), as well as the complex address system of Vietnamese (Vân thị Thanh Trần) and listener responses in extended interaction (Quỳnh Nguyễn). Four of the studies, on requesting, apologizing, complaining, and address terms, are designed as interlanguage pragmatics studies, contrasting the performance of native Vietnamese speakers with that of learners of Vietnamese as a second or foreign language, or, in the case of requesting and address terms, comparing low- and high-proficiency learners with each other. The study on inviting is a cross-cultural pragmatics study, comparing invitations in English and Vietnamese as done by native speakers. The study on listener responses focuses exclusively on Vietnamese as a native language and eschews comparison.

We hope that these studies can inform further research on Vietnamese as well as the learning of Vietnamese as a target language. In particular, the chapters on requesting, apologizing, inviting, and complaining can form the starting points for an investigation of how these and other speech acts are performed sequentially in talk-in-interaction in a variety of settings. Such a research agenda can address questions such as how actions are formulated and negotiated in the moment-to-moment unfolding of talk and how speakers position themselves and others involved through the format of these actions. The chapter on Vietnamese address terms also opens up several possibilities for further research, including how speakers shift address terms in the course of a conversation, when address terms are used and when they are omitted, and what recipients do when an unexpected address term is used. Finally, based on the findings from the chapter on listener responses, future research may explore response practices used in conversations involving equal and asymmetric dyads, in multi-party conversations, and in a range of activities. By investigating these topics on speakers of Vietnamese as both a first and second language, researchers can extend current understanding about Vietnamese pragmatics as well as the challenges and successes experienced by learners of Vietnamese as a target language.

Notes

1 Keeping in mind the caveat about the Vietnamese sources in *Ngôn Ngữ [Language]*.

2 We limit our survey to published sources and exclude unpublished theses.

References

We cite Vietnamese authors by their full names, due to the fact that last names and initials alone are usually not sufficient to identify people in Vietnamese. The Vietnamese names are cited in Vietnamese name order (i.e., family name, middle name, then given name).

Al-Gahtani, S., & Roever, C. (2012). Role-playing L2 requests: Head acts and sequential organization. *Applied Linguistics*. Advance online publication. doi: 10.1093/applin/amr031

Austin, J.L. (1962). *How to do things with words*. Oxford: Oxford University Press.

Beebe, L.M., & Cummings, M.C. (1996). Natural speech-act data versus written questionnaire data: How data collection method affects speech-act performance. In S.M. Gass & J. Neu (Eds.), *Speech acts across cultures* (pp. 65–86). Berlin: Mouton de Gruyter.

Blum-Kulka, S., House, J., & Kasper, G. (Eds.). (1989). *Cross-cultural pragmatics: Requests and apologies*. Norwood, NJ: Ablex.

Brown, P., & Levinson, S.D. (1987). *Politeness: Some universals in language usage*. Cambridge: Cambridge University Press.

Bùi Minh Yến (1990). Xưng hô giữa vợ và chồng trong gia đình người Việt [Address terms between husbands and wives in Vietnamese families]. *Ngôn Ngữ, 79,* 30–37.

Chew Chye Lay, G. (2005). The functions of "được" (OK; possible; can) in business communication in Vietnam. *Journal of Asian Pacific Communication, 15*(2), 229–256.

Chu thị Thanh Tâm (1995). Hành vi mời và đoạn thoại mời [The speech act of inviting and the inviting sequence]. *Ngôn Ngữ, 1,* 47–52.

Clark, M. (1991). Conjunctions as topicalizers: More on Southeast Asian languages. In M. Ratliff & E. Schiller (Eds.), *Papers from the First Annual Meeting of the Southeast Asian Linguistics Society* (pp. 87–107). Temple: Arizona State University.

Clark, M. (1992). Conjunction as topicalizer in Vietnamese. *Mon-Khmer Studies, 20,* 91–109.

Daley, K.A. (1998). *Vietnamese classifiers in narrative texts*. Arlington: The Summer Institute of Linguistics and the University of Texas at Arlington.

Đào Nguyên Phúc (2004). Một số chiến lược lịch sự trong hội thoại Việt ngữ có sử dụng hành vi ngôn ngữ "xin phép" [Some politeness strategies in Vietnamese conversations using the speech act «xin phép»]. *Ngôn Ngữ, 185,* 49–57.

Đào Thanh Lan (2011). Nhận diện hành động mời và rủ trong tiếng Việt [Identifying the speech acts of inviting in Vietnamese]. *Ngôn Ngữ, 262,* 20–25.

Đỗ Thị Thu Hương (2008). Những nhân tố làm chuyển hướng, lệch hướng đề tài trong hội thoại thường ngày (trên tư liệu hội thoại thường ngày giữa bạn bè) [Factors leading to topic shifts and topic changes in ordinary conversations (based on conversations between friends)]. *Ngôn Ngữ, 226,* 18–28.

Golato, A. (2003). Studying compliment responses: A comparison of DCTs and naturally occurring talk. *Applied Linguistics, 24,* 90–121.

Hartford, B.S., & Bardovi-Harlig, K. (1992). Experimental and observational data in the study of interlanguage pragmatics. In L.F. Bouton & Y. Kachru (Eds.), *Pragmatics and language learning* (pp. 33–52). Urbana, IL: DEIL.

Hutchby, I., & Woffitt, R. (2008). *Conversation analysis.* Cambridge: Polity.

Ishida, M. (2009). Development of interactional competence: Changes in the use of ne in L2 Japanese during study abroad. In T.H. Nguyen & G. Kasper (Eds.), *Talk-in-interaction: Multilingual perspectives* (pp. 317–350). Honolulu: University of Hawai'i Press.

Ishida, M. (2011). Engaging in another person's telling as a recipient in L2 Japanese: Development of interactional competence during one-year study abroad. In G. Pallotti & J. Wagner (Eds.), *L2 learning as social practice: Conversation-analytic perspectives* (pp. 44–85). Honolulu, HI: National Foreign Language Resource Center.

Kasper, G. (2006). Speech acts in interaction: Towards discursive pragmatics. In K. Bardovi-Harlig, J.C. Felix-Brasdefer, & A.S. Omar (Eds.), *Pragmatics & language learning* (Vol. 11, pp. 281–314). Honolulu, HI: National Foreign Language Resource Center.

Kasper, G. (2008). Data collection in pragmatics research. In H. Spencer-Oatey (Ed.), *Culturally speaking* (2nd edition, pp. 279–303). London: Continuum.

Kasper, G. (2009). Categories, context and comparison in Conversation Analysis. In H.T. Nguyen & G. Kasper (Eds.), *Talk-in-interaction: Multilingual perspectives* (pp. 1–28). Honolulu, HI: National Foreign Language Resource Center.

Kim, Y. (2009). The Korean Discourse Markers –nuntey and kuntey in native-nonnative conversation: An acquisitional perspective. In T.H. Nguyen & G. Kasper (Eds.), *Talk-in-interaction: Multilingual perspectives* (pp. 317–350). Honolulu, HI: National Foreign Language Resource Center.

Kleifgan, J.A. (2001). Assembling talk: Social alignments in the workplace. *Research on Language and Social Interaction, 34*(3), 279–308.

Kleifgan, J.A., & Lê thị Huỳnh Trang (2007). Vietnamese immigrants' shifting patterns of status display at work: Impressions from Hanoi. *Journal of Asian Pacific Communication, 17*(2), 259–279.

Leech, G. (1983). *Principles of pragmatics.* London: Longman.

Lương Hinh (2010). Các hình thức cảm ơn gián tiếp của người Việt [Forms of indirect thanking by Vietnamese]. *Ngôn Ngữ, 252,* 38–45.

Lương Văn Hy. (1990). *Discursive practices and linguistic meanings: The Vietnamese system of person reference.* Amsterdam: Benjamins.

Lâm Uyên Bá (2010). Khảo sát từ "kẻo" về cú pháp, ngữ nghĩa, và ngữ dụng [Examining the word "kẻo" from grammatical, semantic, and pragmatic perspectives]. *Ngôn Ngữ, 259,* 55–71.

Lưu Quý Hương, & Trần Thị Phương Thảo (2008). Nghi thức lời từ chối một đề nghị giúp đỡ trên cơ sở lý thuyết hành vi ngôn ngữ (tiếng Anh so sánh với tiếng Việt) [Forms of refusals to offers to help from a speech-act perspective (comparison between English and Vietnamese)]. *Ngôn Ngữ, 225,* 13–21.

Martínez-Flor, A., & Usó-Juan, E. (Eds.). (2010). *Speech act performance.* Amsterdam: Benjamins.

Michaelis, L.A. (1994). Expectation contravention and use ambiguity: The Vietnamese connective "cũng." *Journal of Pragmatics, 21*(1), 1–36.

Nguyễn thị Hạnh (2009). The recommendation sequence in Vietnamese family talk: Negotiation of asymmetric access to authority and knowledge. In G. Kasper & H. thi Nguyen (Eds.), *Talk in interaction: Multilingual perspectives.* Honolulu, HI: National Foreign Language Resource Center/ University of Hawai'i Press.

Nguyễn Thị Lương (2010). Các hình thức cảm ơn trực tiếp của người Việt [Forms of direct thanking by Vietnamese]. *Ngôn Ngữ, 250,* 14–24.

Nguyễn Quý Thành (1990). Vài nét về lời rao của những người bán hàng rong [Some notes on peddlers' cries]. *Ngôn Ngữ, 79,* 25–26, 29.

Nguyễn Thị Lương (2010). Các hình thức giới thiệu trực tiếp của người Việt [Forms of direct introduction by Vietnamese]. *Ngôn Ngữ, 257,* 14–23.

Nguyễn Văn Độ (2004). Hành động thỉnh cầu trong tiếng Anh và tiếng Việt [The speech act of request in English and in Vietnamese]. *Ngôn Ngữ, 177,* 30–40.

Nguyễn Đình Thư (2005). Giving and receiving compliments: Viewed from textbooks and respondents. In T. Le (Ed.), *Proceedings of the international conference on critical discourse analysis: Theory into research* (pp. 562–573). Tasmania: University of Tasmania.

Pekarek Doehler, S., & Pochon-Berger, E. (2011). Developing 'methods' for interaction. In J.K. Hall, J. Hellermann, & S. Pekarek Doehler (Eds.), *L2 interactional competence and development* (pp. 206–243). Bristol: Multilingual Matters.

Rosen, V. (1996). The interpretation of empty pronouns in Vietnamese. In T. Fretheim & J.K. Gundel (Eds.), *Reference and referent accessibility* (pp. 251–261). Amsterdam: Benjamins.

Searle, J. (1969). *Speech acts.* Cambridge: Cambridge University Press.

Sophana, S. (2004). Politeness strategies in Hanoi Vietnamese speech. *Mon-Khmer Studies, 34,* 137–157.

ten Have, P. (2007). *Doing conversation analysis* (2nd ed.). London: Sage.

Thanh Hương (1990). Bước đầu tìm hiểu các hành vi giao tiếp mở đầu tương tác bác sĩ–bệnh nhân [Preliminary notes on opening behaviors in doctor-patient interactions]. *Ngôn Ngữ, 79,* 6–8, 13.

Trần Quỳnh Giao (2010). Replying to compliments in English and Vietnamese. *The International Journal of Language, Society and Culture, 30,* 104–130.

Trần Thanh Vân (2011). Những khác biệt giới tính biểu hiện qua hành động mặc cả của người mua ở chợ Đồng Tháp [Gender differences in buyers' negotiating behaviors in Đồng Tháp Market]. *Ngôn Ngữ, 260,* 47–60.

Trần Kim Phượng (2011). Từ *thôi* trong tiếng Việt nhìn từ ba bình diện: Kết học, nghĩa học và dụng học [The word *thôi* in Vietnamese: Syntactic, semantic, and pragmatic perspectives]. *Ngôn Ngữ, 264,* 50–58.

Trần Vũ Mai Yên (2010). Politeness in Vietnamese. *Griffith Working Papers in Pragmatics and Intercultural Communication, 3*(1), 12–21.

Trần thị Hồng Vân, & Thompson, E.A. (2008). The nature of “reporter voice” in a Vietnamese hard news story. In E.A. Thompson & P.R.R. White (Eds.), *Communicating conflict* (pp. 51–65). London: Continuum.

Vũ Thị Nga (2008). Hành vi rào đón và phép lịch sự trong hội thoại Việt ngữ [Hedging behaviors and politeness in Vietnamese conversations], *Ngôn Ngữ, 227,* 44–52.

1 Requesting in Vietnamese as a Second Language

Minh thị Thủy Nguyễn
National Institute of Education
Nanyang Technological University

Helen Basturkmen
The University of Auckland

The study reported in this chapter examines requests by 18 adult learners of Vietnamese as a second language (L2). In particular, it investigates the pragmatic strategies that the learners employ when making requests in Vietnamese and how their proficiency levels and lengths of residence in the target language (TL) environment affect their choice of these strategies. This study lies within the broad domain of interlanguage pragmatics (ILP) research (i.e., "the study of nonnative speakers' use and acquisition of L2 pragmatic knowledge"; Kasper, 1996, p. 145). The rationale for the present study lies in the relative shortage of ILP studies on requests in an Asian language as an L2 (e.g., Byon, 2004; Hassall, 2001, 2003; Ishihara & Tarone, 2009) as opposed to the substantial body of research on requests in an Asian language as a native language (e.g., Byon, 2006; Hassall, 1999; Lee-Wong, 1994; Rue & Zhang, 2008; Upadhyay, 2003; Vu, 1997, 1999; Zhang, 1995a, 1995b) and requests in a Western language as an L2 (e.g., Al-Gahtani & Roever, 2012; Cohen & Shively, 2007; Felix-Brasdefer, 2007; Hendriks, 2008; Otcu & Zeyrek, 2006, 2008; Schauer, 2007, 2008, 2009; Shively, 2011; Taleghani-Nikazm & Huth, 2010; Warga, 2004; Woodfield,

Pragmatics of Vietnamese as a native and target language, pp. 13–75
Carsten Roever & Hạnh thị Nguyễn (Eds.), 2013
Honolulu, HI: University of Hawai'i, National Foreign Language Resource Center

2008). Particularly, requests in Vietnamese as an L2 have not yet been reported in any previous studies. This chapter aims to fill this gap in the literature.

Following Searle (1969), a request is defined as a directive act which is performed to get the hearer (H) to do an act which the speaker (S) wants H to do for S's benefit and which is at a cost to H. From S's point of view, H is able to do this act, but it is not obvious that H will do it in the normal course of events or of H's own accord. A request can be linguistically realized by means of various strategy types and levels of directness (described in further detail below). A strategy is a semantic formula by which the request is expressed (see Blum-Kulka, House, & Kasper, 1989; Takahashi, 1996). The level of directness refers to the extent to which S's intent is made transparent (see Blum-Kulka, 1987). That is, the more direct a request is, the less effort is needed to interpret it, and vice versa. A request may also be mitigated by means of different external and internal modifiers. External modifiers are supportive moves that occur before or after the head act, whereas internal modifiers occur within the head act and form an integral part of it (Kasper, 1981). Our study is informed by previous research on the acquisition of requests as speech acts in a second or foreign language, which we will review in the next sections.

Acquisition of requests in a second or foreign language

Previous studies of L2 requests typically address such issues as how L2 learners perform and learn to perform this speech act over time and what factors might affect their use and acquisition of the speech act. Findings regarding the first issue generally suggest that although learners seem to have access to the same range of requesting strategy types as native speakers (NSs), they tend to show different preferences for particular strategies, mostly due to the influence of their L1 pragmatics. For example, the uninstructed American learners of Spanish in Shively's (2011) study tended to use conventionally indirect strategies in service encounters more frequently and relied on direct strategies less frequently than is expected by the NS norms. This behavior is due to a transfer of pragmatic norms governing their native language use. In other studies, L2 learners were repeatedly found to differ from NSs in their choice of the overall level of directness for their requests. For example, although many English learners were reported to be more direct than their NS counterparts (Beal, 1990, 1994; Chen, 2006; Færch & Kasper, 1989; Fukushima, 1990; Kobayashi & Rinnert, 2003; Tanaka, 1988; Warga 2003, 2004; Woodfield, 2008), learners of other languages such as Hebrew, Spanish, or Japanese were found to be more indirect (Blum-Kulka, 1982, 1983; Kubota, 1996; le Pair, 1996, 2005; Nakahama, 1998; Shively, 2011).

L2 learners, especially those with a low proficiency level, have also been found to be less attentive to contextual factors than NSs when choosing their realization strategies (Ervin-Tripp, Lampert, & Bell, 1987; Felix-Brasdefer, 2007; Fukushima, 1990; Tanaka, 1988; Tanaka & Kawade, 1982). The low-level American learners of Spanish in Felix-Brasdefer's (2007) study, for instance, employed the same direct strategies in all requesting situations, regardless of the relative social status and social distance between themselves and their interlocutors. Similarly, studies on student-to-professor email communication show that as L2 learners failed to recognize the different status between them and their professors, their emails tended to contain inappropriate requests for help from the latter (Blotch, 2002; Biesenbach-Lucas, 2005; Chen, 2006).

Finally, learners in many studies were also observed both to mitigate their requests, especially by means of internal modifiers, to a considerably lesser extent than NSs, and to draw on a narrower range of linguistic resources for doing so (Biesenbach-Lucas, 2007; Færch & Kasper, 1989; Hartford & Bardovi-Harlig, 1996; Hendriks, 2008; Hill, 1997; House & Kasper, 1987; Kasper, 1981; Otcu & Zeyrek, 2006; Woodfield, 2008). This pragmatic behavior is often attributed to learners' limited L2 linguistic competence, their incomplete L2 pragmatic knowledge, and especially their reliance on a synergism of both L1 and L2 pragmatic competence in performing the given speech act (see Blitvich, 2006; V. Cook, 2001; Kecskés & Papp, 2000, for a discussion of intercultural competence).

As far as developmental issues are concerned, a great number of cross-sectional studies comparing learners of different proficiency levels have reported a proficiency effect on learners' use of request realization strategies and mitigating devices (Kasper, 1996). Generally, it has been consistently shown that as learners become more proficient in the TL, they tend to demonstrate more targetlike pragmatic behavior (Felix-Brasdefer, 2007; Hendriks, 2008; Hill, 1997; Otcu & Zeyrek, 2008; Rose, 2000; Scarcella, 1979). Felix-Brasdefer (2007), for example, found that as their proficiency increased, American learners of Spanish drew less on speaker-oriented requests and more on hearer-oriented requests, which was more consistent with NS pragmatic norms. With increasing proficiency levels, the learners also tended to decrease their use of direct strategies and increase their use of conventionally indirect strategies. In a similar vein, Rose (2000) reported a greater use of conventionally indirect requests by higher proficiency Chinese learners of English, thus approximating a targetlike use. As learners improve their levels of proficiency in the L2, they also seem to expand their pragmatic routines and other linguistic means to express their sensitivity to contextual variations. In Scarcella (1979), for instance, the advanced learners were able to vary the syntactic forms of their requests according to context and used imperatives only for equal familiars and subordinates, while their less proficient peers invariably relied on imperatives. In Otcu & Zeyrek (2008), the learners became less likely to rely on formulaic utterances to realize their requests with increasing proficiency levels.

Higher proficiency learners have also been reported to mitigate their requests to a considerably greater extent than their lower proficiency peers thanks to a greater degree of control over the L2 (Felix-Brasdefer, 2007; Hill, 1997; Otcu & Zeyrek, 2006; Rose, 2000; Warga, 2004). For example, Felix-Brasdefer (2007) reported an increasing use of the conditional form to internally modify requests among advanced learners of Spanish, while this form was infrequently used by the intermediate learners and almost absent in the beginners' data. Similarly, Otcu & Zeyrek (2006) found that higher proficiency Turkish learners of English employed internal modifiers more frequently than the lower proficiency group. Warga (2004) found a steady increase in the use of external modifiers by her higher proficiency Austrian learners of French as compared to the less proficient learners, mirroring the findings of Hill (1997) and Rose (2000).

These findings are supported by recent studies on L2 requests from a Conversation Analysis perspective which show that advanced learners were generally able to effectively project an upcoming dispreferred first pair part by making use of prerequest sequences (Al-Gahtani & Roever, 2012; Taleghani-Nikazm & Huth, 2010). Al-Gahtani & Roever (2012) investigated how 26 male Saudi learners of Australian English made requests in three role-play situations. They found that while higher level learners overwhelmingly provided preexpansions, laying the groundwork for the upcoming requests by checking the interlocutor's availability and providing accounts, lower level learners rarely did so. Instead, they tended to produce the requests earlier on, relying on the interlocutor to elicit further information. Similarly, Taleghani-Nikazm & Huth (2010), examining requests in L2 German by 24 advanced American learners, found that although all the participants were able to employ presequences to mediate and negotiate their requests, the weaker ones among them were less successful in doing so.

Findings from longitudinal studies of L2 requests also suggest evidence of pragmatic improvement as learners move along their developmental stages (Achiba, 2003; Barron, 2003; Bataller, 2010; Chen, 2006; Cohen & Shively, 2007; Ellis, 1992; Kasper & Rose, 2002; Owen, 2001; Schauer, 2007, 2008, 2009; Schmidt, 1983; Shively, 2011). Overall, the findings of these studies are congruent with those from the cross-sectional studies discussed above, suggesting a greater use of targetlike routines and fine-tuning through more mitigation and complex lexico-syntactic features with increasing grammatical competence (see Kasper & Rose, 2002).

Chen (2006), for example, observing a Taiwanese graduate student's email practice during her studies in the US for two and a half years, found that her email communication with professors improved over time. Initially, she relied predominantly on displaying both a needy and coercive tone and failing to show status-appropriate politeness. However, gradually she learned how to employ query preparatory strategies and expressed greater sensitivity to speaker-hearer role relationships via effective use of supportive moves and lexico-syntatic modification. Chen attributed these changes to the student's developing knowledge of the email medium, changing conception of identity, evolving pragmalinguistic competence, and importantly, her developing conception of politeness in student-professor interaction and realization of culture-specific politeness as a result of being socialized into the target culture. Similarly, Schauer (2008), observing L2 German learners of English in the UK for one academic year, found that over time the learners increased their use of indirect requests while decreasing their use of direct requests. They also developed a broader repertoire of request strategies, which allowed them to vary their requests according to the context of the interaction.

A number of studies on requests by learners of languages other than English in the study-abroad context have also revealed that learners gradually acquire the pragmatic norms of the TL community. Shively (2011), studying seven American learners of Spanish over one semester of sojourn in Spain, found a shift from speaker- to hearer-oriented requests among the learners when interacting in service encounters, demonstrating a closer approximation to the NS norms. This finding is consistent with earlier findings regarding learners of Spanish (e.g., Felix-Brasdefer, 2007; Pinto, 2002). Shively also found a shift towards more directness among the learners as they learned to adopt the NS requestive behavior in the context of the service encounter. Similarly, Owen (2001) reported a closer approximation to the NS strategy use by American study-abroad learners of Russian compared to those who did not have the same experience. Although some aspects of the learners' requests still remained different from the NS use, Owen concluded that the study-abroad program had a positive impact on the learners' pragmatic abilities.

In addition to the increased use of targetlike strategies, research has also shown an increase in the use of targetlike modification by L2 learners over the course of their sojourn abroad (Barron, 2003; Bataller, 2010; Cohen & Shively, 2007; Schauer, 2007, 2009). Barron (2003), following the pragmatic development of 33 Irish learners of German in a one-year study-abroad program in Germany, found that the learners increased their use of lexico-phrasal modifiers over time, towards the NS norms. However, there was little evidence of development in their use of syntactic modifiers, suggesting that these types of modifiers may be acquired later than the former. Cohen & Shively (2007) found that after staying for one semester in a Spanish- or in a French-speaking country and receiving intervention on language and culture strategies, the learners became more aware of mitigating their requests, although their frequency of use of verbal downgrading still fell short of the NS norms. Similar findings were reported in Schauer (2007, 2009), who found that study-abroad German learners of English developed a much broader range of both internal and external modifiers as compared to at-home learners.

As with studies that suggest a superiority of second language (SL) settings to foreign language (FL) settings (e.g., Bardovi-Harlig & Dörnyei, 1998; Kasper & Rose, 2002; Kitao, 1990; Koike, 1989), the advantages of study-abroad learners in the above reviewed studies might be attributed to a number of factors. First, residency in the TL environment can provide them not only opportunities for noticing and obtaining pragmatic input, but also opportunities for engaging in interaction with NSs and practicing the input, thus developing control over it (Bardovi-Harlig & Dörnyei, 1998; see also Bialystok, 1993, 1994; Schmidt 1993, 1995, 2001, for a discussion of the role of input in L2 pragmatic development). Learning a language outside the context where it is spoken, on the other hand, does not seem to facilitate both contextual familiarity and exposure to the TL patterns (Takahashi & Beebe, 1987), nor does it give learners sufficient opportunities for sustained, meaningful language use. Besides, as Bardovi-Harlig and Dörnyei (1998) pointed out, SL learners who experience successful communication with NSs might be even more motivated to use the language. FL learners, in contrast, are often set back by grammar-based instruction and tests and thus attend more to grammar than language use.

It should be noted, however, that not all studies supported the claim that L2 pragmatic development is less successful in FL settings. Niezgoda and Roever (2001), replicating Bardovi-Harlig and Dörnyei's (1998) study with two other groups of ESL and EFL learners, found that their highly motivated EFL learners indeed demonstrated a fairly high level of pragmatic awareness. In a follow-up to his earlier study (1996), Roever (2001) also found that the most proficient learners who had not stayed in the TL environment reached a high level of comprehension of TL pragmatic routines. The findings of these studies indicate that although FL settings may offer more limited opportunities for L2 learning, pragmatic development is possible if learners are highly motivated (see H. M. Cook, 2001; DuFon, 1999; Kasper, 2009; Kasper & Rose, 2002; Ushioda, 2007) and supported by appropriate instruction (see Alcon-Soler, 2008; Kasper & Rose, 2002; Rose & Kasper, 2001; Taguchi, 2011).

Overall, the growing body of research on L2 requests in the last few decades has contributed greatly to our understanding of how this speech act is performed and acquired by learners in different learning contexts. However, this body of research is not without limitations. First, many earlier studies are based on discourse completion task (DCT) data (see Al-Gahtani & Roever, 2012), which are often criticized for their shortcomings in representing authentic speech and studying interaction (see Kasper, 2008). Interactional data such as natural discourse or role plays are therefore required in future research in order to support a more interactive approach to the study of

L2 pragmatic development. Second, because earlier studies focused on a fairly limited range of TLs, such as English, French, German, or Spanish as an L2, it is not clear how speakers develop pragmatic competence in a wider range of TLs. Future research should therefore aim to expand the range of the TLs under inquiry, thus contributing further to the field of L2 pragmatics acquisition. Finally, although a great number of recent studies have investigated the impact of study abroad on L2 request development, few studies have actually addressed the effects of different lengths of stay (e.g., Schauer, 2008). This question offers important implications for the teaching and learning of L2 pragmatics and certainly deserves future research attention.

Study

Research questions

Informed by the literature on the acquisition of L2 requests above, this study addresses the following three research questions:

1. How do learners of Vietnamese as an L2 make requests in Vietnamese?
2. To what extent do low- and high-proficiency learners vary in the way they make requests in Vietnamese?
3. To what extent does length of residency in the TL environment affect the way the learners make requests?

Methodology

Participants

Eighteen learners of L2 Vietnamese at low- and high-proficiency levels participated in this study. At the time of data collection, the learners were taking Vietnamese courses in language schools in Hanoi. They were selected from a larger pool of 29 learners who responded to the researchers' advertisement for recruitment of research participants. The learners were first grouped according to their proficiency levels. The low-proficiency group (hereafter referred to as "Low Group") comprised 13 learners who were learning Vietnamese at the preintermediate and intermediate levels. The high-proficiency group (hereafter referred to as "High Group") included 16 learners who were enrolled in the upper-intermediate and advanced courses of Vietnamese. Since there were no standardized tests of Vietnamese as L2, the learners' proficiency levels were determined on the basis of the levels of the courses of Vietnamese they were undertaking and by their self-ratings. Each of the learners was then assigned a unique number. Finally, a sample of eight low-proficiency and 10 high-proficiency learners, representing 60% of their respective groups, was randomly drawn and included in the study. Table 1 presents the background information on these learners.

Table 1. Background information on the learner participants

group		high proficiency	low proficiency	total
gender	M	3	4	**7**
	F	7	4	**11**
age	19–25	6	4	**10**
	26–30	1	2	**3**
	over 30	3	2	**5**
length of study	6 months–1 year	0	2	**2**
	1–3 years	8	3	**11**
	over 3 years	2	3	**5**
length of stay	short stay (under 1 year)	3	5	**8**
	long stay (over 1 year)	7	3	**10**

Eleven of the learners were female and seven were male. Their ages ranged from 19 to 44. The learners came from various first language (L1) backgrounds, with five Polish NSs, three Russian NSs, one French NS, one Laotian NS, four NSs of different dialects of Chinese, and four NSs of different varieties of English. The learners also varied greatly in their lengths of study of Vietnamese. Two had been learning Vietnamese for less than one year; 11 had been learning the language between one and three years; and 5 had been learning it from three years onward. The learners' lengths of residency in Vietnam also varied greatly between 6 months and 11 years. Eight learners who had been staying for less than one year were streamed into the 'Short-stay' group, and 10 who had been staying for more than one year were placed into the 'Long-stay' group. The learners' bio-data revealed that many of them had had substantial exposure to Vietnamese use outside the classroom, mostly via interaction with Vietnamese NS friends and mass media such as Vietnamese TV programs and newspapers. Informal communication with the learners revealed that many of them were not explicitly taught how Vietnamese NSs make requests in different scenarios.

Data collection

In this study, six role-play (RP) scenarios were designed to elicit learners' requests (Appendices A and B), and the learners' performances were audio recorded. The RP was selected because on the one hand, it allows for impromptu speech production in conversational sequences, thus sharing a number of similarities with natural speech production (Kasper, 2008). On the other hand, unlike naturally occurring discourse, it allows us to observe how context factors such as power, distance, and imposition (see Brown & Levinson, 1987) affect the speaker's choice of pragmatic strategies. Its other strength is that it can yield a large corpus of data in a relatively short time. We acknowledge, however that RPs are fundamentally different activities from natural interaction because RPs are pretence without consequences for the participants. However, Okada (2010) argues that in RPs participants draw on their interactional competencies by default. This justifies the use of RPs in teaching/training and testing, and cautious use in research.

The scenarios, some of which were adapted from Blum-Kulka and Olshtain (1984) and Hassall (2003), varied in the relative power between S and H but not in the social distance between them. They included (1) borrowing a computer from a friend, (2) borrowing lecture notes from a classmate, (3) asking a roommate to return a book to the library, (4) asking a teacher to write a letter of recommendation, (5) asking a teacher for a deadline extension, and (6) asking a supervisor to change the date of an upcoming meeting. Situations 1 through 3 described an equal power relationship (friend-friend), and the relationship described in Situations 4 through 6 is characteristic of an unequal power (request directed at a lecturer/supervisor). The social distance, however, was kept constant: All the situations described a close relationship between S and H. In order to avoid the researcher's subjectivity as much as possible, before the role play took place,[1] the scenarios were given to the learner participants to rate the degree of imposition exerted on H, using a Likert 5-point scale. Results showed that the degree of imposition was rated 'low' in Situations 1 (Computer) and 2 (Lecture Notes; means falling below 3.0); 'medium' in Situations 3 (Library), 5 (Assignment), and 6 (Meeting; means between 3.0 and 3.5); and 'high' in Situation 4 (Letter of Reference; mean over 3.5). Table 2 summarizes the information about these six role-play scenarios.

All the scenarios contained a complicating factor that prompted the participants to produce more requests (see Al-Gahtani & Roever, 2012). This factor was known only to the interlocutor and was kept confidential from the participants. In Scenario 1 (Computer), the participant wanted to use the interlocutor's computer, but the complication was that the interlocutor was chatting with her boyfriend who was celebrating his birthday alone in another town. In Scenario 2 (Lecture Notes), the participant wanted to borrow the interlocutor's lecture notes, but the interlocutor was working on assignments at the moment and needed the notes at hand. In Scenario 3 (Book), the participant asked the interlocutor to return a book to the library on the way to school. However, the interlocutor had other commitments. In Scenario 4 (Letter of reference), the participant urgently needed a letter of reference from the interlocutor, but the interlocutor would not be able to write the letter immediately. In Scenario 5 (Extension), the interlocutor was going away soon and would prefer the participant to submit her or his draft before the interlocutor left. Finally, in Scenario 6 (Appointment) the interlocutor was fully booked and would not be able to see the participant another day unless she or he could come after office hours.

All scenarios were written in simple Vietnamese and translated into English to facilitate the participants' comprehension (Appendix B). Before being used for the present study, the role plays were piloted with a group of NSs of Vietnamese. Adjustments were then made to the instruction and scenario descriptions to enhance their comprehensibility. Also, because participants may find it difficult to perform in a role play if the tasks are not realistic (see Bonikowska, 1988; Kasper, 2008), before the role play took place, the participants were asked to rate the extent to which they felt they were able to imagine themselves in each scenario, using a Likert 5-point scale. Results indicated that the learners scored quite highly on all scenarios (means varying from 3.9 to 4.6), suggesting that they were familiar enough with the situations. Based on this result, all scenarios were kept for data collection. Each learner then role-played all six scenarios in Vietnamese in a random order for approximately one hour with the Vietnamese researcher or a Vietnamese research assistant, who was carefully trained in the procedure. We collected 108 role-play conversations, which contained 312 requests.

Table 2. Interpretation of learners' ratings of the role-play scenarios

situation	social distance	relative power	degree of imposition
asking a friend to lend you her computer	close	equal	low
asking a classmate to lend you her lecture notes	close	equal	low
asking a roommate to return a book to the library for you	close	equal	medium
asking a lecturer to write you a letter of reference	close	low to high	high
asking a lecturer to extend the deadline for submitting your assignment	close	low to high	medium

asking your supervisor to change the date of your next meeting	close	low to high	medium

Analytical procedure

The role-play conversations were transcribed and data were then coded, using Blum-Kulka, House, & Kasper's (1989) taxonomy with slight adaptations to cater for the specific features of politeness in Vietnamese (see details below). According to Vũ (1997), politeness in modern Vietnamese incorporates what she terms *lịch sự lễ độ* [respectful politeness] and *lịch sự chiến lược* [strategic politeness]. Respectful politeness indexes social relationship and is characteristic of, in Vũ's terms, *lễ phép* [respectfulness] and *đúng mực* [propriety]. Respectfulness involves showing respect to people of higher power, whereas propriety involves showing proper respect to people of equal and lower power and keeping distance vs. solidarity in conformity with the nature of the given speaker-hearer relationship. Thus, 'respectfulness' politeness is necessarily normative. Linguistic devices that help to convey this kind of politeness, according to Vũ, include address terms, honorifics, or lexical means with similar function. Interlocutors make these linguistic choices depending on the relative power and social distance between themselves. For example, when addressing an older person (i.e., having higher power in Vietnamese culture), a younger person is not expected to use a 'no-naming' style but needs to choose appropriate address terms to indicate his or her lower status and acknowledge the other person's higher status (e.g., *em – anh/chị* [younger sibling – elder sister/brother], *cháu – chú/cô/bác* [niece/nephew – uncle/aunt], *cháu – ông/bà* [grandson/granddaughter – grandfather/grandmother]). Choices outside of these expected pairs will most likely invoke other participation frameworks.

The other dimension, strategic politeness, on the other hand, is bound to specific communicative intents, though still constrained by social relationships. This type of politeness involves what Vũ terms *khéo léo* [delicacy] and *tế nhị* [tact] and functions as a means of minimizing the disadvantages and maximizing the advantages of the situation so that participants can achieve their communicative goals. Linguistic means that help to achieve 'strategic' politeness include indirectness and lexical items with mitigation functions such as *làm ơn* [doing a favor], *xin lỗi* [excuse me], *hộ/giúp/giùm* [help], *có thể* [maybe/may], and so on (Vũ, 1997).

Using the above frameworks, requests were coded according to their (1) levels of directness, (2) strategy types, and (3) modifiers. The Vietnamese researcher and the Vietnamese research assistant coded the data independently and achieved an agreement rate of 90%. The coding categories of request perspectives, strategy types, and modifiers are presented in the lists below. They are illustrated with examples from the NS pilot data (symbol "NS") and the learner data (symbol "L"). Modifications were counted each time they occurred in the requests.

Categories of direct, conventionally indirect, and nonconventionally indirect requests

1. Direct

1.1. Imperative: Mood derivable structures in full or elliptical form.

Example 1

```
(NS) Thế  cho  tớ           mượn,  cuối  giờ
     DisM give me (casual)  borrow end   lesson
     So let me borrow, after class

     cho  tớ           mượn   vở       nhé
     give me (casual) borrow notebook AlignM
     let me borrow your notes, OK?
```

Example 2

```
(L)  Làm ơn,   cô giáo            cho  thêm  thời gian
     do favor  teacher (female)  give more  time
     Please, give me more time

     để   viết  xong
     for  write complete
     to finish writing
```

1.2. Performative: Containing performative verbs that denote the request such as *đề nghị* [request], *bảo* [tell], *nhờ* [ask for help], *xin* [beg], etc., with or without hedges (e.g., *muốn* [would like/want]).

Example 3

```
(NS) Thế thì  em               muốn nhờ[2]
     So  then younger sibling  want ask for help
     So I'd like to ask you to help me

     chị          là chị          đi  đến
     older sister that older sister go  arrive
     when you get to

     trường thì  chị          tạt qua   thư viện
     school then older sister drop by  library
     school, please stop by the library

     trả     sách  hộ   em              với
     return book  help younger sibling AlignM
     and return a book for me.
```

Example 4

```
(L)  Em           nhờ          cô giáo
     I (student) ask for help teacher (female)
     I'd like to ask you to help

     chuyển   nộp    luận văn
     transfer submit thesis
     move my thesis submission (deadline)
```

1.3. Obligation & necessity: Containing verbs that denote obligation and necessity such as *nên* [should], *cần (phải)* [need to], and *phải* [have to].

Example 5

```
(L)  Cô                phải viết  thư    này
     Teacher (female) must  write letter this
     You have to write this letter

     cho  em  để   em được  nộp    thư    này
     for  me  for I  PosM  submit letter this
     for me so I can include it in my application

     và  được học bổng(L)
     and PosM scholarship
     and get scholarship
```

1.4. Want statement: Containing verbs that denote S's needs, wishes, and desires such as *muốn* [want], *cần* [need], and *phải* [have to].

Example 6

```
(NS) Em           chỉ  cần    thầy
     I (student) only need   teacher
     I just need you

     cho   em nửa tiếng
     give  me half hour
     to give me half an hour
```

Example 7

```
(L)  Em                muốn chị
     Younger sibling  want older sister
     I want you

     trả    quyển sách của em
     return book       of  younger sibling
     to return my book

     vào thư viện
     into  library
     to the library
```

2. Conventionally indirect

2.1. Suggestory formula: Utterances beginning with *Thế thì* [so], *Không thì* [if not then], or *Hay là* [or] and pronounced in a rising intonation. Suggestions often come after an initial failure to get H to perform the act.

Example 8

```
(NS) Không thì  chị            nói   chuyện
     No    then older sister  speak story
     How about you talk

     với  anh ấy một lát nữa
     with him    a bit   more
     to him a bit more

     rồi  chị          nói   xong   thì
     then older sister speak finish then
     and then when you're done

     cho  em              mượn
     give younger sibling borrow
     you can lend it to me

     một tý  được     không?
     one bit possible no?
     for a moment?
```

Example 9

```
(L) Thế thì  em                sẽ   copy bài    này
    So  then younger brother  will copy lesson this
    How about I copy the notes

    và  trả    vở       cho chị?
    and return notebook to  older sister?
    and  then give them back to you?
```

2.2. Query preparatory: S refers to the preparatory condition for the realization of a request. For example, S checks H's ability/willingness to perform the act, or asks for permission to perform the act. Very often, the utterance takes the form of a question.[3]

Example 10

```
(NS) Em                muốn hỏi chị          xem
     Younger brother   want ask older sister see
     I'd like to ask if

     chị          có thể cho  em              mượn
     older sister can    give younger brother borrow
     you can lend me

     máy tính  một lát được     không?
     computer  one bit possible no?
     your computer for a moment?
```

Example 11

```
(L) Nếu em          gặp cô
    If  I (student) see teacher (female)
    Is it possible if I see you

    lúc 9 giờ  được     không?
    at  9 hour possible no?
    at 9 o'clock?
```

3. Nonconventionally indirect

3.1. Hints: S's intent can be inferred thanks to his or her reference to the precondition for the realization of the request (e.g., H's availability) or to the reason for the request. Unlike a query preparatory, a hint is not conventionalized.[4]

Example 12

```
(NS) Em          xin lỗi    em           chưa
     I (student) apologize  I (student)  not yet
     I'm sorry I did not

     làm bài tập về nhà.
     do  homework
     do my homework.

     Tuần trước em          bị   ốm.
     Week last  I (student) NegM sick
     I was sick last week.

     Em           có   giấy chứng nhận
     I (student)  have certificate
     I have a doctor's note

     của bác sĩ đây  cô               ạ
     of  doctor here teacher (female) PolM
     here with me
```

Categories of request modifiers

1. External modifiers: Supportive moves that occur before or after the head act.

1.1. Steers: Phrases that S uses to prepare H for the request. S may do so by checking if H is available to perform the request. Steers are used to avoid being abrupt and inconsiderate.

Example 13

```
(NS) Chị          ơi
     Older sister vocative
     Sister,

     đang làm gì   đấy?
     Prog do  what there?
     what are you doing
```

Example 14

```
(L)  Bạn    ơi       hôm nay
     Friend vocative today
     My friend,

     bạn    có  bận  không?
     friend yes busy no
     are you busy today?
```

1.2. Presequences: S announces that she or he is going to make a request or checks if H is willing to hear the request.

Example 15

```
(NS) Cô                ơi       em          có   việc
    Teacher (female) vocative I (student) have matter
    Teacher, there's something

    muốn nhờ          cô
    want ask for help teacher (female)
    I need your help with

    một tý được    không ạ?
    a bit possible no    PolM?
    is it OK?
```

Example 16

```
(L) Cô                ơi       em          có
    Teacher (female) vocative I (student) have
    Teacher, I have to ask you

    việc   một chút ạ
    matter a bit    PolM
    about something
```

1.3. Grounders: Excuses, reasons, or explanations that S uses to justify the request and thus appear reasonable.

Example 17

```
(L)Chị           ơi        em              có thể
   Older sister vocative younger sibling can
   Sister, could I

   sử dụng máy tính chị          mấy  tiếng không?
   use     computer older sister few  hours no?
   use your computer for some hours?

   Máy tính em bị   hỏng
   Computer me NegM broke down.
   Mine broke down.
```

1.4. Disarmers: Utterances that S uses to show awareness of the pressure that the request may place on H. S might want to acknowledge the pressure and/or apologize.

Example 18

```
(NS) Chị          ơi       em              có   việc
     Older sister vocative younger sibling have matter
     Sister, I have to ask you about something

     này  phiền  chị          quá  nhưng mà
     this bother older sister much but
     I know it is very inconvenient for you but

     buộc   phải hỏi chị
     forced must ask older sister
     I have no other choice
```

Example 19

```
(L) Vâng em          biết cô giáo          rất  bận
    PolM I (student) know teacher (female) very busy
    I know you are very busy

    nhưng em          muốn cô giáo
    but   I (student) want teacher (female)
    but I want you to

    viết  hộ   em
    write help I (student)
    write the letter for me
```

1.5. Imposition minimizers: Utterances that S uses to free H from the imposition of the request.

Example 20

```
(L) Nếu bạn    đi học
    If friend  go study
    If you go to school,

    tớ          có thể nhờ          bạn
    I (casual) can    ask for help friend
    can I ask you to help

    trả     hộ    tớ không?
    return help me no?
    return the book?
```

1.6. Committers: S may want to minimize the cost for H by expressing compromise with H's conditions or offering to make it easier for H to perform the act.

Example 21

```
(NS) Thật  ra  nếu em          cố gắng
     Truth out if  I (student) try
     Actually, if I try hard

     sắp xếp thời gian để          đưa cho thầy
     arrange time      in order to give to teacher
     to arrange my time to give it to you

     thứ năm  này  có  được     không?
     Thursday this yes possible no?
     this Thursday, is it possible?

     Sớm   một ngày so       với   hẹn
     Early one day  compare with  deadline
     It's a day earlier than the due date,

     hơi   vất vả cho em
     a bit hard   for me (student)
     which is a bit hard for me

     nhưng em          sẽ   cố gắng
     but   I (student) will try
     but I will try
```

1.7. Understatement: S may want to understate the request so as to convince H of the minimal cost of the act. Understatements normally occur when H shows hesitation to help.

Example 22

```
(NS) Cái này chỉ  mười phút   thôi mà   cô
     This    just ten  minutes only StaM teacher (female)
     It should take just only ten minutes
```

1.8. Offer of compensation: S may also reduce the cost for H by offering H compensation or a reward.

Example 23

```
(NS) Thôi em                trả    hộ   chị
     DisM younger sibling return help older sister
     Alright, you return

     quyển sách chiều     chị           nấu cơm cho
     book       afternoon older sister cook    for
     the book for me, I will cook for you this afternoon
```

1.9. Sympathy seekers: S may want to appeal for H's sympathy so as to increase the chance of success of the request. This category is absent in Blum-Kulka et al. (1989) but has been added to fit our data.

Example 24

```
(NS) Thôi cô                 thông cảm
     DisM teacher (female) sympathize
     Please understand.
```

Example 25

```
(L)  Nếu em            không gửi
     If  I (student) not   send
     If I don't submit it now

     thì  ngày mai em           sẽ   có
     then tomorrow I (student) will have
     I will have

     rất  nhiều vấn đề
     very many  problem
     a lot of problems tomorrow
```

1.10. Smoothers: S may want to appeal for H's willingness to perform the act by offering H a compliment/appreciation or by emphasizing H's role.

Example 26

```
(L) Bạn    tốt bụng      lắm  mà
    Friend kind-hearted very EmM
    You're such a kind person, aren't you
```

1.11. Thanking: S may want to increase the benefit for H by expressing gratitude to H for the act.

2. Internal modifiers: Occur within and form part of the head act.

2.1. Address terms: Address terms help to express the speaker-hearer relationship (i.e., respectful politeness). The wrong choice of address term may threaten H's face and thus might be associated with a lack of politeness. Blum-Kulka et al. (1989) do not categorize address terms as request modifiers but because these linguistic features function as markers of respectful politeness in Vietnamese, we classify them as a type of internal modifier.

2.2. Politeness markers: Particles, honorifics, and verbs that express respect to H (e.g., *vâng, dạ, ạ* [honorifics], *làm ơn* [do favor], *xin* [beg], *cho* [give], *hộ* [help]). This category is absent in Blum-Kulka et al. (1989) but has been added to fit our data.

2.3. Downgraders: Adverbial modifiers that help S to downgrade the act (e.g., *một chút, một tý* [one bit]).

2.4. Downtoners: Verbs and sentence modifiers that S uses to reduce the pressure the request may place on H such as *có lẽ, có thể, chắc là* [perhaps, possibly, maybe/may, probably], etc.

2.5. Appealers: Particles or phrases S uses to call for H's understanding and sympathy (e.g., *nhé, với, đi, cái* [alignment markers], *được không?* [possible no?]).[5] This category is absent in Blum-Kulka et al. (1989) but has been added to fit our data.

Results and discussion

How do learners of Vietnamese as an L2 make requests in Vietnamese?

The majority of learners' requests were made up of both direct and conventionally indirect strategies (41% and 50%, respectively), suggesting that they did not have a clear preference for either level of directness. However, the learners tended to opt for nonconventionally indirect requests with a relatively low frequency (9% of the time), probably because they perceived the levels of imposition in most role-play situations as being relatively low and medium (Figure 1).

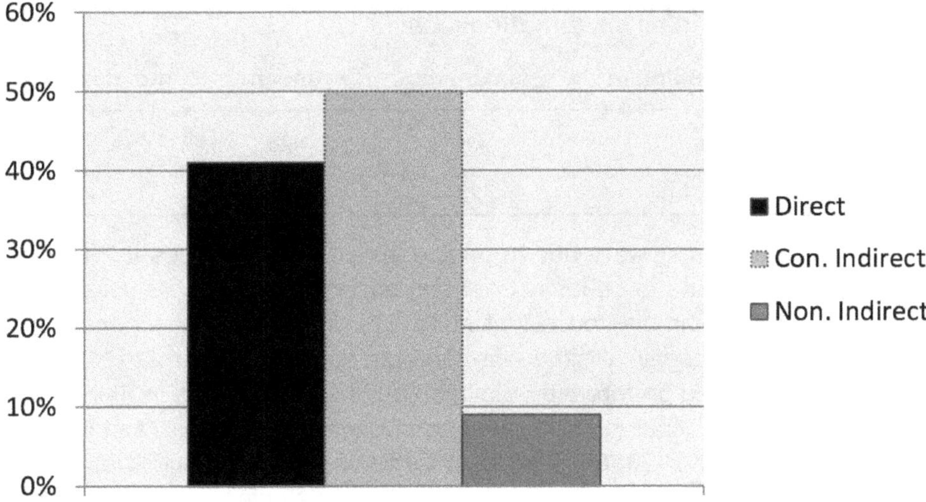

Figure 1. Distributions of learners' direct, conventionally indirect, and nonconventionally indirect requests in all six scenarios.

A close look at the learners' uses of individual strategy types also indicated that they did not prefer one single strategy. Rather, they tended to spread their choices over different types, quite unlike NSs of Vietnamese, who show far less variety in their choice of request strategy (cf. Vũ, 1997, 1999 – discussed below). For example, 29% of the learners' requests were made up of query preparatory formulas, 21% of suggestory formulas, 20% of want statements, and 14% of imperatives. The other formulas were also employed from time to time. What is more, Table 3 shows that the standard deviation computed for each strategy type was quite large, suggesting that the learners seemed to vary largely among themselves in their choice of a particular strategy type.

Table 3. Descriptive statistics for individual strategy types used by learners in all six situations

strategy types	minimum	maximum	mean	std. deviation
imperative	.00	.42	.14	.14
performative	.00	.24	.05	.07
want statement	.00	.80	.21	.22
obligation	.00	.11	.01	.03
suggestory	.07	.39	.19	.09

continued...

Table 3. Descriptive statistics for individual strategy types used by learners in all six situations *(cont.)*

strategy types	minimum	maximum	mean	std. deviation
query preparatory	.00	.64	.28	.17
hints	.00	.23	.08	.06

The above findings were not surprising, as in many previous ILP studies, L2 learners were found to be less consistent performers than NSs. House and Kasper (1987), for example, found that while NSs of British English consistently chose query preparatory in all situations, German and Danish learners of English showed a more varied preference. Similar results were reported in Blum-Kulka (1982), Færch and Kasper (1989), Kasper and Blum-Kulka (1993), and Niki and Tajika (1994). Nguyễn (2008b), finding a large variability among Vietnamese learners of English in their choice of realization strategies for criticizing and responding to criticism, argued that because the learners were uncertain of the appropriate norms of "doing things with words" in the TL, there seemed to be no common rule of choice within the group. The same argument could be made concerning the lack of homogeneity within the present group of learners. The learners' variability could also be explained by the fact that they came from different L1 backgrounds, which might have different pragmatic norms.

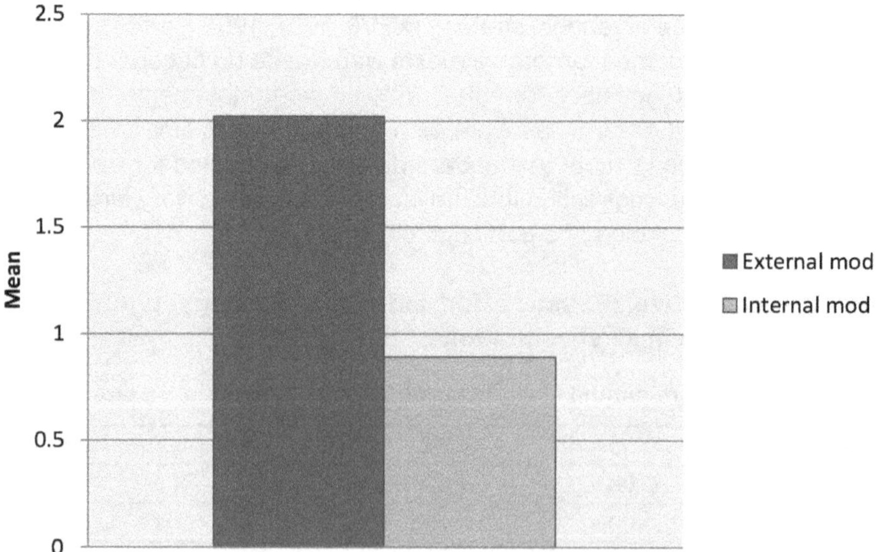

Figure 2. Distribution of learners' external and internal modifiers.

Figure 2 shows that the learners tended to draw more heavily on external modifiers (*M*=2.02, *SD*=.51) than on internal modifiers (*M*=.88, *SD*=.50) when softening their requests in Vietnamese. Again, this finding supported previous studies (mentioned above) showing that high-intermediate and advanced learners tended to prefer supportive moves mostly for their explicit politeness function and their easy accessibility. Internal modifiers, on the other hand, might have caused learners greater difficulty because their pragmatic meanings were less noticeable and because they added more structural complexity to the speech act, thus requiring more processing effort (Hassall, 2001).

The findings of the present study suggest that internal modifiers might be challenging not only for learners of inflected languages such as English and German (as reported in Faerch & Kasper, 1989; Hendriks, 2008; House & Kasper, 1987; Nguyễn, 2008a; Woodfield, 2008), but also for learners of an isolating language like Vietnamese, in which the addition of internal modifiers does not result in morphological changes to the structure. The difficulty in the latter case might stem from the fact that internal modifiers perhaps do not operate, both formally and functionally, in the same way in the learners' L1s and the TL (see Hassall, 2001, for further discussion).

For example, verb tenses (e.g., past tense with present time reference) typically function as internal modifiers in English (Nguyễn, 2008a). However, this is not the case for Vietnamese, in which verb tenses only indicate or emphasize the time factor. As Vũ (1997, 1999) pointed out, Vietnamese NS requests are more typically 'internally' modified by means of address terms, politeness markers (including such verbs as *làm ơn* [do a favor], *xin* [beg], *cho* [give], *hộ* [help], and the honorific *ạ*), and appealers that are alignment markers (e.g., *nhé, với, cái, đi*), which might not be the case for English requests. Another example is the case of the politeness expression *làm ơn* [doing a favor], which is more or less functionally equivalent to the English *please*. However, while *please* can occur literally anywhere in the head act (e.g., *Can you please pass the salt? Please, can you pass the salt? Can you pass the salt, please?*), *làm ơn* can occur only between the subject and the verb in the head act.

As competent L1 users, adult learners enjoy knowledge of pragmatic universals (Kasper, 1992), and thus might already be very well aware that a speech act can be 'internally' modified. However, the different formal and functional operations of internal modifiers and the different form-function mappings in learners' L1s and the L2s might present certain challenges. Therefore, as Nguyễn (2008a) argued, learners might be driven to rely on external modifiers for expressing politeness in an attempt to compensate for their difficulty with internal modifiers.

Concerning the effects of situational variation on learners' requests, the results of chi-square tests showed that learners generally did not opt for differential levels of directness in situations varying in relative power [$\chi 2(1, N=312)=.56$, $p>.05$, *n.s.*] and degrees of imposition [$\chi 2(2, N=162)=2.41$, $p>.05$, *n.s.*]. However, looking at individual strategy types, it seemed that learners employed more imperatives in equal power situations but more hints in unequal power situations [$\chi 2(5, N=329)=34.5$, $p<.001$]. The other strategies (i.e., want statements, suggestory formulas, and query preparatory), on the other hand, were used more or less invariably in all situations. Although there is no easy explanation for this behavior, we might assume that perhaps learners' decisions were influenced by their perceptions of the pragmatic properties of the given strategies. Put differently, because imperatives are mood derivable, they tend to express the most direct type of requests. Hints, on the other hand, represent the act the most subtly due to a complete absence of transparency in S's intent. The learners might rely on this knowledge to discriminate their contexts of use. For the other strategies, because they are not found at the two extreme ends of the directness continuum like imperatives and hints, but rather in between the ends (see Blum-Kulka et al., 1989), learners might have more difficulty mapping them onto the appropriate contexts of use in the L2.

Finally, the learners did not vary their requesting strategies in situations varying in degrees of imposition [$\chi 2(6, 171)=6.0$, $p>.05$, *n.s*). This was probably because from the learners' points of view, the situations did not differ greatly in this aspect. Indeed, their scores on the degrees of imposition in the six situations did not show much discrimination (ranging between 2.7 and 3.7).

To what extent do low- and high-proficiency learners vary in the way they make requests in Vietnamese?

The High and Low Groups did not differ in their frequencies of use of direct [$t(16)=1.74$, $p>.05$, *n.s.*] and nonconventionally indirect requests [$t(16)=.86$, $p>.05$, *n.s.*]. However, the High Group opted for conventionally indirect requests considerably more often than their less proficient peers [$t(16)=2.44$, $p<.05$] (Table 4). Looking at individual strategy types, the two groups differed only in their use of imperatives [$t(16)=2.51$, $p<.05$] and want statements [$t(16)=3.60$, $p<.05$]. Specifically, the Low Group employed a greater number of want statements, whereas the High Group relied significantly on imperatives (Figure 3).

Table 4. Distribution of direct, conventionally indirect, and nonconventionally indirect requests by proficiency levels[6]

	low proficiency			high proficiency			*t*	*P* value
	f	*Mean*	*SD*	*f*	*Mean*	*SD*		
direct requests	66/130	.51	.21	63/182	.35	.19	1.74	.101

conven-tionally indirect requests	51/130	.39	.19	105/182	.57	.17	2.44	.027
nonconven-tionally indirect requests	13/130	.10	.08	14/182	.08	.05	.86	.402

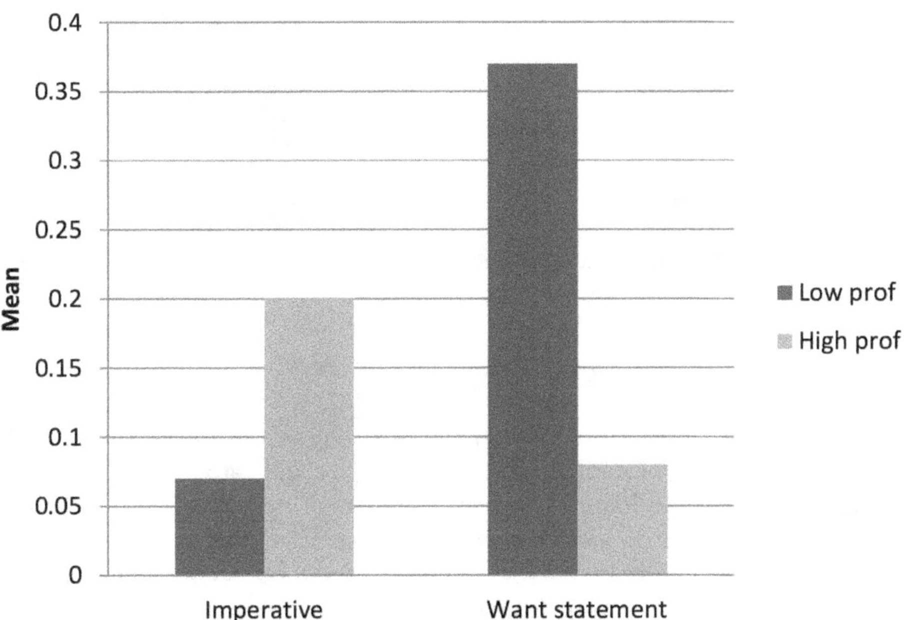

Figure 3. Distribution of imperatives and want statements by proficiency levels.

The High Group's preference for conventionally indirect requests confirms the findings of many earlier ILP studies reviewed above. However, what is striking is these learners' over-use of imperatives. Indeed, this group employed imperatives almost as frequently as suggestory formulas and query preparatory strategies, and even more frequently than hints (Figure 4). We would expect learners at this proficiency level to rely no longer on such direct, formulaic requests, which, in fact, are characteristic of a much earlier stage of development (Achiba, 2003; Ellis, 1992; Felix-Brasdefer, 2007; Kasper & Rose, 2002; Schauer, 2008; Schmidt, 1983).

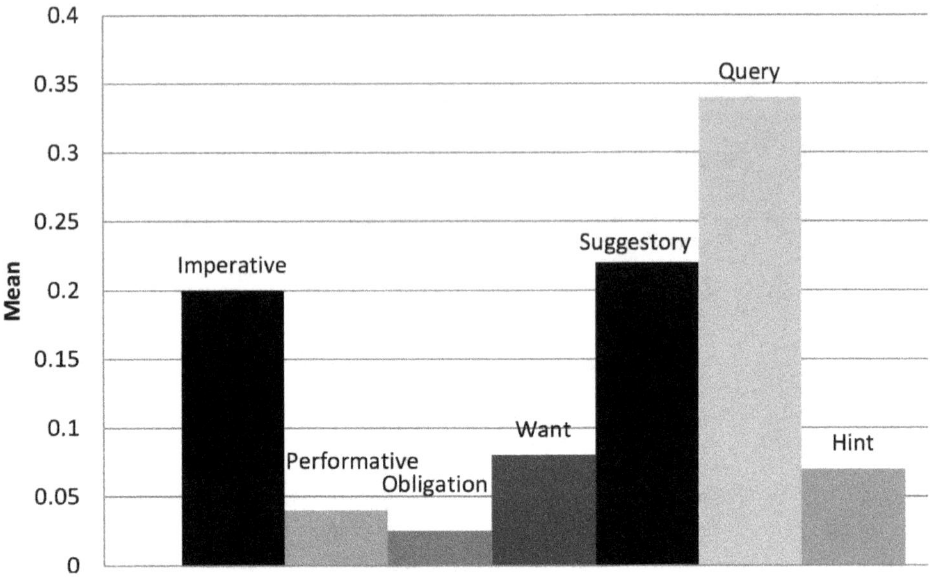

Figure 4. Strategy types by high-proficiency learners.

Nonetheless, looking at Vietnamese NS requests, it becomes clear that the High Group's choice of imperatives might reflect targetlike behavior. Vũ (1997, 1999) collected naturally occurring requests by a group of Vietnamese NSs of Hanoi dialect as they were communicating in various social contexts. She found a striking preference for directness by her participants. For example, more than 90% of the requests she gathered were imperatives. Also, 76.7% of the Vietnamese NS respondents in her study did not consider barely mitigated imperatives inappropriate while 64% deemed mitigated imperatives to be polite. When comparing her own data with Blum-Kulka's (1989) data on requests in a number of L1s, Vũ concluded that Vietnamese NSs tended to prefer direct requests to a considerably greater extent than NSs of many languages. Therefore, the frequent use of 'imperative requests' by the High Group in the present study, though still far behind the NS level of use (20%, as opposed to 90.5% as reported in Vu, 1999), seemed to display a closer approximation to the NS tendency, in comparison to the Low Group.

This NS approximation becomes more evident when we consider the politeness strategies that the High Group employed in realizing imperative requests. The analysis of their imperative samples shows that the learners tended to take into account both respectful and strategic politeness, just like any NS of Vietnamese, and in fact successfully achieved both types of politeness. For example, they correctly added address terms and honorifics in conformity to the speaker-hearer relationship. They effectively added supportive moves that help minimize the imposition of the requests such as disarmers, imposition minimizers, sympathy seekers, and those that help maximize the benefits to H such as offers of compensation and smoothers (see examples of the categories in the section on analytical procedures). They also successfully employed politeness markers and appealers with similar mitigation functions. Indeed, their imperatives show strikingly similar features to the NS sample (taken from the pilot data). Examples 27–28 compare how a High learner and a NS used external modifiers to support their imperatives, and examples 3–13 illustrate how High learners and NSs used internal modifiers.

Example 27: High learner sample, request to borrow class notes

```
(L: learner; I: interlocutor):

01 L: hôm qua   bạn    có  đi học  không?
      yesterday friend yes go study no?
      did you go to class yesterday?

02 I: ừ   có
      yes yes
      yes, I did

03 L: thế  cô giáo          có  cho  nhiều à  cho
      DisM teacher (female) yes give much  ah give
      did the teacher assign

      về nhà nhiều bài tập không?
      return home much homework no?
      a lot of homework?

04 I: nhiều, làm bò ra
      much,  do  on all legs
      heaps, we have heaps to do

05 L: thế à   cho  tớ           mượn   vở       cái!
      really, give me (casual) borrow notebook AlignM
      really? let me borrow your notes, then!

06 I: nhưng mà cần dùng cần  lắm  vì
      but        need use need much because
      but I really need to use them now

      xem  mới   làm được    bài
      look CondM do  possible homework
      because I can only do my homework with the notes

07 L: thì tớ           mượn   một tý thôi
      EmM I (casual)  borrow a bit  only
      wWell, I'll just borrow them for a short time,

      chỉ  chép nhanh   thôi xong giả   luôn       mà
      just copy quickly only then return right away StanM
      I'll just copy them and return them right away
```

08 I: ui cậu chép lâu lắm
oh you (casual) copy long vey
oh but you copy so slowly

09 L: đâu tớ chép nhanh
StaM I (casual) copy quickly
oh but I can copy it down quickly

10 I: không
no
no

11 L: tớ chép nhanh xong tớ
I (casual) copy quickly finish I (casual)
I'll tmake very quick notes and I

12 I: mượn người khác đi
borrow another person AlignM
you can ask other people, can't you?

13 L: tớ mượn nhiều người lắm rồi
I (casual) borrow many people very already
I have asked so many people

nhưng mà không ai cho toàn ky bo
all mean but nobody give
but nobody lent me their notes, they're so stingy

tớ biết bạn là không như thế mà ((laughs))
I(casual)know friend are not like that EmM
I know you're not like that ((laughs))

14 I: ((laughs))

15 L: bạn tốt bụng lắm mà ((giggles))
friend kind-hearted very EmM
I know you are such a kind person

16 I: nhưng mà chép thì lâu lắm
but copy EmM slow very
but it takes a lot of time to copy the notes

17 L: không không lâu đâu nhanh
no not slow StaM quick
oh no, it doesn't take that long, it'll be quick

18 I: hay thôi chạy ù ra photo
or DisM run quickly out photocopy shop
or you make a quick run to the photocopy shop

19 L: ừ được rồi tớ chạy ra phô tô
yes ok already I(casual) run out photocopy shop
yes okay I'll dash to the photocopy shop

20 I: nhanh nhé, không được làm mất
quick AlignM not possible make lose
be quick, then, and don't lose

trang nào đâu đấy
page any StaM AffM
a single page, OK?

21 L: rồi 5 phút là giả luôn
ok 5 minute then return right away
ok, 5 minutes and I'll return them right away

22 I:
nhớ nhé
remember AlignM
remember that, OK?

23 L: ừ cảm ơn
yes thank you
yes, thank you

Example 28: NS, request to return a book

(P: participant; I: interlocutor)

01 P: hôm nay ấy đến trường lúc mấy giờ đấy?
today you(casual) go school at what time EmM?
what time are you going to school today?

02 I: tí nữa đi bây giờ, sao?
a bit more go now why?
very soon, why?

03 P: tí nữa đi bây giờ.
a bit more go now
very soon.

ừ thế cho tớ gửi quyển sách
yes so give me (casual) send book
uh so let me ask you to take a book

gửi trả thư viện.
send return library
to return to the library.

hôm nay đến hạn trả rồi
today arrive due return already
it's due today

04 I: thế sao cậu không lên?
DisM why you not go up?
but why don't you go to the library yourself?

05 P: ừ hôm nay đang mệt, không đi được
yes today prog. tired not go possible
I'm so tired today, I can't go

06 I: thế nhưng mà tớ, nhưng mà
DisM but I (casual) but
but I, but

phải trả lúc mấy giờ?
must return what time?
what time is it due?

07 P: chỉ đi qua thư viện bỏ vào,
just go pass library drop enter
just go by the library and drop it

bỏ vào thư viện thôi mà, có gì đâu
drop in library only StaM nothing StaM
drop it off at the library, that's it

08 I: nhưng mà trả lúc mấy giờ
but return what time
but what time is it due,

vì tớ học đến 3 giờ cơ,
because I (casual) study until 3 hour EmM
because I have a class until 3

lớp tớ đến 3 giờ cơ
class me (casual) until 3 hour EmM
my class goes until 3

09 P: thì lúc nào qua cũng được,
EmM anytime pass EmM possible
any time would do

lúc nào cũng được
anytime EmM possible
any time

10 I: thôi được rồi, thế thì đi học sớm
DisM ok already so then go study early
ok then, so I'll go to school early

đưa qua cũng được
pass by EmM ok
and return it

11 P: ừ tớ cảm ơn
yes I (casual) thank you
yes thank you

Example 27 shows that the learner did not convey her intentions abruptly. Instead, she opened the conversation with 'steers' (Blum-Kulka et al.,1989) in turns 1 and 3, leading H into the topic naturally. This was similar to the way the NS in Example 28 approached his interlocutor (turn 1). When initially refused, the learner employed strategies such as understating the trouble involved in the request (i.e., understatement, turns 7, 9, 11, 17, 21), justifying her action (i.e., grounder, turn 13), complimenting her interlocutor (i.e., smoother, turns 13, 15), and immediately agreeing to this person's suggestion (i.e., committer, turn 19), so as to get this person to agree to her request. These were similar to the way the NS led the conversation to achieve his intention in Example 28 (e.g., grounder in turn 5, understatement in turn 7, and imposition minimizer in turn 9).

Examples 29–39 show that the High learners were able to substantially reduce the threat of their imperative requests by employing targetlike internal modifiers.

High learner samples:

Example 29

Em   mượn   máy tính của chị   một chút!
Young sister borrow computer of elder sister a bit!
Please let me borrow your computer for just a moment!

Example 30

Bạn   ơi   cho tớ   mượn
Friend vocative give me (casual) borrow
My friend, please let me borrow

máy   bạn   cái!
computer friend AlignM
your computer!

Example 31

Chị   giúp em   đi!
Elder sister help younger sibling AlignM
Sister, please help me!

Example 32

Anh   xin mượn   nhé!
Elder brother beg borrow AlignM
Please let me borrow it!

Example 33

Cô   viết giúp cho em   nhé!
Teacher (female) write help for I (student) AlignM
Teacher, please write it for me!

Example 34

Cô   chỉ viết em   sinh viên
Teacher (female) just write I (student) student
You only need to write that I'm

giỏi nhất trong lớp   thôi cô   ạ!
best   in   class only teacher (female) PolM
the best student in the class!

NS samples:

Example 35

```
Mày             ơi         mày             cho
You (intimate) vocative you (intimate) give
Hey buddy, let

tao            mượn   cái máy tính cái
me (intimate) borrow computer     AlignM!
me borrow your computer!
```

Example 36

```
Vâng cho  em               dùng một tiếng nhé!
PolM give younger sibling use  one hour  AlignM
Yes, please let me use it for just one hour!
```

Example 37

```
Bạn    ơi       tớ           mượn   vở       cái!
Friend vocative I (casual) borrow notebook AlignM!
My friend, please let me borrow your notebook!
```

Example 38

```
Thôi, em             trả    hộ
DisM younger sibling return help
oh please return

chị          quyển sách!
elder sister book
the book for me!
```

Example 39

```
Cô                cho  em
Teacher (female) give me (student)
Please let me have

xin một tuần đi!
beg one week AlignM!
one week!
```

The High learners addressed higher status interlocutors respectfully (Examples 29, 31, 33, 34) and equal and lower status interlocutors properly (Examples 30, 32), just like the NSs in Examples 35–39 addressed their partners in corresponding relationships. In particular, they were able to put more weight on solidarity and power factors to tailor the degree of their respectful politeness to different higher status people. For example, they used honorifics for their teacher (Example 34), but not for an older friend (Examples 29, 31). Generally speaking, honorifics would be desirable when a lower status person addresses a higher status person; however, in cases where the status difference is not too large (e.g., a younger friend to an older friend, a junior colleague to a senior colleague) and especially if the relationship is close, their use would be considered unnecessarily ceremonious (*khách sáo*) and distant (*xa cách*). The High learners, while showing sufficient respect to their older friends by using appropriate address terms, successfully saved themselves from going unnecessarily formal in a close relationship. What is more, like the NSs in Examples 35–39, they were able to appeal for H's cooperation and support by using appealers in the form of alignment markers such as *cái*, *đi*, *nhé*, and politeness markers such as *giúp*, *xin*, thus avoiding giving H the impression that they were imposing their will on H. As Vũ (1997) pointed out, address forms and appealers (termed *modal particles* in her study) constitute a majority of Vietnamese politeness devices (65% and 12%, respectively) and are ranked higher by NSs on the politeness continuum as compared to other devices. The High learners employment of these modifier types therefore represented a NS approximation. Therefore, what we can assume from the High Group's successful use of imperatives is a higher level of pragmatic development as compared to their less proficient peers.

In contrast, the Low Group's under-use of imperatives as compared to strategies such as want statements, suggestory formulas, query preparatory, and hints (Figure 5) appeared to be consistent with their current stage of development, which was no longer characterized by a reliance on unanalyzed formulas. However, this behavior suggested a deviation from the NS distribution. Most likely, the learners' linguistic competence allowed them to have full access to this strategy type, but due to their incomplete knowledge of Vietnamese sociopragmatics, they did not use it as appropriately as did their more proficient peers, who had more advanced knowledge of the TL norms.

Overall, the learners' differential levels of use of imperatives at different stages of development seemed to suggest that like grammar learning, L2 pragmatics learning also involves much constructing and reconstructing of IL knowledge. In this study, the high-proficiency learners had long passed the stage of development where imperatives are predominant. However, in light of the newly acquired L2 pragmatics knowledge, they did not seem to hesitate to use this strategy, although they had acquired sufficient means to express their communicative intentions in a more indirect manner and thus did not seem to hesitate to 'fall back' on it.

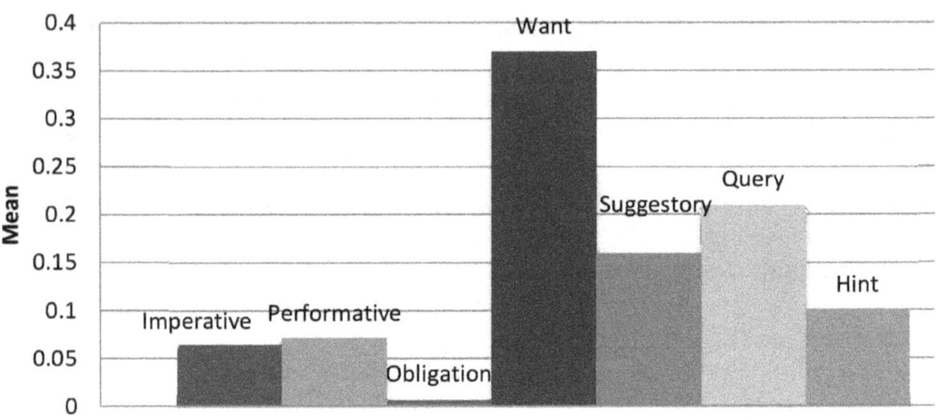

Figure 5. Strategy types by low-proficiency learners.

The Low Group's heavy reliance on want statements is also consistent with previous studies (e.g., Felix-Brasdefer, 2007; Hassall, 2003; Koike, 1989; Rintell, 1981; Schauer, 2008). Low-proficiency learners have been repeatedly found to make use of statements of personal desire and needs to a greater extent than their more advanced fellow learners and NSs (Hassall, 2003). Koike (1989) attributed this behavior to learners' strong concern for clarity. In other words, learners tend to prefer formulas that can help to clearly convey their messages. This explanation seemed plausible for the Low Group in the present study, especially when we considered the instances where the learners repeated the strategy a few times to make their intentions explicit (examples 40, 41) or where their initial, more subtle requests were not noticed by H (Examples 42, 43).

Example 40: Low learner, request for a letter of recommendation

```
01 L: chào         cô giáo
      greetings, teacher (female)
      hello, teacher

02 I: chào         em
      greetings, you (student)
      hello

03 L: em            muốn cô giáo            viết   thư
      I (student) want teacher (female) write  letter
      I want you to write me a letter

      giới thiệu    của em
      introduction of  me
      of recommendation
```

04 I: gì hả em?
What QuesM you (student)
what is it?

05 L: vì em muốn học bổng,
because I (student) want scholarship
because I want a scholarship

em phải à ba ngày nữa
I (student) must ah three days more
I must ah

là hết hạn nộp đơn
be due date submit form
the application deadline is in three days

06 I: viết thư giới thiệu á?
write letter introduction QuesM?
write a letter of recommendation?

07 L: vâng em biết cô giáo rất bận
yes I(student) know teacher (female) very busy
yes I know you are very busy

nhưng em muốn cô giáo viết hộ
but I (student) want teacher (female) write help
but I want you to help me and write

em em à em đã
I (student) I(student) ah I (student) Past.
that I was

là sinh viên nhất lớp
be student best class
the best student in the class

Example 41: Low learner, request for a letter of recommendation

01 L: em chào cô ạ
I (student) greet teacher (female) PolM
hello, teacher

02 I: ừ chào em
yes greetings you (student)
hello

03 L: hôm nay em muốn à nhờ
today I (student) want ah ask for help
today I want uh to ask

cô giúp em một việc
teacher (female)help me (student) one matter
for your help with something

04 I: ừ? việc gì?
yes, matter what?
ok, what is that?

05 L: em muốn xin học bổng
I (student) want ask scholarship
I want to apply for a scholarship

```
06 I: học bổng    à?    thế à? sao mình lại  xin được
      scholarship QuesM really Why I    StaM ask possible
      a scholarship? how come I can

      cho  bạn  học bổng?
      give you scholarship?
      get you a scholarship?

07 L: vì      em           cảm thấy em           học giỏi
      because I (student) feel     I (student) study well
      because I feel that I'm a good student

08 I: nhưng mà sao em             lại  bảo mình
      but      why you (student) StaM say  I
      but how come you're saying that

      giúp em            học bổng    là thế nào?
      help you (student) scholarship be how?
      I can get a scholarship for you? What do you mean?

09 L: à em            muốn cô                 à cho
      ah  I (student) want teacher (female) ah give
      uh I want you uh to give


      em           à  một cái    chứng minh thư  là à
      me (student) uh one Class. proof      card be ah
      me uh an identity card uh


10 I: chứng minh thư  á?
      proof      card QuesM?
      an identity card?



11 L: chứng minh à  chứng minh em
      prove      ah prove      I (student)
      ah proof that I'm

      là học sinh giỏi
      be student excellent
      a good student

12 I: à  chứng minh bằng cách nào bây giờ?
      ah prove      how           now?
      ah how can I do that?

      Em           nộp    bảng điểm  của em            ý!
      you (student) submit form grade of  you (student) EmM
      you just submit your academic transcript!

13 L: à  bảng điểm
      ah form grade
      ah academic transcript

14 I: ừ   bảng điểm  ý
      yes form grade EmM
      yes, your academic transcript

15 L: bảng điểm
      form grade
      academic transcript

16 I: ừ, thế sao lại   liên quan gì   đến mình
      yes so why StaM  related   what to me
      yes, but why does this have to do with me?
```

17 L: nhưng mà có điểm cô thì
but have grade teacher (female) then
but with your grade

xin học bổng sẽ dễ hơn
ask scholarship will easy more
it will be easier to get a scholarship

18 I: có cái gì cơ nhỉ?
have what EmM AlignM?
with exactly what, dear?

19 L: *có điểm cô*
have grade teacher (female)
your grade

20 I: có điểm rồi, nhưng mà
have grade already but
the grade are already there but

sao có chuyện gì nhỉ
why have matter what AlignM?
what is happening?

mình chưa hiểu ý em
I not yet understand idea you (student)
I don't get your point

21 L: chưa hiểu ý ạ
not yet understand idea PolM?
you didn't get my point?

22 I: ừ
yes
no I didn't

23 L: em muốn à cô chứng minh cho ah
I (student) want uh teacher (female) prove for ah
I want ah you to prove ah

24 I: chứng minh à? tức là làm cái gì?
prove QuesM meaning do what?
prove? what does that mean?

chứng minh bằng cách nào?
prove by way which?
and how can I prove it?

25 L: viết một giấy à một tờ giấy
write one paper ah one paper
write a paper ah a sheet of paper

26 I: một tờ giấy?
one sheet paper
a paper?

27 L: một tờ giấy chứng minh
one paper prove
a certification

28 I: à
ah
ah

```
29 L: để    giới thiệu à
      for   introduce ah
      to introduce ah

30 I: tức là   giới thiệu
      meaning introduce?
      so you mean to introduce

31 L: giới thiệu em          là à  một sinh viên giỏi
      introduce  I (student) am ah one student   excellent
      introduce me as a good student

32 I: à  tức là    thư    giới thiệu
      ah meaning  letter recommendation
      ah you mean a letter of recommendation
```

Example 42: Low learner, request for a letter of recommendation

```
01 L: xin chào  cô,                xin lỗi cô
      greetings teacher (female) apology teacher (female)
      hello teacher, excuse me

02 I: chuyện gì   hả     em?
      matter what QuesM  you (student)
      yes, what's up?

03 L: em           mới  biết thông tin
      I (student) just know information
      I just learned some information

      về    một học bổng
      about one scholarship
      about a scholarship

      và  muốn à  muốn nộp    đơn  xin học bổng    đó
      and want ah want submit form ask scholarship that
      and I want to apply for it

04 I: à thế     à  tốt  quá
      ah really ah good very
      ah that's very good,

      em            học   giỏi thế thì xin đi
      you (student) study well so then ask AlignM
      you are a good student, so go for it

05 L: à  nhưng em          cần  gấp      à
      ah but   I (student) need urgently ah
      ah but I urgently need uh

      em          cần gấp
      I (student) need urgently
      I urgently need

      thư    giới thiệu     của cô                à
      letter recommendation of  teacher (female) ah
      your letter of reference ah

      vì      vài  ngày  nữa  là
      because some days  more  be
      because the application deadline
```

```
hết  hạn      nộp    đơn          và
end  due date submit application  and
closes in a few days and

em          không biết là   em          không biết
I (student) not   know that I (student) not know
I don't know uh I don't know

viết   thư    giới thiệu     này  thế nào
write letter recommendation this how
how to write this letter of recommendation
```

Example 43: Low Learner, request to borrow a computer

```
01 L: chị          ơi
      older sister vocative
      hey sister

02 I: ừ   có   chuyện gì   hả    em?
      yes have matter what QuesM younger sibling?
      hey, what's up?

03 L: máy tính của em bị   hỏng
      computer of  me NegM broken
      my computer broke down

04 I: ừ   thế à     thế em              sửa    chưa?
      yes so QuesM so younger sibling repair yet?
      oh really? did you get it repaired?

05 L: em              muốn mượn   máy tính để  à
      younger sibling want borrow computer for ah
      I want to borrow your computer for uh

      vì      em                   phải viết
      because I (younger sibling) must write
      because I have to write

      ba    trang bài luận
      three page  essay
      a three-page essay
```

In Example 40, the learner requested a letter of reference from his teacher by explicitly stating his needs (turn 3) but the teacher did not seem to understand at first (turn 4). Therefore, the learner stated his needs again in turn 5 (*I want a scholarship*) and turn 7 (*I want you to help me and write that I was the best student*), obviously in hope of expressing his message more clearly to the teacher. Example 41 presents the same scenario. The learner had some difficulty explaining her request to the teacher due to limited linguistic competence (turns 5 through 31). She repeatedly resorted to want statements (turns 9, 23) perhaps because she found the formula easy to express while still having clarity. In both Examples 42 and 43, the learners first approached their interlocutors with an indirect, subtle request (turn 3 in both conversations). However, because their request was not noticed by H (evidenced by H's responding only to the propositional meaning of the utterances), they probably decided to announce their needs more explicitly.

In contrast to the Low Group, the High Group did not make frequent use of want statements (37% vs. 8% of the time, respectively). While every learner in the Low Group selected this strategy for at least one scenario, only five out of ten learners in the High Group did so. Presumably, they had acquired a wider range of linguistic means to express their meanings in a less face-threatening manner, and perhaps also developed better control over the processing of these means, which enabled them to attend to both message and politeness at the same time (see Nguyễn, 2008b, for further discussion). The Low Group, due to their lower level of fluency in the TL, might have had more restricted access to complex, mitigated requests, and thus had to rely on explicit formulas at the expense of politeness (see Nguyễn, 2008b, for a discussion of reduction of modality by low-proficiency learners). This finding seemed to suggest some interplay between grammatical competence and pragmatic competence. In other words, better control over language processing seemed to enable the highly proficient learners to achieve their propositional and pragmatic meanings more efficiently, but a lack of fluency in the TL seemed to inhibit the low-proficiency learners from doing both successfully at the same time.

Regarding the learners' choices of other major strategies such as suggestory formula and query preparatory, hardly any evidence of pragmatic development was found. In fact, both learner groups tended to show a deviation from the NS norms. As indicated earlier, Vietnamese NSs tend to prefer a high level of directness in making requests (evidenced in their exclusive reliance on imperative formulas) and rely more considerably on supportive elements with politeness effects such as alignment markers, emphasis markers, and stance markers rather than on indirectness for expressing politeness (Vũ, 1997). Indirectness is also considered a politeness device; however, it does not rank as high as mitigated directness on the politeness continuum, and in fact, indirect requests only account for a fairly small percentage in Vietnamese NS request samples (9.5% as opposed to 90.5%; Vũ, 1997). Vũ's study also indicated that over 60% of her NS respondents rated the use of query preparatory formulas (e.g., *Can/could H tell S what time is it, please?*) as 'rarely found' in unfamiliarity contexts (e.g., between strangers), and over 70% rated the use of this strategy as 'unapplicable' for family members.

The learners' use of conventional indirectness suggested an opposite tendency to the NSs. Both High and Low Groups tended to use suggestory formulas and query preparatory with relatively high frequencies (see Figures 4 and 5). For the High Group, suggestory formulas accounted for

23.6% of the total number of requests made, and query formulas accounted for 34%. For the Low Group, 18% of their requests were suggestory formulas, and 21% were query preparatory. No significant differences were found for the two groups in their frequencies of use of these strategies although the High Group was found to opt for a significantly higher level of conventional indirectness ($t=.000$, $p<.05$, see Table 6). The learners' employment of conventionally indirect strategies in Vietnamese, although seemingly consistent with their current stages of IL development (see Kasper & Rose, 2002), was in fact not consistent with the NS use. Their choice of these strategies might therefore be attributed to incomplete knowledge of Vietnamese sociopragmatics and perhaps a reliance on their L1 pragmatic rules, at least in the case of English-speaking background (ESB) learners. Indeed, a close examination into these learners' query preparatory suggested that they might have transferred the structure from English. In Vietnamese, the presence of the modal verb *có thể* (more or less equivalent to English modal verbs *can/could/may/might*) is optional in ability/ permission requests, and the main carrier of the structure's propositional meaning is the final interrogative expression *được không*? [possible no?]. However, due to the influence of English grammar, the ESB learners tended to add *có thể* to many of their ability/permission requests. For example, a High learner produced (44) and a Low learner produced (45).

Example 44: High learner

Em muốn hỏi cô
I (student) want ask teacher (female)
I'd like to ask

có thể giúp em được không?
can help me possible no
if you can help me

Example 45: Low learner

Sau đó làm bài tập chị
After that do homework elder sister
After you're done with your homework,

có thể cho mượn vở được không?
can give borrow notes possible no?
can you lend me your notes?

An important finding is that the frequent use of targetlike modifiers by the learners offered evidence of pragmatic development (Table 5). Specifically, the number of politeness devices used overall by the High Group significantly exceeded the number used by the Low Group

[$t(16)=2.48$, $p<.05$]. The High Group employed a significantly greater number of targetlike internal modifiers than their less proficient peers [$t(16)=2.35$, $p<.05$]. They did not, however, employ more external modifiers than the latter. This finding seemed to support the claim made in previous ILP studies that internal modifiers might present more problems to L2 learners as they carry less noticeable pragmatic meanings and tend to increase the structural complexity of the utterance, thus requiring more processing attention (see Hassall, 2001; Nguyễn, 2008a). In the present study, as the learners reached a higher level of proficiency, they also developed better control over internal modifiers and perhaps became more aware of their pragmatic meanings as used by NSs. Therefore, they began to draw more on this type of modifier. On the other hand, this study found no difference in the use of external modifiers by the High and Low Groups. Perhaps this was because external modifiers were generally more easily added to the speech act, and at the preintermediate and intermediate levels, the Low learners had sufficient linguistic resources to express supportive moves as much as did their higher proficiency fellow learners.

Table 5. Distribution of modifiers by proficiency levels

	low proficiency		high proficiency		*t*	*P* value
	Mean	*SD*	*Mean*	*SD*		
external modifiers	1.9	.61	2.1	.43	1.05	.309
internal modifiers	.60	.29	1.1	.53	2.35	.032
total number	**2.5**	**.71**	**3.2**	**.58**	**2.48**	**.025**

Concerning the situational variation effects, it was found that the High Group preferred directness in equal power situations and indirectness in lower-to-higher power situations [$\chi2(1, N=182)=3.97$, $p<.05$], whereas the Low Group did not show any discrimination [$\chi2(1, N=130)=1.11$, $p>.05$, *n.s.*]. The High Group also tended to employ more 'imperatives' in equal power situations [$\chi2(4, N=182)=30.1$, $p<.05$], but their contextual distribution of other strategies was less clearly evident. The Low Group, on the other hand, used all strategies with variation, regardless of the differential representation of the power factor in each situation. This finding is consistent with previous studies (see Kasper & Rose, 2002), adding further evidence of the higher level of sensitivity to sociocultural cues by higher proficiency learners when making speech acts in the TL. Finally, both the learner groups were not found to vary their strategies according to the levels of imposition [$\chi2(2, N=94)=2.11$, $p>.05$, *n.s.* for the High Group; $\chi2(2, N=69)=1.59$, $p>.05$, *n.s.* for the Low Group]. This was, again, because the situations in fact did not vary greatly in terms of the degree of imposition.

To what extent do the learners' lengths of residency in the TL environment affect the way they make requests?

The learners were also compared in terms of the length of time they had spent in the TL community, in an attempt to examine the effects of this learning context on their pragmatic development. Results showed the Long-stay and Short-stay groups tended to differ significantly only in their frequencies of use of imperatives and want statements and their distributions of imperatives in situations varying in the power factor.

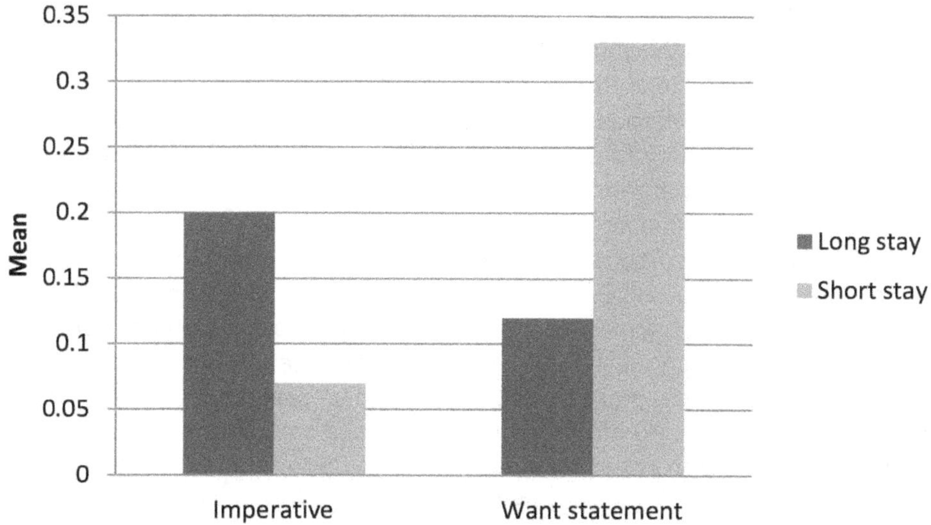

Figure 6. Distributions of imperatives and want statements by lengths of residence.

First, the Long-stay group was found to employ a significantly greater number of imperative requests than their Short-stay peers [M=.20, SD=.16 as opposed to M=.07, SD=.06, $t(16)=2.17$, $p<.05$, see Figure 6]. This finding seemed to reflect a similar tendency to the High Group and the NSs, who also made frequent use of the given strategy. The Short-stay group, on the other hand, employed significantly more want statements [M=.33, SD=.26 vs. M=.12, SD=.14, $t(16)=2.21$, $p<.05$], suggesting a similar tendency to the Low Group.[7]

Second, there were differences between the two groups in terms of use of request realization strategies in relation to contextual variables. The Long-stay group used more imperative requests in equal power scenarios than in scenarios where S had a lower status than H [$\chi2(4, N=176)=20.7$, $p<.05$]. However, the

Short-stay group did not seem to be affected by this contextual variation [$\chi2(2, N=95)=2.44$, $p>.05$, *n.s.*]. Again, the Long-stay group was found to behave in a similar way to the native speakers (see Vu, 1997, 1999).

Overall, the above results might suggest a positive impact of length of residency in the TL culture on pragmatic development. Specifically, as the learners spent more time in the context where the language is spoken, they began to come closer to the NSs in their use of imperative requests. The learners who had spent less time in the TL community, on the other hand, seemed to use different pragmatic strategies from the NSs and appeared to be less responsive to contextual variables when expressing their meanings. This finding is not surprising since the SL learning context has been documented to facilitate both the contextual familiarity and the acquisition of TL pragmalinguistics (see Kasper & Rose, 2002; Schauer, 2009). The reasons are obvious: In addition to formal language learning, learners in the SL context also benefit from numerous opportunities for using the language outside the classroom. Thus, if they take full advantage of the opportunities presented to them, perhaps they can achieve a near-native level over time. This finding is also congruent with findings from the few available studies on the effects of different lengths of residency on pragmatic development in the study-abroad context (see Schauer, 2008 for a review). In these studies, nine months may be a critical period for achieving near-native pragmatic competence. Similarly, the present study suggests that a long stay of at least one year in the TL environment produces more impact on learners' pragmatic abilities than a shorter stay. This finding offers important implications regarding the planning of study-abroad programs to maximize learning opportunities for L2 learners.

Conclusion

This chapter has reported the results of a cross-sectional study of requests in Vietnamese as an L2 with a view to understanding how this speech act is learned and used by an under-researched population of learners. First, the findings show that the types of requests produced by the learners are successfully captured by the Cross-Cultural Speech Act Realization Project (CCSARP) taxonomy although slight modifications are needed to cater for the specific features of politeness in Vietnamese. The findings also support the claim of previous studies that learning L2 pragmatics is a challenging task for many learners, especially those with a lower proficiency level in the L2. For example, the low-proficiency learners tended to employ nontargetlike request strategies and were unable to vary their strategies according to different contextual cues. The learners' difficulty most likely resulted from their limited L2 linguistic competence, their incomplete L2 pragmatic knowledge, and especially their reliance on a combination of some sort of both L1 and L2 pragmatic competence in performing the given speech act.

The findings also provided some evidence of pragmatic development for both groups of learners who achieved a higher level of proficiency in Vietnamese and who stayed in the TL culture for a longer period of time, although they still experienced certain difficulties in making requests in the TL. Particularly, as the learners became more proficient in the TL and their length of residency increased, they tended to follow the NSs more closely in their use of imperative requests, a predominant strategy type in Vietnamese NS request data. They also showed more sensitivity to contextual variations and were more likely to vary their strategies accordingly. The high-proficiency learners were also able to modify their requests to a greater extent than their less proficient peers, perhaps because of both a more advanced knowledge of L2 pragmatics and a better control over attention to language processing. This latter finding has led to an argument that learning L2 pragmatics necessarily involves both the learning of new pragmatic knowledge and the development of control over this knowledge (see Bialystock, 1993).

Traditionally, L2 classrooms have placed a great emphasis on developing linguistic rather than pragmatic competence. Pragmatic components are also treated inadequately in L2 textbooks and course materials (see Nguyễn, 2011; Vellenga, 2004). Research has shown that pragmatic features, when not deliberately taught, are learned slowly (see Kasper & Rose, 2002; Rose, 2005). Therefore, pragmatic instruction is both necessary and desirable. In this chapter we have shown that learning internal modifiers for expressing respectful politeness is a daunting task for learners of Vietnamese, especially those with a lower level of proficiency and a short period of residence in the TL country. Unlike English NSs, Vietnamese NSs tend to prefer a high level of directness in making requests and rely more considerably on supportive elements with politeness effects such as alignment markers, emphasis markers, and stance markers rather than on indirectness for expressing politeness. Learners should be made aware of these politeness strategies so that they can make informed pragmatic decisions that do not break down communication and that allow learners to maintain their cultural identities.

Notes

1 We acknowledge that this rating task might prompt learners to tap into their metapragmatic knowledge when selecting pragmatic strategies; however, this choice making is not different from what people do in real-life communication.

2 Although this sentence contains both *muốn* and *nhờ*, *nhờ* is the main verb. *Muốn* in this case only functions as a politeness device, making this phrase equivalent to the English "I would like/want to ask," which Blum-Kulka & Olshtain categorized as "hedged performative."

3 Note that the Vietnamese language has the modal verb *có thể*, which denotes ability, possibility, and permission (equivalent to *can, could, may, might* in English) but this verb is only optional in ability/permission requests. Vietnamese ability/permission requests are more often expressed via the structure "*S+V … được không?*" [is it ok …?]. *Có thể* in this case only functions as a modifier.

4 Note that an utterance can be coded as a 'hint' only when it occurs alone in an exchange (not together with another strategy type). Otherwise, it would be more suitably coded as a supportive move rather than the head act.
Consider the following example produced by native speakers:
(I=interlocutor, P=Participant)

```
01 I: Mời        vào
      Invite     in
      Come in, please

02 P: Em            chào  cô                ạ.
      I (student) greet teacher (female) PolM
      Hello, teacher.

      Em            xin lỗi    em            chưa     làm
      I (student) apologize I (student) not yet do
      I'm sorry I did not do

      bài về nhà. Tuần trước em            bị   ốm.
      homework     Week last  I (student) NegM sick
      my homework. I was sick last week.

      Em            có    giấy  chứng nhận của bác sĩ
      I (student) have paper certify     of  doctor
      I have the doctor's note

      đây  cô                ạ.
      here teacher (female) PolM
      here with me.

03 I: Nhưng mà hôm nay là thứ Ba     rồi
      But       today   be Tuesday  already
      But today is already Tuesday.

      mà    thứ Sáu là phải nộp     rồi,
      StaM Friday  be must submit already
      and Friday is the due date

      nguyên tắc là phải xin trước  một tuần cơ, thế thì
      principle  be must ask before one week EmM so then
      The rule is you have to ask one week in advance

04 P: Vâng ạ     nhưng mà em            ốm     đột xuất
      Yes  PolM but        I (student) sick  suddenly
      Yes, but I was sick all of a sudden

05 I: Nhưng mà như thế là phải bị    trừ     20% điểm
      But       so       be must NegM reduce 20% mark
      But then there'll be a 20% deduction from your grad

07 P: Thế thì  cũng được ạ
      So  then EmM  okay PolM
      That'll be ok.
```

In this conversation S did not make an explicit request but only referred to her condition and the reason she did not complete her assignment. H interpreted S's utterance as a request for an extension and S did not correct H. This means H's interpretation was accurate. Thus, in this case, S's utterance is coded as a request rather than a prerequest supportive move.

5 Note that *được không* is coded as an appealer only when it is not part of the syntactic structure of the request but is an independent element that functions as an agreement seeker, such as in the example below:
(I=Interlocutor, L: Learner)

```
01 L: Chị          sẽ   giúp tôi nhiều khi  phải trả
      Elder sister will help I   much  when must return
      You will help me a lot if you return

      cuốn sách và  có thể em              giúp chị
      book      and maybe  younger sibling help elder sister
      this book and maybe I will help you

      cuối tuần này làm  sạch sẽ phòng ngủ
      weekend  this make clean   bedroom
      tidy up your bedroom this weekend

      hay là làm  nấu  món ăn
      or     make cook food
      or do the cooking

02 I: ((giggles))

03 L: Được không?
      possible no
      is that OK?
```

6 Here we are using proportions to investigate whether there are differences in the relative strategy preferences between the groups, corrected for total number of strategies.

7 Length of stay overlaps to some extent with proficiency. Therefore, the results reported in this section should be treated with caution.

References

Achiba, M. (2003). *Learning to request in a second language: Child interlanguage pragmatics*. Clevedon: Multilingual Matters.

Alcon-Soler, E. (Ed.). 2008. *Learning how to request in an instructed language learning context.* Bern: Lang.

Al-Gahtani, S., & Roever, C. (2012). Proficiency and sequential organization of L2 requests. *Applied Linguistics, 33,* 42–65.

Bardovi-Harlig, K., & Dörnyei, Z. (1998). Do language learners recognize pragmatic violations? Pragmatic versus grammatical awareness in instructed L2 learning. *TESOL Quarterly, 32,* 233–262.

Barron, A. (2003). *Acquisition in interlanguage pragmatics: Learning how to do things with words in a study abroad context.* Amsterdam: Benjamins.

Bataller, R. (2010). Making a request for a service in Spanish: Pragmatic development in the study abroad setting. *Foreign Language Annals, 43*(1), 159–174.

Béal, C. (1990). It's all in the asking: A perspective on problems of cross-cultural communication between native speakers of French and native speakers of Australian English in the workplace. *Australian Review of Applied Linguistics Series S7,* 16–32.

Béal, C. (1994). Keeping the peace: A cross-cultural comparison of questions and requests in Australian English and French. *Multilingua, 13*(1–2), 35–58.

Bialystok, E. (1993). Symbolic representation and attentional control in pragmatic competence. In G. Kasper & S. Blum-Kulka (Eds.), *Interlanguage pragmatics* (pp. 43–59). New York, NY: Oxford University Press.

Bialystok, E. (1994). Analysis and control in the development of second language proficiency. *Studies in Second Language Acquisition, 16,* 157–168.

Biesenbach-Lucas, S. (2005). Communication topics and strategies in email consultation: Comparison between American and international university students. *Language Learning & Technology, 9*(2), 24–46.

Biesenbach-Lucas, S. (2007). Students writing emails to faculty: An examination of e-politeness among native and nonnative speakers of English. *Language learning and Technology, 11*(2), 59–81.

Blitvich, P. (2006). Interlanguage pragmatics: A response to Andrew Cohen's "Strategies for learning and performing L2 speech acts" published in Vol. 2, No.3 of Intercultural Pragmatics. *Intercultural Pragmatics, 3*(2), 213–223.

Bloch, J. (2002). Student/teacher interaction via email: The social context of Internet discourse. *Journal of Second Language Writing, 11,* 117–134.

Blum-Kulka, S. (1982). Learning how to say what you mean in a second language: A study of the speech act performance of learners of Hebrew as a second language. *Applied Linguistics, 3,* 29–59.

Blum-Kulka, S. (1983). Interpreting and performing speech acts in a second language: A cross-cultural study of Hebrew and English. In N. Wolfson & E. Judd (Eds.), *Sociolinguistics and language acquisition* (pp. 36–55). Rowley, MA: Newbury House.

Blum-Kulka, S. (1987). Indirectness and politeness in requests: Same or different? *Journal of Pragmatics, 11,* 131–146.

Blum-Kulka, S. (1989). Playing it safe: The role of conventionality in indirectness. In S. Blum-Kulka, J. House, & G. Kasper (Eds.), *Cross-cultural pragmatics: Requests and apologies* (pp. 37–70). Norwood, NJ: Ablex.

Blum-Kulka, S., & Olshtain, E. (1984). Requests and apologies: A cross-cultural study of speech act realisation patterns (CCSARP). *Applied Linguistics, 5,* 196–213.

Blum-Kulka, S., & Olshtain, E. (1986). Too many words: Length of utterance and pragmatic failure. *Journal of Pragmatics, 8,* 47–61.

Blum-Kulka, S., House, J., & Kasper, G. (1989). *Cross-cultural pragmatics: Requests and apologies*. Norwood, NJ: Ablex.

Bonikowska, M. (1988). The choice of opting out. *Applied Linguistics, 9,* 169–181.

Brown, P., & Levinson, S. (1987). *Politeness: Some universals in language usage*. Cambridge: Cambridge University Press.

Byon, A. (2004). Sociopragmatic analysis of Korean requests: Pedagogical settings. *Journal of Pragmatics, 36*(9), 1673–1704.

Byon, A. (2006). The role of linguistic indirectness and honorifics in achieving linguistic politeness in Korean requests. *Journal of Politeness Research, 2*(2), 247–276.

Chen, C. (2006). The development of e-mail literacy: From writing to peers to writing to authority figures. *Language Learning & Technology, 10*(2), 35–55.

Cohen, A., & Shively, R. (2007). Acquisition of requests and apologies in Spanish and French: Impact of study abroad and strategy-building intervention. *The Modern Language Journal, 91*(2), 189–212.

Cook, V. (2001). *Second language learning and teaching*. London: Arnold.

Cook, H.M. (2001). Why can't learners of Japanese as a foreign language distinguish polite from impolite speech styles? In K.R. Rose & G. Kasper (Eds.), *Pragmatics in language teaching* (pp. 80–102). Cambridge: Cambridge University Press.

DuFon, M.A. (1999). The acquisition of linguistic politeness in Indonesian as a second language by sojourners in a naturalistic context. *Dissertation Abstracts International, 60,* 3985.

Ellis, R. (1992). Learning to communicate in the language classroom: A study of two learners' requests. *Studies in Second Language Acquisition, 14,* 1–23.

Ervin-Tripp, S., Lampert, M., & Bell, N. (1987). Understanding requests. *Linguistics, 25,* 107–143.

Færch, C., & Kasper, G. (1989). Internal and external modification in interlanguage request realisation. In S. Blum-Kulka, J. House, & G. Kasper (Eds), *Cross-cultural pragmatics: Requests and apologies* (pp. 221–247). Norwood, NJ: Ablex.

Felix-Brasdefer, C. (2007). Pragmatic development in the Spanish as a FL classroom: A cross-sectional study of learner requests. *Intercultural Pragmatics*, *4*(2), 253–286.

Fukushima, S. (1990). Offers and requests: Performance by Japanese learners of English. *World Englishes, 9,* 317- 325.

Hartford, B.S., & Bardovi-Harlig, K. (1996). At your earliest convenience: A study of written student requests to faculty. In L.F. Bouton (Ed.), *Pragmatics and language learning* (Vol.7, pp. 55–71). Urbana-Champaign: University of Illinois, Division of English as an International Language.

Hassall, T. (1999). Request strategies in Indonesian. *Pragmatics, 9*(4), 585–606.

Hassall, T. (2001). Modifying requests in a second language. *International Review of Applied Linguistics in Language Teaching, 39,* 259–283.

Hassall, Y. (2003). Requests by Australian learners of Indonesian. *Journal of Pragmatics, 35,* 1903–1928.

Hendriks, B. (2008). Dutch English requests: A study of request performance by Dutch learners of English. In M. Puetz & J. Neff van Aertselaer (Eds.), *Developing contrastive pragmatics: Interlanguage and cross-cultural perspectives* (pp. 335–354). Berlin: Mouton de Gruyter.

Hill, T. (1997). *The development of pragmatic competence in an EFL context.* (Unpublished doctoral dissertation). Temple University, Tokyo, Japan.

House, J., & Kasper, G. (1987). Interlanguage pragmatics: Requesting in a foreign language. In W. Lörscher & R. Schulze (Eds.), *Perspectives on language in performance* (pp. 1250–1288). Tübingen: Narr.

Ishihara, N., & Tarone, E. (2009). Subjectivity and pragmatic choice in L2 Japanese: Emulating and resisting pragmatic norms. In N. Taguchi (Ed.), *Pragmatic competence in Japanese as a second language* (pp. 101–128). Berlin: Mouton de Gruyter.

Kasper, G. (1981). *Pragmatische aspekte in der interimsprache [Pragmatic aspects in interlanguage].* Tübingen: Narr.

Kasper, G. (1990). Linguistic politeness: Current research issues. *Journal of Pragmatics, 14*(2), 193 – 218.

Kasper, G. (1992). Pragmatic transfer. *Second Language Research, 8*(3), 203–231.

Kasper, G. (1996). Introduction: Interlanguage pragmatics in SLA. *Studies in Second Language Acquisition, 18,* 145–148.

Kasper, G. (2008). Data collection in pragmatic research. In H. Spencer-Oatey (Ed.), *Culturally Speaking: Culture, Communication and Politeness Theory* (2nd revised edition, pp. 279–303). New York, NY: Continuum.

Kasper, G. (2009). L2 pragmatic development. In W. Ritchie & T. Bhatia (Eds.), *The new handbook of language acquisition* (2nd revised edition, pp. 259–293). Bingley: Emerald Group.

Kasper, G., & Rose, K. (2002). *Pragmatic development in a second language.* Oxford: Blackwell.

Kecskés, I., & Papp, T. (2000). *Foreign language and mother tongue.* Mahwah, NJ: Erlbaum.

Kitao, K. (1990). A study of Japanese and American perceptions of politeness in requests. *Doshida Studies in English, 50,* 178–210.

Kobayashi, H., & Rinnert, C. (2003). Coping with high imposition requests: High vs. low proficiency EFL students in Japan. In A. Martínez-Flor, E. Usó-Juan, & A. Fernández (Eds.), *Pragmatic competence in foreign language teaching* (pp. 161–184). Castelló de la Plana: Servei de Publicacions de la Universitat Jaume I.

Koike, D.A. (1989). Pragmatic competence and adult L2 acquisition: Speech acts in interlanguage. *The Modern Language Journal, 73,* 279–289.

Kubota, M. (1996). Acquaintance or fiancee: Pragmatic differences in requests between Japanese and Americans. *Working Papers in Educational Linguistics, 12*(1), 23–38.

le Pair, R. (1996). Spanish request strategies: A cross-cultural analysis from an intercultural perspective. *Language Sciences, 18*(3–4), 651–570.

le Pair, R. (2005). Politeness in the Netherlands: Indirect requests. In L. Hickey & M. Stewart (Eds.), *Politeness in Europe* (pp. 66–81). Clevedon: Multilingual Matters.

Lee-Wong, S. (1994). Imperatives in requests: Direct or impolite – Observations from Chinese. *Pragmatics, 4*(4), 491–515.

Nakahama, Y. (1998). Requests in L1/L2 Japanese and American English: A cross-cultural investigation of politeness. In L.F. Bouton (Ed.), *Pragmatics and language learning,* (Vol. 9, pp. 1–29). Urbana-Champaign: University of Illinois, Division of English as an International Language.

Nguyễn Thị Thủy Minh (2008a). Modifying L2 criticisms: How learners do it? *Journal of Pragmatics, 40*(4), 768–791.

Nguyễn Thị Thủy Minh (2008b). Criticizing in an L2: Pragmatic strategies used by Vietnamese EFL learners. *Intercultural Pragmatics, 5*(1), 41–66.

Nguyen, Thị Thủy Minh (2011). Learning to communicate in a globalized world: To what extent do school textbooks facilitate the development of intercultural pragmatic competence? *RELC Journal, 42*(1), 17–30.

Niezgoda, K., & Roever, C. (2001). Pragmatic and grammatical awareness: A function of the learning environment? In K. Rose & G. Kasper (Eds.), *Pragmatics in language teaching* (pp.63–79). Cambridge: Cambridge University Press.

Niki, H., & Tajika, H. (1994). Asking for permission vs. making requests: Strategies chosen by Japanese speakers of English. In L.F. Bouton & Y. Kachru (Eds.), *Pragmatics and language learning* (Vol. 5, pp. 110–124). Urbana-Champaign: University of Illinois, Division of English as an International Language.

Okada, Y. (2010). Role play in oral proficiency interviews: Interactive footing and interactional competencies. *Journal of Pragmatics, 42,* 1647–68.

Otcu, B., & Zeyrek, D. (2006). Requesting in L2: Pragmatic development of Turkish learners of English. In *LAUD Series A: General & Theoretical Papers, LAUD 2006.* Essen: Universitat Duisburg-Essen.

Otcu, B., & Zeyrek, D. (2008). Development of requests: A study on Turkish learners of English. In M. Puetz & J. Neff van Aertselaer (Eds.), *Developing contrastive pragmatics: Interlanguage and crosscultural perspectives* (pp. 265–300). Berlin: Mouton de Gruyter.

Owen, J.S. (2001). *Interlanguage pragmatics in Russian: A study of the effects of study abroad and proficiency levels on request strategies.* (Unpublished doctoral dissertation). Bryn Mawr College, Bryn Mawr, PA.

Pinto, D. (2002). Perdóname, ¿llevas mucho esperando? *Conventionalized language in L1 and L2 Spanish.* (Unpublished doctoral dissertation). University of California, Davis.

Rintell, E. (1981). Sociolinguistic variation and pragmatic ability: A look at learners. *International Journal of Sociology and Language, 27,* 11–34.

Rose, K., & Kasper, G. (Eds.). (2001). *Pragmatics in language teaching.* New York, NY: Cambridge University Press.

Rose, K. (2000). An exploratory cross-sectional study of interlanguage pragmatic development. *Studies in Second Language Acquisition, 22*(1), 27–67.

Roever, C. (2001). A web-based test of interlanguage pragmalinguistic knowledge: Speech acts, routines, implicatures. *Dissertation Abstracts International, 62,* 2095.

Rue, J., & Zhang, G. (2008). *Request strategies: A comparative study in Mandarin Chinese and Korean.* Amsterdam: Benjamins.

Scarcella, R. (1979). On speaking politely in a second language. In C.A. Yorio, K. Perkins, & J. Schachter (Eds.), *On TESOL'79* (pp. 275–287). Washington DC: TESOL.

Schauer, G.A. (2007). Finding the right words in the study abroad context: The development of German learners' use of external modifiers in English. *Intercultural Pragmatics, 4*(2), 193–220.

Schauer, G.A. (2008). Getting better in getting what you want: Language learners' pragmatic development in requests during study abroad sojourns. In M. Puetz & J. Neff van Aertselaer (Eds.), *Developing contrastive pragmatics: Interlanguage and cross-cultural perspectives* (pp. 399–426). Berlin: Mouton de Gruyter.

Schauer, G.A. (2009). *Interlanguage pragmatic development: The study abroad context.* London: Continuum.

Schmidt, R. (1983). Interaction, acculturation, and the acquisition of communicative competence: A case study of one adult. In N. Wolfson & E. Judd (Eds.), *Sociolinguistics and language acquisition* (pp.137–174). Rowley, MA: Newbury House.

Schmidt, R. (1993). Consciousness, learning, and interlanguage pragmatics. In G. Kasper & S. Blum-Kulka (Eds.), *Interlanguage pragmatics* (pp. 21–42). New York, NY: Oxford University Press.

Schmidt, R. (1995). Consciousness and foreign language learning: A tutorial on the role of attention and awareness in learning. In R. Schmidt (Ed.), *Attention and awareness in foreign language learning* (pp. 1–63). Honolulu: University of Hawai'i, National Foreign Language Resource Center.

Schmidt, R. (2001). Attention. In P. Robinson (Ed.), *Cognition and second language instruction* (pp. 3–32). Cambridge: Cambridge University Press.

Searle, J. (1969). *Speech acts.* Cambridge: Cambridge University Press.

Shively, R. (2011). L2 pragmatic development in study abroad: A longitudinal study of Spanish service encounters. *Journal of Pragmatics, 43*(6), 1818–1835.

Taguchi, N. (2011). Teaching pragmatics: Trends and issues. *Annual Review of Applied Linguistics, 31,* 289–310.

Takahashi, S. (1996). Pragmatic transferability. *Studies in Second Language Acquisition, 18,* 189–223.

Takahashi, T., & Beebe, L. (1987). The development of pragmatic competence by Japanese learners of English. *JALT Journal, 8,* 131–155.

Taleghani-Nikazm, C., & Huth, T. (2010). L2 requests: Preference structure in talk-in-interaction. *Multilingua, 29,* 185–202.

Tanaka, N. (1988). Politeness: Some problems for Japanese speakers of English. *JALT Journal, 9,* 81–102.

Tanaka, S., & Kawade, S. (1982). Politeness strategies in second language acquisition. *Studies in Second Language Acquisition, 5,* 18–33.

Upadhyay, S. (2003). Nepali requestive acts: Linguistic indirectness and politeness reconsidered. *Journal of Pragmatics, 35*(10–11), 1651–1677.

Ushioda, E. (2007). Motivation and language. In J. Östman, J. Verschueren, & E. Versluys (Eds), *Handbook of pragmatics.* Amsterdam: Benjamins.

Vellenga, H. (2004). Learning pragmatics from ESL & EFL textbooks: How likely? *TESL-EJ 8*(2). Retrieved from http://www-writing.berkeley.edu/TESL-EJ/ej30/a3.html

Vũ Thị Thanh Hương (1997). *Politeness in modern Vietnamese: A sociolinguistic study of a Hanoi speech community.* (Unpublished doctoral dissertation). University of Toronto, Toronto, Canada.

Vũ Thị Thanh Hương (1999). Gián tiếp và lịch sự trong lời cầu khẩn tiếng Việt [Indirectness and politeness in Vietnamese requests]. *Ngôn ngữ, 1*(112), 34–43.

Warga, M. (2003). Neigen Lernende zum 'Labern'? Eine Untersuchung zum Französischen als Lernersprache. [Do learners tend to 'waffle'? An investigation of French as a foreign language.] In H.J. Krumm & P.R. Portmann-Tselikas (Eds.), *Theorie und Praxis: Österreichische Beiträge zu Deutsch als Fremdsprache in Österreich* (pp. 227–241). Innsbruck: StudienVerlag.

Warga, M. (2004). *Pragmatische Entwicklung in der Fremdsprache. Der Sprechakt 'Aufforderung' im Französischen* [Pragmatic development in the foreign language. The speech act 'request' in French.] Tübingen: Gunter Narr Verlag.

Woodfield, H. (2008). Interlanguage requests: A contrastive study. In M. Puetz & J. Neff van Aertselaer (Eds.), *Developing contrastive pragmatics: Interlanguage and cross-cultural perspectives* (pp. 231–264). Berlin: Mouton de Gruyter.

Zhang, Y. (1995a). Strategies in Chinese requesting. In G. Kasper (Ed.), *Pragmatics of Chinese as native and target language* (pp. 23–68). Honolulu: University of Hawai'i Press.

Zhang, Y. (1995b). Indirectness in Chinese requesting. In G. Kasper (Ed.), *Pragmatics of Chinese as native and target language* (pp. 69–118). Honolulu: University of Hawai'i Press.

Appendix A: Role-play cards, Vietnamese version

Chỉ Dẫn Cho Người Tham Gia

Anh/Chị sẽ hội thoại với nghiên cứu viên trong những tình huống đóng vai sau đây. Đề nghị Anh/Chị **sử dụng tiếng Việt** khi hội thoại. Anh/Chị hãy đọc kỹ các tình huống trước khi hội thoại. Mỗi tình huống có hai câu hỏi. Anh/Chị cần trả lời hai câu hỏi này trước khi đóng vai. Hãy cố gắng tưởng tượng mình ở trong các tình huống đó và hội thoại một cách tự nhiên nhất có thể.

Điều quan trọng là Anh/Chị phải hiểu các tình huống. Vì vậy trước khi hội thoại, Anh/Chị hãy đặt câu hỏi cho nghiên cứu viên nếu như có vấn đề gì chưa hiểu.

Hội thoại đóng vai của Anh/Chị sẽ được thu âm với sự đồng thuận của Anh/Chị. Cảm ơn Anh/Chị đã giúp đỡ.

Tình huống 1:

Anh/Chị đang viết ba trang bài luận cho giáo viên. Hôm nay là hạn nộp. Anh/Chị vừa viết xong đoạn đầu tiên thì bỗng nhiên máy tính của Anh/Chị bị hỏng. Anh/Chị thấy người bạn cùng nhà đang dùng máy tính để nói chuyện trực tuyến với một ai đó. Hai người là bạn tốt của nhau. Vì vậy **Anh/Chị hỏi mượn máy tính để viết nốt bài. Anh/Chị cần thuyết phục được người bạn cùng nhà đồng ý cho mượn máy.**

Câu hỏi 1: Anh/Chị có hình dung được ra tình huống này không?

Hãy khoanh tròn con số phù hợp nhất với câu trả lời của Anh/Chị.

1	2	3	4	5
Hoàn toàn KHÔNG				Hoàn toàn CÓ

Câu hỏi 2: Anh/Chị nghĩ lời đề nghị của mình có gây áp lực cho người nghe không?

Hãy khoanh tròn con số phù hợp nhất với câu trả lời của Anh/Chị.

1	2	3	4	5
Hoàn toàn không				Rất gây áp lực

Hãy bắt đầu hội thoại đóng vai bằng tiếng Việt. Nghiên cứu viên sẽ đóng vai người bạn cùng nhà của Anh/Chị.

Tình huống 2:

Tuần trước Anh/Chị bị ốm và bỏ mất một buổi học quan trọng. Bây giờ Anh/Chị đang đọc lại giáo trình nhưng không hiểu lắm. Một người bạn của Anh/Chị có đi học hôm đó và ghi chép bài đầy đủ. Hai người là bạn tốt của nhau. Vì vậy Anh/Chị tin rằng người bạn đó sẽ không ngần ngại cho Anh/Chị mượn vở. Anh/Chị gặp người bạn đó và hỏi mượn vở. **Anh/Chị cần thuyết phục được người bạn đó cho mượn vở.**

Câu hỏi 1: Anh/Chị có hình dung được ra tình huống này không?

Hãy khoanh tròn con số phù hợp nhất với câu trả lời của Anh/Chị.

1	2	3	4	5
Hoàn toàn KHÔNG				Hoàn toàn CÓ

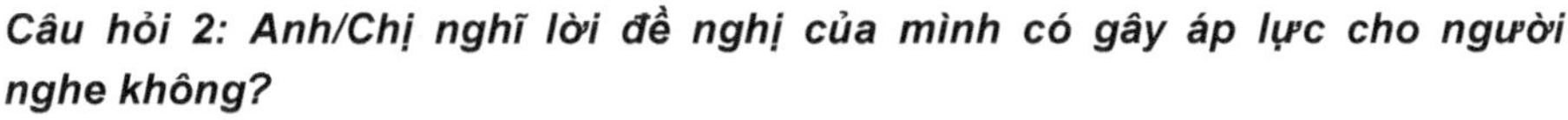

Câu hỏi 2: Anh/Chị nghĩ lời đề nghị của mình có gây áp lực cho người nghe không?

Hãy khoanh tròn con số phù hợp nhất với câu trả lời của Anh/Chị.

1 2 3 4 5

Hoàn toàn không — Rất gây áp lực

Hãy bắt đầu hội thoại đóng vai bằng tiếng Việt. Nghiên cứu viên sẽ đóng vai người bạn cùng nhà của Anh/Chị.

Tình huống 3:

Anh/Chị phải trả thư viện một cuốn sách trong ngày hôm nay. Đêm hôm qua Anh/Chị mới dùng xong. Anh/Chị chỉ đến trường những hôm có giờ học vì Anh/Chị sống tương đối xa. Hôm nay Anh/Chị không có giờ. Người bạn cùng nhà của Anh/Chị có lớp sáng nay, vì vậy **Anh/Chị nhờ người bạn đó trả hộ cuốn sách. Anh/Chị cần thuyết phục được người bạn đó giúp đỡ.** Hai người là bạn tốt của nhau.

Câu hỏi 1: Anh/Chị có hình dung được ra tình huống này không?

Hãy khoanh tròn con số phù hợp nhất với câu trả lời của Anh/Chị.

1 2 3 4 5

Hoàn toàn KHÔNG — Hoàn toàn CÓ

Câu hỏi 2: Anh/Chị nghĩ lời đề nghị của mình có gây áp lực cho người nghe không?

Hãy khoanh tròn con số phù hợp nhất với câu trả lời của Anh/Chị.

1 2 3 4 5

Hoàn toàn không — Rất gây áp lực

Hãy bắt đầu hội thoại đóng vai bằng tiếng Việt. Nghiên cứu viên sẽ đóng vai người bạn cùng nhà của Anh/Chị.

Tình huống 4:

Anh/Chị mới biết thông tin về một học bổng và muốn nộp đơn xin học bổng đó. Anh/Chị cần gấp thư giới thiệu của thầy/cô giáo vì vài ngày nữa là hết hạn nộp đơn. Anh/Chị có một cô giáo đã dạy Anh/Chị một vài học kỳ và Anh/Chị luôn là một trong những sinh viên giỏi nhất trong lớp. Cô giáo của Anh/Chị rất bận nhưng Anh/Chị tin rằng cô giáo sẽ ủng hộ Anh/Chị. Sau giờ học Anh/Chị đến gặp cô giáo và nhờ cô viết hộ thư giới thiệu. **Anh/Chị rất muốn có được học bổng đó nên Anh/Chị cần thuyết phục được cô giáo giúp đỡ.**

Câu hỏi 1: Anh/Chị có hình dung được ra tình huống này không?

Hãy khoanh tròn con số phù hợp nhất với câu trả lời của Anh/Chị.

1 2 3 4 5

Hoàn toàn KHÔNG — Hoàn toàn CÓ

Câu hỏi 2: Anh/Chị nghĩ lời đề nghị của mình có gây áp lực cho người nghe không?

Hãy khoanh tròn con số phù hợp nhất với câu trả lời của Anh/Chị.

1 2 3 4 5

Hoàn toàn không — Rất gây áp lực

Hãy bắt đầu hội thoại đóng vai bằng tiếng Việt. Nghiên cứu viên sẽ đóng vai người bạn cùng nhà của Anh/Chị.

Tình huống 5:

Anh/Chị đang viết luận văn. Hôm nay Anh/Chị có hẹn với cô giáo hướng dẫn để nộp một chương luận văn. Tuy nhiên, tuần trước Anh/Chị bị ốm nên chưa viết xong. Anh/Chị cần thêm thời gian. Hôm nay khi gặp cô giáo hướng dẫn Anh/Chị xin cô gia hạn thêm một thời gian. Anh/Chị muốn cô đọc và góp ý càng sớm càng tốt nên sẽ cố gắng hoàn thành sớm. **Anh/Chị cần thuyết phục được cô giáo cho thêm thời gian để viết.**

Câu hỏi 1: Anh/Chị có hình dung được ra tình huống này không?

Hãy khoanh tròn con số phù hợp nhất với câu trả lời của Anh/Chị.

1 2 3 4 5

Hoàn toàn KHÔNG Hoàn toàn CÓ

Câu hỏi 2: Anh/Chị nghĩ lời đề nghị của mình có gây áp lực cho người nghe không?

Hãy khoanh tròn con số phù hợp nhất với câu trả lời của Anh/Chị.

1 2 3 4 5

Hoàn toàn không Rất gây áp lực

Hãy bắt đầu hội thoại đóng vai bằng tiếng Việt. Nghiên cứu viên sẽ đóng vai người bạn cùng nhà của Anh/Chị.

Tình huống 6:

Hôm nay là thứ Hai. Anh/Chị có hẹn với cô giáo hướng dẫn vào 10 rưỡi sáng thứ Sáu tuần này. Anh/Chị muốn nộp luận văn đã sửa lại cho cô giáo xem. Nhưng hôm nay một giáo viên khác thông báo muốn dạy bù cho buổi học bị nghỉ tuần trước. Không may là phần lớn sinh viên trong lớp lại chọn học vào buổi 10h-12h sáng thứ Sáu tuần này. Anh/Chị không muốn bỏ buổi học này vì chủ đề lần này rất khó và quan trọng. Vì vậy Anh/Chị gặp cô giáo hướng dẫn và nhờ cô chuyển buổi hẹn sang ngày khác. **Anh/Chị cần thuyết phục được cô giáo cho gặp sớm** vì Anh/Chị phải nộp luận văn trong vòng vài tuần nữa.

Câu hỏi 1: Anh/Chị có hình dung được ra tình huống này không?

Hãy khoanh tròn con số phù hợp nhất với câu trả lời của Anh/Chị.

1 2 3 4 5

Hoàn toàn KHÔNG Hoàn toàn CÓ

Câu hỏi 2: Anh/Chị nghĩ lời đề nghị của mình có gây áp lực cho người nghe không?

Hãy khoanh tròn con số phù hợp nhất với câu trả lời của Anh/Chị.

1 2 3 4 5

Hoàn toàn không Rất gây áp lực

Hãy bắt đầu hội thoại đóng vai bằng tiếng Việt. Nghiên cứu viên sẽ đóng vai người bạn cùng nhà của Anh/Chị.

Chỉ Dẫn Cho Người Dẫn Dắt Vai

Anh/Chị sẽ hội thoại **bằng tiếng Việt** với mỗi học viên trong những tình huống đóng vai sau đây. Anh/Chị hãy đọc kỹ các tình huống trước khi hội thoại. Điều quan trọng là Anh/Chị phải hiểu các tình huống. Vì vậy trước khi hội thoại, Anh/Chị hãy đặt câu hỏi cho nghiên cứu viên nếu như có vấn đề gì chưa hiểu.

Hội thoại đóng vai của Anh/Chị sẽ được thu âm với sự đồng thuận của Anh/Chị. Cảm ơn Anh/Chị đã giúp đỡ.

Tình huống 1:

Bạn cùng phòng với Anh/Chị đang viết bài luận cho giáo viên. Bỗng nhiên máy tính của cô ấy/anh ấy bị hỏng và cô ấy/anh ấy đề nghị được mượn máy tính của Anh/Chị. Anh/Chị đang chat trực tuyến với người yêu đang sống ở thành phố khác. Hôm nay là sinh nhật của anh ấy/cô ấy. Nhưng nếu bạn cùng phòng cần máy tính gấp và nếu cô ấy/anh ấy không giữ máy đến một tiếng đồng hồ, Anh/Chị sẵn lòng cho mượn. Hai người là bạn tốt của nhau.

Tình huống 2:

Tuần trước bạn cùng lớp của Anh/Chị bị ốm và bỏ lỡ một buổi học quan trọng. Anh/Chị đi học và ghi chép đầy đủ. Cô ấy/anh ấy muốn mượn vở ghi chép của Anh/Chị. Anh/Chị đang làm bài tập nên cần đến những ghi chép này. Tuy nhiên, nếu cô ấy/anh ấy có thể phô-tô-cóp-pi nhanh và trả lại Anh/Chị trong vòng một giờ, Anh/Chị sẵn lòng cho cô ấy/anh ấy mượn vở. Hai người là bạn tốt của nhau.

Tình huống 3:

Bạn cùng phòng với Anh/Chị phải trả một cuốn sách cho thư viện. Hôm nay Anh/Chị sẽ đến trường. Vì vậy cô ấy/anh ấy đề nghị Anh/Chị trả hộ cuốn sách. Anh/Chị có lớp từ 9 đến 12h trưa ở tòa nhà cách xa thư viện. Sau đó Anh/Chị phải đi làm bán thời gian ở nơi khác. Giờ làm của Anh/Chị bắt đầu lúc 12:30 trưa, do đó Anh/Chị sẽ rất vội. Nhưng nếu cuốn sách đến hạn phải trả hôm nay thì Anh/Chị có thể đi học sớm hơn và trả hộ cuốn sách trước khi vào học.

Tình huống 4:

Anh/Chị là giảng viên đại học. Một sinh viên trong lớp Anh/Chị muốn nộp đơn xin học bổng và nhờ Anh/Chị viết thư giới thiệu. Anh/Chị đã dạy người sinh viên này vài học kì và em ấy luôn là một trong những sinh viên giỏi nhất trong lớp. Anh/Chị sẵn lòng giúp đỡ nhưng Anh/Chị đang có một vài việc phải hoàn thành gấp. Vì thế nếu em ấy không vội, tuần sau Anh/Chị sẽ viết thư.

Tình huống 5:

Anh/Chị là giảng viên đại học và đang hướng dẫn luận văn cho một sinh viên. Anh/Chị hẹn em ấy nộp một chương hôm nay. Tuy nhiên em ấy bị ốm và không thể hoàn thành được chương phải nộp. Em ấy muốn xin gia hạn ngày nộp. Anh/Chị có thể cho em ấy thêm thời gian. Tuy nhiên, hai tuần nữa Anh/Chị sẽ đi công tác. Nếu em ấy có thể nộp trong tuần này, Anh/Chị mới có thời gian để đọc và góp ý trước khi đi công tác. Nếu không, Anh/Chị sẽ cần nhiều thời gian hơn vì có những việc bận khác.

Tình huống 6:

Anh/Chị là giảng viên đại học. Anh/Chị hẹn gặp sinh viên lúc 10:30 sáng thứ Sáu tuần này để thảo luận bản sửa luận văn của em ấy. Anh/Chị là người hướng dẫn luận văn này. Tuy nhiên, hôm nay em ấy ghé qua văn phòng của Anh/Chị và xin phép chuyển buổi hẹn sang ngày khác hoặc giờ khác vì em ấy có buổi học khẩn cấp. Anh/Chị bận từ nay đến hai tuần nữa, nhưng nếu em ấy có thể đến gặp sau giờ làm việc, Anh/Chị có thể thu xếp để gặp.

Appendix B: Role-play cards, English translation

Instruction Sheet For Participants

You will talk with the researcher in the following role-play situations. **Use Vietnamese when you talk.** Take some minutes to read the descriptions of the situations. There are two questions for each situation that you need to answer before role-playing. Try to imagine yourself in the situations and respond to them as you would do in real life.

It is important that you understand these situations completely, so before you start you are encouraged to ask questions if you find something you do not understand.

Your role-play conversations will be tape-recorded with your consent. Thank you for your cooperation.

Situation 1:

You are typing up a three-page essay for your lecturer. It is due today. You have just finished the first paragraph when suddenly, your computer stops working. You see your flatmate chatting online at the moment. You two are good friends. So you ask her to lend you her computer so that you can finish your work. **It is important that you get her to agree to lend you the computer.**

Question 1: Can you imagine yourself in this situation?

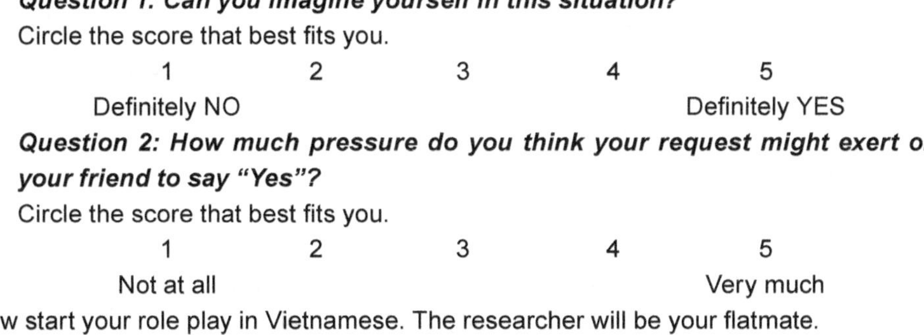

Circle the score that best fits you.

1 2 3 4 5

Definitely NO Definitely YES

Question 2: How much pressure do you think your request might exert on your friend to say "Yes"?

Circle the score that best fits you.

1 2 3 4 5

Not at all Very much

Now start your role play in Vietnamese. The researcher will be your flatmate.

Situation 2:

You were sick and missed an important class last week. Now you are reading the class materials but it is difficult to understand them by yourself. Luckily, your friend attended the class and took careful notes. You two are good friends so you believe she would not mind lending you her notes. You approach your friend and ask for the favour. **It is important that you get her to agree to lend you the notes.**

Question 1: Can you imagine yourself in this situation?

Circle the score that best fits you.

1 2 3 4 5

Definitely NO Definitely YES

Question 2: How much pressure do you think your request might exert on your friend to say "Yes"?

Circle the score that best fits you.

1	2	3	4	5
Not at all				Very much

Now start your role play in Vietnamese. The researcher will be your friend.

Situation 3:

You have to return a book to the library by today. You were still using it until last night. You go to school only on the day you have a class because you live quite far. Today you do not have a class. Your flatmate is having a class this morning, so you ask her to drop the book for you. **It is important that you get her to agree to help you.** You two are good friends.

Question 1: Can you imagine yourself in this situation?

Circle the score that best fits you.

1	2	3	4	5
Definitely NO				Definitely YES

Question 2: How much pressure do you think your request might exert on your friend to say "Yes"?

Circle the score that best fits you.

1	2	3	4	5
Not at all				Very much

Now start your role play in Vietnamese. The researcher will be your flatmate.

Situation 4:

You have just learned about a scholarship, which you would like to apply for. You need a reference letter from your lecturer urgently because the application closes in a few days' time. There is a lecturer who has been teaching you for quite a few semesters and you have always been one of the best students in her class. You know she is very busy but believe she would be supportive enough to write you a reference letter. So after class you approach her and ask for the favour. You really want the scholarship so **it is important that you get her to agree to help you.**

Question 1: Can you imagine yourself in this situation?

Circle the score that best fits you.

1	2	3	4	5
Definitely NO				Definitely YES

Question 2: How much pressure do you think your request might exert on the lecturer to say "Yes"?

Circle the score that best fits you.

1	2	3	4	5
Not at all				Very much

Now start your role play in Vietnamese. The researcher will be the lecturer.

Situation 5:

You are writing your thesis. You are having a meeting with your supervisor today and you are supposed to give her a chapter draft. However, last week you were sick and not able to complete the chapter. You would need some more time. At the meeting you ask your supervisor for an extension. You want to have her feedback as soon as possible so you will try to finish the chapter in the soonest time possible. **It is important that you get her to agree to give you the extension.**

Question 1: Can you imagine yourself in this situation?

Circle the score that best fits you.

1	2	3	4	5
Definitely NO				Definitely YES

Question 2: How much pressure do you think your request might exert on your supervisor to say "Yes"?

Circle the score that best fits you.

1	2	3	4	5
Not at all				Very much

Now start your role play in Vietnamese. The researcher will be your supervisor.

Situation 6:

Today is Monday. You have an appointment with your supervisor at 10:30 a.m. Friday this week. You want to show her your revised thesis. However, another lecturer wants to make up for his missed class last week and unluckily, 10–12 a.m. this Friday is the only time slot that is suited to most students in the class. You do not want to miss this class because it is going to cover a difficult and important topic. So you drop in your supervisor's office and ask if she can move the appointment to another date or time. **It is important that you get your supervisor to agree to see you as soon as she can** because the deadline for submission of your thesis is coming in a few weeks' time.

Question 1: Can you imagine yourself in this situation?

Circle the score that best fits you.

1	2	3	4	5
Definitely NO				Definitely YES

Question 2: How much pressure do you think your request might exert on your supervisor to say "Yes"?

Circle the score that best fits you.

1	2	3	4	5
Not at all				Very much

Now start your role play in Vietnamese. The researcher will be your supervisor.

Instruction Sheet For Interlocutor

You will converse **in Vietnamese** with each student in six role-play situations, which are described in each card. Read the descriptions of the situations carefully and act accordingly.

It is important that you understand the situations completely; therefore, you are encouraged to ask questions if you find something you do not understand.
Your conversations with the students will be tape-recorded with your consent for the purpose of the study.
Thank you for your cooperation.

Situation 1:

Your flatmate is typing a three-page essay for her/his lecturer. Suddenly her/his computer stops working and s/he asks you to lend her/him your computer. You are chatting online with your boyfriend, who is in another town at the moment. Today is your boyfriend's birthday. But if it is urgent and your friend is not going to use the computer for an hour, you are willing to lend it to her/him. You two are good friends.

Situation 2:

Your friend was sick and missed an important class last week. You attended the class and took careful notes. So s/he approaches you and asks if you mind lending her/him your notes. You are working on your assignments right now and need the notes at hand. However, if s/he can make a quick photocopy and give you back within an hour, you are willing to lend her/him the notes. You two are good friends.

Situation 3:

Your flatmate has a book to return to the library. You are going to school today. So your flatmate asks you to drop the book for her. You are having a class from 9am to 12pm in a building quite far from the library. After that you have a part-time job on another campus. Your job starts at 12:30pm, so you will be in a hurry. But if the book is due today, you can go to school some minutes earlier and drop off the book for your flatmate first thing in the morning.

Situation 4:

You are a university lecturer. A student in your class is applying for a scholarship and wants you to write her/him a reference letter. You have been teaching this student for quite a few semesters and know s/he is one of your best students. You would be happy to write her/him a reference letter but you have some deadlines at the moment. So if it is not urgent, you will write it next week.

Situation 5:

You are a university lecturer and supervising a student's thesis. The student that you are supervising is supposed to submit a chapter draft to you when you two have a meeting today. However, s/he was sick and not able to complete it. At the meeting s/he asks for an extension. You can give her/him as much time as s/he needs. However, you are taking a sabbatical leave in two weeks' time. If s/he can give you the chapter within the next week, you can read it and give your comments before you go. If not, it may take a longer while for you to get back to her/him because you have other commitments.

Situation 6:

You are a university lecturer. You have an appointment with your student at 10:30 a.m. Friday this week. S/he wants to show you her/his revised thesis. You are her/his supervisor. However, today s/he drops in your office and asks if you can move the appointment to another date or time because s/he has an urgent class. You are fully booked until two weeks after but if the student can come after your office hour tomorrow, you are willing to see her/him then.

2 Apologizing in Vietnamese as a Native and a Target Language

Lê Gia Anh Hồ
National University of Singapore

Introduction

For maintaining social harmony, apologies are perhaps among the most important speech acts in any culture (Robinson, 2004). Indeed, this type of speech act has sparked a great deal of interest among pragmatics researchers and has been the second most studied speech act, after requests (Jung, 2004; Kasper, 2008; Maeshiba, Yoshinaga, Kasper, & Ross, 1996). Most studies to date have investigated apologies in a number of European languages (Bergman & Kasper, 1993; Clyne, Fernandez, & Muhr, 2003) with much emphasis on English as a native and a target language (Bataineh & Bataineh, 2006; Chang, 2010; Jung, 2004; Kondo, 2010; Robinson, 2004, to name just a few). A growing body of research on Asian cross-cultural apologies focuses on languages such as Japanese (Barnlund & Yoshioka, 1990; Long, 2010; Tanaka, Spencer-Oatey, & Cray, 2008; Wagatsuma & Rosette, 1986), Korean (Hatfield & Hahn, 2011; Kim, 2008; Lee & Park, 2011), or Mandarin Chinese (Chang & Haugh, 2011). Other Asian languages are as yet under-represented in the literature.

The present study is an endeavor to investigate a relatively unexplored aspect of apologies in Vietnamese, a much under-studied language. More specifically, this study aims at documenting an inventory of apology strategies in Vietnamese as a native and a target language as well as examining the effects of

Pragmatics of Vietnamese as a native and target language, pp. 77–110
Carsten Roever & Hạnh thị Nguyễn (Eds.), 2013
Honolulu, HI: University of Hawai'i, National Foreign Language Resource Center

two social variables—social distance and power—on the apology performance of native speakers and learners of this language.

Apology strategies and the acquisition of apologies

Apology strategies

Fraser (1981) was probably the first researcher to propose some specific apology strategies. Based on Fraser's categorization of nine strategies, Olshtain and Cohen (1983) developed an apology speech-act set that consists of a number of semantic formulas, and Trosborg (1986) classified apology strategies into seven types, ordered by their degrees of directness. A more recent classification was proposed by Bergman and Kasper (1993), which was later modified by Trosborg (1995) to include five apology strategies and three strategies for remedial support: *Illocutionary force indicating device (IFID), Acknowledgement of responsibility, Explanation or account, Distracting from the offense, Deflecting blame, Expressing concern for the hearer, Promise of forbearance,* and *Repair.* Trosborg's classification will be used in the present study and is discussed in detail in the section on coding below.

Although there has been mounting evidence from the literature to support the existence of a universal apology speech-act set, it should be noted that sequential organization of apologies (Robinson, 2004), evaluation of politeness of apology strategies (Chang & Haugh, 2011; Hatfield & Hahn, 2011), and illocutionary meanings of apology strategies (Kim, 2008) differ from culture to culture. Therefore, there is a need to teach the speech act of apology for a specific culture to raise learners' cross-cultural awareness (Kondo, 2010) for effective intercultural communication.

Factors influencing the selection of apology strategies

Factors influencing the selection of strategies encompass both context-internal and context-external factors (Bergman & Kasper, 1993; Holmes, 1989; Maeshiba et al., 1996; Olshtain, 1989). According to Robinson (2004), prior research has focused on how apologies are affected by variables such as degree of relational closeness, degree and type of offense, power, gender, and social status (p.292).

Among the context-internal factors, the nature of the offense (i.e., the severity of the offense) is believed to have the strongest influence on apology realization. Tanaka (1991) found that both native speakers of Japanese and Australian English increased apology intensification and formality of apologetic formulae with higher offense severity. However, it is worth bearing in mind that although the severity of the offense affects apology realization, judgments of severity vary according to culture, gender, and individual preference. In Bergman and Kasper's (1993) study, for instance, the same offenses were rated at different levels of severity by their Thai and American informants. Also, Holmes (1989) found that men and women weigh offenses differently, and Kuha (2003) found a great deal of unaccounted variance in her apology data.

With regard to context-external factors, apology performance is affected mostly by such factors as social power and social distance (Blum-Kulka, House, & Kasper, 1989; Maeshiba et al., 1996). For example, Kim (2008) found social power, especially age, and social distance to be important determining social factors in the choice of *IFID* in South Korea. The outcome of Olshtain's (1989) study indicates that the lower the offender's status, the more apologetic force is intensified. However, the results from studies by Holmes (1989), Vollmer and Olshtain (1989), and Trosborg (1995) do not support this claim. Holmes (1989) found a nonsignificant relationship between social power and apology in her New Zealand data. At the same time, Vollmer and Olshtain (1989) reported a weak correlation between social power and their informants' choice of *IFID*. Similarly, in Bergman and Kasper's (1993) study, social power did not greatly influence their American and Thai informants' selection of apology strategies.

The second context-external factor, social distance, is also an important variable in apology realization. According to Wolfson's (1989) theory of social interaction—"the Bulge"—the speech behaviors of strangers and status unequals resemble those of intimates, but differ markedly from the speech behaviors of status-equal friends and acquaintances. When analyzing data collected as part of the Cross-Cultural Speech-Act Realization Project (Blum-Kulka, et al., 1989), she found one example of a Bulge pattern in that at the two extremes of social distance, less than 40% did not use *Explanation or account*, while at the middle of the continuum this number was 70% (Wolfson, Marmor, & Jones, 1989, p. 137). However, Olshtain (1989) found a negative correlation between the use of *IFIDs* and social distance. Her Hebrew speakers used more *IFIDs* with strangers than with friends or acquaintances. Bergman and Kasper (1993) found that the closer the relationship between the offender and the offended person, the more likely the offender was to explicitly express *Acknowledgement of responsibility*. Barnlund and Yoshioka (1990) found some cultural differences in the way their Japanese and American participants apologized to people of different status in that "Japanese employed a wider variety of apologies in adapting to the status of partners while Americans tended to rely on the same narrow repertoire of apologies regardless of the status of their companions" (p.202). The influence of the nature of the relationship on Asian respondents' apologetic behavior was also observed by Wouk (2006), who reported that Lombok Indonesians used deference strategies with higher status addressees and resorted to solidarity strategies with social intimates.

In sum, it is clear that context factors do exert an influence on apology use, but this influence is only partially accounted for by social relationships.

Acquisition of apologies

A number of interlanguage pragmatics studies have examined the production of the apology speech act by learners (mostly of English) at different proficiency levels from various language backgrounds (for example, Bataineh & Bataineh, 2006; Bergman & Kasper, 1993; Chang, 2010; Cohen, Olshtain, & Rosenstein, 1986; Jung, 2004; Maeshiba et al., 1996; Rose, 2000; Trosborg, 1986, 1995; Yang, 2002). Studies on interlanguage apologies, following either longitudinal or cross-sectional design, using native speaker speech-act realization as baseline data, provide some information regarding the extent to which learners at different proficiency levels can approximate native speaker norms in apologizing.

In an early study on Hebrew and English, Cohen and Olshtain (1981) found that nonnative speakers differed from native speakers not only as a result of transfer but also because of their inadequate second language proficiency. Cohen et al. (1986) compared the apology performance of native speakers of American English and advanced Hebrew-speaking EFL learners. They did not find many differences between native speakers and learners with regard to main strategies for apologizing; however, natives and nonnatives differed markedly in various modifications of such strategies.

Trosborg (1995) investigated apology speech-act realization by Danish EFL learners at three proficiency levels. Her findings show that the three groups of Danish EFL learners could perform all the apology strategies used by English native speakers. However, there were significant differences between the learners and the native speakers in the frequency of strategies (especially in *Minimizing the degree of offense* and *Explanation or account*) as well as in the use of internal modification.

In a more recent study on interlanguage apologizing, Jung (2004) compared apology performance of advanced Korean learners of English with that of native English speakers. She found that advanced L2 learners differed from L1 speakers with regard to both pragmatic and lexico-grammatical appropriateness. She explained that some of the contributing factors to these differences were L2 learners' verbosity, L1 linguistic and pragmatic knowledge transfer, lack of awareness of appropriate L2 social norms, as well as lack of L2 linguistic forms.

In a recent study on the development of L2 apology of Chinese learners of English, Chang (2010) found a positive correlation between the L2 learners' repertoires of apology strategies and proficiency levels. The findings of this study supported the developmental patterns of L2 apologies reported in the literature.

In a review of cross-sectional interlanguage pragmatics studies, Kasper and Rose (1999) concluded that most of the studies investigating the production of speech acts found that learners have access to the same range of speech-act realization strategies as native speakers, irrespective of proficiency levels; however, they differ from native speakers in the way they implement strategies linguistically (p. 86). The results from interlanguage pragmatics studies of apologies reviewed above, to a certain extent, lend support to this claim.

Apologies in Vietnamese

Most of the limited pragmatics research studies in Vietnamese are in the tradition of cross-cultural pragmatics, which contrast the realization patterns of speech acts such as requests (T. M. T. Đỗ, 2000), compliments and compliment responses (Q. Nguyễn, 1998), and complaints (V. Nguyễn, 1999) in Vietnamese with those of other languages, particularly English. Like studies on other speech acts, apology studies in Vietnamese also follow the descriptive and contrastive pragmatics tradition. To date, there are three studies (all unpublished theses) on this speech act, by Phạm (1995), Đặng (1999), and Kiều (2000).

Phạm (1995) was the first to document the Vietnamese formulae of greeting, thanking, and apologizing. She found seven structures of apology in Vietnamese as follows: (1) Explicit expressions of apology through the verb *xin lỗi* [apologize]; (2) *Acknowledgement of responsibility*, for example, *em có lỗi với anh* [I owe you an apology]; (3) Request for the hearers' sympathy and forgiveness such as *thông cảm nhé* [please sympathize with me] or *tha lỗi cho anh nhé* [please forgive me]; (4) Expression of regret such as *tiếc qúa* [it's a pity], *mình rất tiếc là mình không giúp gì được* [I regret not being able to help you]; (5) Complaints (i.e., The speaker complains about his or her doing which causes trouble for the hearer) for example, *em làm phiền anh quá!* [I have caused you so much trouble!]; (6) Explanation or account; and (7) Formulaic expressions such as *nói anh đừng giận* [don't be upset with me but ...], or the formulaic expressions *nói vô phép* [this may be impolite to say but...], or *hỏi khí không phải* [this may not be appropriate but may I ask...]. However, the validity of Phạm's data is potentially questionable as she collected data for her study from two sources: The first was written conversations in novels, short stories, magazines, newspapers, and Vietnamese textbooks; the second was oral conversations in movies, dramas, and short plays recorded from television, and everyday conversation (Phạm, 1995). Although she claimed to have some data recorded from everyday conversation, the majority of her data was still from literary works; therefore, it is doubtful how representative her data are of conversational practices in authentic contexts.

Unlike Phạm's (1995) purely descriptive study, Đặng (1999) had a cross-cultural pragmatic focus. In his study, Đặng compared the similarities and differences between English and Vietnamese apologies and apology responses. Survey questionnaires with three different situations were employed as the data collection method. The findings from this study showed that there were differences in Vietnamese and English in terms of levels of directness in both informal and formal settings. In addition, it was found that English speakers used more lexico-modal markers such as intensifiers, downtoners, and hedges than their Vietnamese counterparts. This study is quite significant in being the first to examine cross-cultural differences between Vietnamese and English in the realization of apology strategies. Furthermore, the study was the first to look at responses to apologies in Vietnamese. A shortcoming of the study was that Đặng (1999) only examined apology strategies in terms of directness and indirectness.

Another cross-cultural study on apologies in English and Vietnamese is that by Kiều (2000). In this study, Kiều examined the realization patterns of apology in English and Vietnamese with respect to strategy, remedial support, and internal modification in relation to variation of three context-external factors (power, distance, and the hearer's age) and one context-internal factor (offender's face loss). Two types of questionnaires (metapragmatic questionnaire and discourse completion task) were used to elicit data from native speakers of English and native speakers of Vietnamese. The discourse completion task (DCT) data were analyzed using a coding scheme based on a combination of the Cross-Cultural Speech-Act Realization Project (CCSARP) coding system (Blum-Kulka et al., 1989) and the one used by Trosborg (1995). Further, Kiều also investigated one important context-external factor in Vietnamese: the age of the hearer (H). She found that H's age, as well as power and distance, had an effect on Vietnamese native speakers' apology realization. However, the effect of these context-external factors was much less notable in her English data.

To sum up, the literature on apology studies in Vietnamese shows that (1) all of the studies to date are in the tradition of descriptive and cross-cultural pragmatics, and interlanguage pragmatics has not yet been researched; and (2) no studies have been carried out to examine Vietnamese native speakers' norms in apologies. The present study was conducted in an attempt to fill these gaps.

Research questions

In order to fill the existing gaps in the literature the following exploratory research questions were put forward:

1. What are the most commonly used apology strategies among native speakers (NSs) of Vietnamese? What are the most commonly used apology strategies among nonnative speakers (NNSs)?
2. What are the similarities and differences between the native and nonnative apologies?
3. What effects do the two social variables—social power and social distance—have on the apology realization of the NSs and the NNSs?

Methodology

Study design

This study follows both a descriptive and comparative design. It is in the tradition of descriptive pragmatics that the study aims at documenting the most common features of apologies by NSs of Vietnamese. In addition, this study is comparative in that the performance of learners of Vietnamese is compared to that of NSs. The study investigates the interlanguage pragmatics of learners of Vietnamese, paying particular attention to exposure (length of residency in Vietnam) and proficiency. Due to time constraints and limited scope, this study follows a cross-sectional study design.

Participants

A total of 13 NSs of Vietnamese (six females and seven males) volunteered to participate in this study. The participants were between the ages of 26 and 42. The majority of them were overseas postgraduate Vietnamese students (12/13) who had been in Australia for time periods from a few months to up to 15 months.

The learner group consisted of seven male Australian English (AusE) speakers, aged from 35 to 52. At the time of the study, none of the participants were attending a Vietnamese language course, but all of them had had some formal training in Vietnamese in the past. Although there was no standardized test to assess the Vietnamese proficiency of the NNSs, from their self-ratings and from my native speaker perception of their language production, the participants had proficiency levels ranging from low intermediate to advanced.

Instruments

Open role plays

The issue of data collection methodology in pragmatics research is fraught with recent calls for a move away from speech act coding of elicited data and greater reliance on authentic data and conversation analytic methods of data analysis (Kasper, 2006; Meier, 1998). However, the use of authentic data makes it difficult to control participant background variables (such as native language, exposure, or target language proficiency) and manipulate independent variables of interest (such as social context variables). Conversation analytic methods are strongly associated with the use of authentic data and their use with elicited data is traditionally considered inappropriate (see Huth, 2010; Okada, 2010, for arguments supporting the use of elicited data). This study takes a compromise position by using open role plays and applying speech-act coding to the role-play data. Open role plays, while a social practice in their own right and therefore not analogous to natural data, at least involve extended, real-time discourse. Speech-act coding, although not reflecting sequential organization, has the advantage of enabling the description of the inventory of apology strategies in a target language and a comparison to learners' inventories. Further, using a coding scheme allows the current study to be comparable to previous apology studies, which have overwhelmingly used speech-act coding.

Six open role-play scenarios were designed to elicit apologies from the participants. In all six scenarios, the role relationships between the two interlocutors varied along two parameters postulated by Brown and Levinson (1987)—social power (P) and social distance (D). Due to the limited scope of this study, the context-internal factor—the severity of the offense—was omitted.

Social power in this study varies along three dimensions:

P+ Speaker (S) is of higher power/social status than the hearer (H)
P– S is of lower status than H
P= S and H are of equal status

Social distance varies along two dimensions:

D+ S and H are strangers
D– S and H know each other well

Some of the scenarios were created based on those used in previous studies (Blum-Kulka et al., 1989; Trosborg, 1995) but adapted to a Vietnamese context. Also, from the author's experience and from her discussions with other Vietnamese speakers, some scenarios with a high frequency of occurrence in a Vietnamese context (e.g., Scenario 6) were also included. All six scenarios were designed with a combination of the two parameters as follows:

Scenario 1 Forgot to grade an assignment (P+ D–)
Scenario 2 Late for an interview (P+ D+)
Scenario 3 Breaking a valuable dish (P– D–)
Scenario 4 Spilling water over some important documents (P– D+)
Scenario 5 Breaking a CD player (P=D–)
Scenario 6 Motorbike scratch (P=D+)

For a full description of the role-play scenarios, please see Appendix A.

Questionnaires

Questionnaires were distributed to the NNSs of Vietnamese to collect personal information regarding their age, their proficiency level, when they started learning Vietnamese, the length of time they had spent learning the language, and whether or not they had been to Vietnam (see Appendix B).

Data collection procedure

In all role plays, the author played the role of the potential recipient of the apology (Trosborg, 1995) while the participants played the role of the potential apologizer. In most of the scenarios (four out of six), the author took the first turn of the conversation, whereas in the spontaneous scenarios (three and four), the first turn was left open. The reason was that in order to closely simulate authentic situations, an action like spilling some water and dropping something on the floor was actually done, and in that case it was usually the participants (as 'offender') who took the first turn.

All the role plays were audio-recorded in Melbourne, Australia, over a period of two months. For the NS participants, the role plays were tape-recorded at the University of Melbourne or at the participants' houses at their convenience. Almost all the NNSs' role plays were tape-recorded at the University of Melbourne. The participants were given a language statement to keep and a consent form to sign. All the role plays took 10 to 15 minutes to complete. For the nonnative group, the role plays and questionnaires took about 25 minutes. All the role plays were transcribed using transcription conventions put forward by Du Bois, Schuetze-Coburn, Cummings, and Paolonio (1993). Examples of the open role plays are presented in Appendix C.

Analytical procedure

Coding

The coding scheme was initially based on the schemes by Blum-Kulka et al. (1989) and Trosborg (1995) but was adjusted to fit the data by adding three substrategies: *Request for sympathy*, *Request for repair suggestion*, and *Request for the hearer's help*.

The revised coding scheme consists of nine main categories. Following Trosborg (1995), categories 1 to 5 are main apology strategies and categories 6 to 8 are remedial support strategies.

***Category 1: Illocutionary force indicating devices** (IFIDs)*

Substrategies

1.1. Expression of apology
1.2. Expression of regret
1.3. Request for sympathy
1.4. Request for forgiveness

Category 2: Acknowledgement of responsibility

Substrategies

2.1. Expression of self-deficiency
2.2. Lack of intent
2.3. Expression of embarrassment
2.4. Explicit acceptance of the blame or self-blame
2.5. Explicit acknowledgement of responsibility
2.6. Implicit acknowledgement of responsibility

Category 3: Explanation or account

Substrategies

3.1. Implicit explanation or account
3.2. Explicit explanation or account
3.3. Admission of facts

Category 4: Distracting from the offense
Substrategies
4.1. Minimizing the degree of the offense
4.2. Querying preconditions
4.3. Pretending not to notice the offense
4.4. Appeaser

Category 5: Deflecting blame
Substrategies
5.1. Explicit denial of responsibility
5.2. Implicit denial of responsibility
5.3. Explicitly blaming the hearer
5.4. Blaming someone else
5.5. Implicitly blaming the hearer

Category 6: Expressing concern for the hearer

Category 7: Promise of forbearance

Category 8: Repair
Substrategies
8.1. Implicit offer of repair
8.2. Explicit offer of repair
8.3. Request for repair suggestion
8.4. Request for the hearer's help

Category 9: Intensifiers of the apology
Substrategies
9.1. *IFID* internal – intensifying adverbs
9.2. Emotional expressions/exclamations

For a full coding scheme with examples, see Appendix D.

Method of analysis

The author and another native speaker of Vietnamese coded the data, according to the revised coding scheme, and disagreements were resolved through consensus coding. After that, the author listed all of the strategies used by each participant in each scenario, and then tabulated all the manifestations of the strategies of each group. For example, in Scenario 1, the 13 NSs produced altogether 85 manifestations of apology categories, of which 16 belong to the *IFIDs* category. Therefore, *IFIDs* was described as accounting for 19% in this scenario.

Results

Inventory of strategies in native and nonnative apology

In the following section, apology strategies by native and nonnative speakers of Vietnamese will be reported in descending order of occurrence frequency. The

NSs produced altogether 604 manifestations of eight strategies. With the only exception of category 7, *Promise of forbearance,* all the other eight categories were present in the data. Table 1 presents NSs' strategies according to their frequency of use across the six scenarios.

Table 1. Native speakers' apology strategies

strategy	scenario						total	percent
	1	2	3	4	5	6		
Repair	23	15	28	26	30	19	141	23.3
IFIDs	16	24	32	30	9	28	139	23.0
Acknowledgement of responsibility	13	10	30	24	4	7	88	14.6
Explanation or account	16	18	3	4	21	21	83	13.7
Intensifiers of the apology	7	12	19	25	3	11	77	12.8
Expressing concern for the hearer	6	10	4	8	0	14	42	7.0
Deflecting blame	0	1	0	1	11	10	23	3.8
Distracting from the offense	4	1	0	0	0	6	11	1.8
total	**85**	**91**	**116**	**118**	**78**	**116**	**604**	**100**

As can be seen in Table 1, *Repair* was the most frequently used strategy among the NSs at 23.3% (*n=141*). The second most common strategy was *IFIDs*, which accounted for 23% (*n=139*). In addition to the three types of expressions also found in other studies, *Expression of regret, Offer of apology,* and *Request for forgiveness,* the Vietnamese NSs also used *Request for sympathy* as a substrategy. The third most chosen strategy was *Acknowledgement of responsibility*, at 14.6% (*n*=88). *Explanation or account* was similarly frequent, and accounted for 13.7% (*n*=83). Other strategies that the NSs used across the six scenarios included *Intensifiers of the apology, Expressing concern for the hearer, Deflecting blame*, and *Distracting from the offense* (12.8%, 7%, 3.8%, and 1.8%, respectively).

The NSs frequently used a combination of different strategies in one turn. For example, the most common trend was to combine three strategies in the order of *Intensifiers of the apology*, *IFIDs*, and then *Acknowledgement of responsibility*, as can be seen in Scenario 3 below.

Example 1

Ôi chết cháu xin lỗi bác   cháu làm vỡ mất rồi.
oh die niece sorry   uncle niece break lose already.
Oh gosh I am sorry I accidentally broke it.

Another common combination was *Intensifiers of the apology*, *IFIDs*, and *Explanation or account* as seen in Scenario 2.

Example 2

```
Anh            thành thật xin lỗi em
Older brother sincere    sorry   younger sibling
I am really sorry

về    việc   anh           đã   đến    muộn hôm nay
about matter older brother Past come late  today
for the fact that I came late today

vì      nói  thật  với  em              là
because tell true  with younger sibling that
because to tell you the truth

trong thời gian vừa qua bọn  anh
in    time      recent  PluM older brother
recently we

có   nhiều cuộc   họp     quá… hôm vừa rồi thì
have many  Class. meeting so…  day recent  TopM
have had so many meetings… the other day

giám đốc có   triệu tập cuộc   họp     đột xuất
manager  have summons   Class. meeting urgent
my manager called an urgent meeting

em              ạ.
younger sibling PolM
you know
```

The most common strategy, *Repair*, was either used alone or together with other strategies such as *IFIDs*, and/or *Explanation or account,* as seen in Scenario 6.

Example 3

```
Vâng xin lỗi chị          em              đang
yes  sorry   older sister younger sibling Prog.
Oh I am sorry I am

phải vội     đến     cơ quan
must hurry   arrive  office
in a hurry to go to work

hôm nay có     cuộc   họp     sớm…  hay là bây giờ
today   have   Class. meeting early or  be now
today I have an early meeting…  how about now

hai   chị          em            mình đi đến
two   older sister younger sister us  go to
we go to

hiệu sửa   xe   đằng kia   chị          nhá.
shop repair bike over there older sister AlignM
the bike repair shop over there?
```

The NNSs showed a similar distribution of strategies though with some interesting differences, as summarized in Table 2. Compared with the NSs, the NNSs produced far fewer manifestations of the eight strategies (*n*=222). All of the strategies with their frequency of occurrence across all six scenarios are presented in Table 2.

Table 2. Nonnative speakers' apology strategies

strategy	scenario						total	percent
	1	**2**	**3**	**4**	**5**	**6**		
IFIDs	6	7	19	17	8	13	70	31.5
Repair	9	2	6	13	13	8	51	23
Intensifiers of the apology	0	2	10	11	3	5	31	14
Explanation or account	8	6	2	1	10	4	31	14
Acknowledgement of responsibility	4	0	6	3	2	5	20	9
Expressing concern for the hearer	1	3	2	1	1	5	13	5.8
Distracting from the offense	0	0	0	0	0	4	4	1.8
Deflecting blame	0	0	0	0	2	0	2	0.9
total	**28**	**20**	**45**	**46**	**39**	**44**	**222**	**100**

As shown in Table 2, *IFIDs* was used most frequently by the NNSs with 31.5% (*n*=70). The second most common strategy was *Repair,* which accounted for 23% (*n*=51). Both *Explanation or account* and *Intensifiers of the apology* came in third place with 14% (*n*=31). Other strategies chosen by the NNSs were *Acknowledgement of responsibility, Expressing concern for the hearer, Distracting from the offense*, and *Deflecting blame* (9%, 5.8%, 1.8%, and 0.9%, respectively).

The most common strategy, *IFIDs*, was used together with other strategies, for example, *Explanation or account* or *Acknowledgement of responsibility.* In Scenario 3, for instance, one NNS used *Intensifiers of the apology, IFIDs*, and *Acknowledgement of responsibility* as follows.

Example 4

```
Trời ơi         cháu  xin lỗi bác    ạ    cháu  mới bể
Sky  vocative niece sorry   uncle PolM niece new break
Oh my gosh I am sorry I have just broken

ký…    một ký..  chén hay đĩa  gì   của bác    ạ…
Class. one Class. bowl or  dish what of  uncle PolM
the… one of your bowls or dishes

cháu   xin lỗi bác   nghe…
niece  sorry   uncle AlignM
I am so sorry uncle…
```

In Scenario 2, *IFIDs* was used together with *Explanation or account.*

Example 5

```
Anh            xin lỗi em              anh…
Older brother sorry   younger sibling older brother
I am sorry I…

anh             đến   muộn  vì…
older brother   come  late  because
I am late because

anh            đã   có     cuộc   họp
older brother  Past have   Class. meeting
I had a meeting
```

The second most common strategy, *Repair,* was used with another strategy, for instance, *Explanation or account,* as seen in Scenario 5.

Example 6

```
Có    nhưng mà có    một vấn đề  vấn đề  là
yes   but       have one problem problem be
Yes, but there's a problem, the problem is

hôm qua     anh           đã   phát hiện ra  rằng
yesterday   older brother Past find      out that
yesterday I found out that

đĩa  cái    đài đĩa   của em              bị   hỏng
disc Class. CD player of  younger sibling NegM break
your CD player was broken

anh           đã   mua một
older brother Past buy one
I have bought a

cái    mới cho em.
Class. new for younger sibling
new one for you.
```

There are a number of similarities between the two groups in their apology performances across the scenarios. Overall, *IFIDs* and *Repair* were the most favored strategies, followed by *Acknowledgement of responsibility*, *Explanation or account*, and *Intensifiers of the apology.* The least favored strategies were *Expressing concern for the hearer, Deflecting blame*, and *Distracting from the offense.* Specifically, in Scenario 1, both the NSs and NNSs used *Repair, Explanation or account*, and *IFIDs* most frequently. In Scenario 2, *IFIDs* and *Explanation or account* were the most commonly chosen strategies. In both Scenario 3 and 6, *IFIDs* accounted for the highest frequency. In Scenario 4, both the NSs and NNSs resorted to *IFIDs, Repair*, and *Intensifiers of the apology* most often. In Scenario 5, both the two groups utilized *Repair* and *Explanation or account* most frequently.

When the two groups are compared, some differences can also be detected. First, on average each NS produced much longer apologies and with more different manifestations of the apology strategies than each NNS (604/13 vs. 222/7). Second, with regard to selection of apology strategies, the NSs used a wider range of strategies than the NNSs. Apart from Scenario 5 (the NNSs had more strategies than the NSs), and Scenario 3 (both groups used the same number of strategies: six), a larger number of apology strategies were found in the NS data. Two strategies employed by many NSs but not chosen by any NNSs were *Distracting from the offense* (in Scenario 1) and *Deflecting blame* (in Scenario 6). There were also some differences in the overall preferences for strategies between the two groups. The NNSs used *IFIDs* with much higher frequency than the NSs, and clearly preferred them to *Repair*, whereas the NSs used both strategies nearly equally. The NSs were also more likely to use *Acknowledgement of responsibility* than the NNSs, who preferred *Intensifiers* and *Explanation or account.*

Although this study only analyzed the main apology strategy categories, it is noteworthy that the NSs used two substrategies—*Expression of self-deficiency* (Substrategy 2.1) and *Request for repair suggestion* (Substrategy 8.3).

Influence of social context factors

The context factors social power and social distance had an impact on apology speech-act realization by the NSs and NNSs. The influence of these factors was more evident in the native than nonnative speaker data.

With regard to social power, NS apologies were longer, more direct, and more intense in the P– setting compared to the P+ and P= settings. Specifically, the NSs used more *Intensifiers of the apology*, more *IFIDs*, more *Acknowledgement of responsibility*, and their apologies were longer when they were in lower power positions. In addition, it is worth noting here that the NSs used more informal forms of *IFIDs* in the P= setting, while they used more formal forms in the P– setting. For the NNSs, they used much more *Intensifiers of the apology* in the P– setting.

In relation to social distance, for the NSs the effect of this variable only showed up in the P= setting where they produced many more apology manifestations, resorting to many more different strategies and using *IFIDs* twice as frequently in D+ as in D–. In other words, the NSs used more direct strategies when conversing with unfamiliar interlocutors than when conversing with familiar ones. For the NNSs, there were only evident differences between D–and D+ in the P– setting. The NNSs used more *IFIDs* when conversing with someone at a high social distance than with someone with great familiarity.

To sum up, I have described some differences in native and nonnative apology behavior caused by varying social power and social distance settings. While social variable effects could be observed in the six scenarios, it should be noted that there may have been situational effects and effects of the perceived severity of the offense as well.

Discussion

Universality and culture specificity of apology strategies

The findings from this study support Olshtain and Cohen's (1983) idea of a universal apology speech-act set. With the exception of *Promise of forbearance* (which was absent in the data), in this study the participants used all four main semantic formulae postulated by Olshtain and Cohen (1983). Furthermore, the participants also used two more strategies and various modifications of the apologies by using intensifiers similar to those used in Trosborg's (1995) study.

However, the findings from this study also show that apology speech-act realization is subject to culture specificity. The Vietnamese native speakers' preferences for some strategies over others or their use of substrategies in this study reflect cultural characteristics of Vietnamese communicative styles discussed elsewhere by researchers (Phạm, 1995; Trần, 1995) such as preferences for implicitness over explicitness, sentimentality-oriented communicative style, and humility and deference.

The Vietnamese native speakers' inclination towards indirectness is shown by the lower frequency of *IFIDs* compared with *Repair.* This finding is consistent with those from Đặng (1999) and Phạm (1995). In Vietnamese culture, *IFIDs* (especially, an explicit expression of apology through the word *xin lỗi*) are seen as direct and formal; therefore, they are more often used in formal situations, with nonintimates, or with interlocutors of higher status. Instead of *IFIDs*, the Vietnamese would opt for *Repair* or *Explanation or account*, which is considered an implicit apology (Phạm, 1995), especially in informal and status-equal settings. This is reflected in the high frequency of *Explanation or account* in Scenarios 5 and 6 in the data.

Second, the use of *Request for sympathy* is a specific semantic formula in Vietnamese that reflects a sentimentality-orientated approach to interaction (i.e., one communicative goal of the Vietnamese in interaction is to maintain sympathy and understanding with their interlocutors; Phạm, 1995).

Third, the Vietnamese communicative style values modesty, humility, respect, and deference (Phạm, 1995). This is shown in the high frequency of substrategies – *Request for sympathy* (Category 1), *Expression of self-deficiency* (Category 2), *Request for repair suggestion* (Category 8), together with the use of honorifics, especially in the P– setting. This finding is consistent with findings from Kiều (2000).

Intergroup variation

When comparing the NSs and NNSs, the similarities between the groups are striking. The existence of a "universally valid apology speech-act set" (Bergman & Kasper, 1993, p. 84) can be used to account for a number of similarities in the implementation of apology strategies between the two groups. According to Kasper and Rose (1999), adult language learners can access "universal pragmatic knowledge" (p. 87). The NNSs of Vietnamese may have drawn on the universal pragmatic knowledge to perform their apologies in a way similar to the NSs. Another factor to account for the similarities in apology realization of the natives and the nonnatives is the high proficiency and high exposure of most NNSs in the study (6/7 NNSs had been to Vietnam many times and had lived there for at least three years).

However, there were also some differences between the groups, and proficiency effects, individual differences, language socialization, and pragmatic transfer are the potential factors that may account for these differences.

Previous studies (Chang, 2010; Scarcella, 1979; Trosborg, 1987; cited in Kasper & Schmidt, 1996) have shown that there is a positive correlation between learners' proficiency and their repertoires of pragmatic routines and other linguistic means of speech-act realization. In this study, only very highly proficient NNSs could utilize all of the apology realization strategies employed by the NSs. Low-proficiency learners are more likely to differ from NSs and contribute to variation between the groups.

In addition, individual preferences also account for the selection of one strategy over the other and the length of responses. Research has shown that learner subjectivity does play a role in second language sociolinguistic performance (Siegal, 1996). Kasper and Rose (1999) have also pointed out that "there is mounting evidence that divergence from native norms does not always stem from pragmatic or linguistic incompetence but may be a more or less deliberate choice on the part of the learner not to participate in target practices" (p. 97). This point can be elaborated by one comment from a NNS who said that even though he was aware of the hierarchy of the Vietnamese culture and language, he could not see himself conforming to the norms because he did not feel comfortable with them. Another NNS noted that his response to the role plays reflected his personality, which would also determine his reaction to real life situations.

Moreover, language socialization may also play a part in the NNSs' deviation from the NS norms. Although all of the NNSs had some formal training in the Vietnamese language, most of them reported having exposure mainly to colloquial Vietnamese. As a result, they did have some difficulties responding to Scenarios 1, 2, and 4, which required fairly formal Vietnamese. In other words, they were not socialized into a sufficiently wide variety of different language situations to be able to master different registers of the target language.

Furthermore, L1 linguistic and pragmatic transfer may also account for the nonnative apology performance. Jung (2004) found that advanced Korean learners of English differed from target language speakers due to a variety of factors, amongst which is transfer of their L1 linguistic and pragmatic knowledge. The findings from the present study lend support to Jung (2004). The higher frequency of *IFIDs* among the NNSs (compared to the NSs) can be attributed to their L1 pragmatic transfer. All the nonnative participants mentioned that in English people use many more *IFIDs* than in Vietnamese. They also commented that one of the mistakes that Westerners (especially those from English-speaking backgrounds) make in speaking Vietnamese is that they use the substrategy *Expression of apology* too often.

To sum up, the native and nonnative differences in apology performance may have been caused by a number of factors such as proficiency, individual differences, language socialization, and pragmatic transfer. Further studies with larger numbers of participants would be desirable in order to investigate the causes for the nonnative Vietnamese speakers' differences from the target language apologizing norms.

Social variable effects

Three important findings emerged in relation to the effects of the two social variables in this study. The first finding that the two social variables had a role in the participants' apology performance was consistent with findings from apology speech-act studies in Vietnamese (Kiều, 2000) and in other languages (Olshtain, 1989; Reiter, 2000; Wouk, 2006) and was consistent with findings for other speech acts in Vietnamese like complaints (H. T. T. Đỗ, this volume). The effects of the two variables were reflected in the participants' selections of apology strategies, and in their use of address forms and honorifics. However, the unclear patterns (i.e., social distance only had clear effects in the P+ and P= settings for the NSs and in the P– setting for the NNSs) may be attributed to the interplay between the two variables with the severity of the offense (which could not be investigated in this study). According to Kuha (2003), participants' perceptions of the seriousness of the offense had various effects on their speech-act realization patterns. In this study, although the severity of the offense could not be investigated, the participants may have had different assessments of this context-internal factor, which may have caused variations in their responses to the same social power and social distance setting.

The second finding that there were differing effects of the two social variables on the natives and the nonnatives might be explained by an assumption that the natives had a more finely tuned ability to vary their apology performance according to each situation (Cohen et al., 1986). Native speakers usually have access to a greater variety of language registers and different linguistic repertoires. More specifically, in speech-act performance, native speakers possess a broader range of strategies, and they have been socialized more widely in many different situations. As a result, native speakers are more able than nonnative speakers to adjust their language use to the situation.

Conclusion and directions for further research

The present study investigates apologies in Vietnamese using data elicited from six role-play scenarios. The study uses the NSs' apology realization as baseline data to which that of the NNSs is compared. The study shows that the participants used a wide range of apology strategies with differing frequencies depending on each situation, and it identified a number of similarities and differences in the native and nonnative apology performance. It also detected somewhat diffuse effects of the two social context variables on the participants' apology performance. Overall, findings support the existence of a universal apology speech-act set but indicate culture-specific differences in the preference for certain strategies and a pronounced effect of native speaker status on the elaborateness and breadth of apology realizations.

Further research should address apologies in Vietnamese as a native and target language by investigating issues such as the role of address forms and honorifics; the effect of the context variables imposition, age, and gender; as well as the role of paralinguistic features including tone, voice, and prosody. Of particular developmental interest would be longitudinal studies investigating the pragmatic development of interlanguage apologizing by learners of Vietnamese from different language backgrounds such as Chinese, English, French, or Korean, as well as the effect of pragmatic instruction. Finally, comparisons between apology sequences in role-play data and naturally occurring data would contribute to the assessment of different methodological approaches to pragmatics research.

References

Barnlund, D.C., & Yoshioka, M. (1990). Apologies: Japanese and American styles. *International Journal of Intercultural Relations, 14,* 193–206.

Bataineh, R.F., & Bataineh, R.F. (2006). Apology strategies of Jordanian EFL university students. *Journal of Pragmatics, 38*(11), 1901 – 1927.

Bergman, M.L., & Kasper, G. (1993). Perception and performance in native and nonnative apology. In G. Kasper & S. Blum-Kulka (Eds.), *Interlanguage pragmatics* (pp. 82–107). New York, NY: Oxford University Press.

Blum-Kulka, S., House, J., & Kasper, G. (1989). *Cross-cultural pragmatics: Requests and apologies.* Norwood, NJ: Ablex.

Brown, P., & Levinson, S. (1987). *Politeness: Some universals in language usage.* Cambridge: Cambridge University Press.

Chang, W.M., & Haugh, M. (2011). Evaluations of im/politeness of an intercultural apology. *Intercultural Pragmatics, 8*(3), 411–442.

Chang, Y. (2010). 'I no say you say is boring': The development of pragmatic competence in L2 apology. *Language Sciences, 32*(3), 408–424.

Clyne, M., Fernandez, S., & Muhr, R. (2003). Communicative styles in a contact situation: Two German national varieties in a third country. *Journal of Germanic Linguistics, 15*(2), 95–154.

Cohen, A.D., & Olshtain, E. (1981). Developing a measure of sociolinguistic competence: The case of apology. *Language Learning, 31*(1), 113–134.

Cohen, A.D., Olshtain, E., & Rosenstein, D.S. (1986). Advanced EFL apologies: What remains to be learned? *International Journal of the Sociology of Language, 62,* 51–74.

Đặng T.P. (1999). *A cross-cultural study on apologizing and responding to apologies in Vietnamese and English.* (Unpublished master's thesis). Vietnam National University, Hanoi.

Đỗ T.M.T. (2002) *Some English-Vietnamese cross-cultural differences in requesting.* (Unpublished master's thesis). Vietnam National University, Hanoi.

Đỗ T.T.H. (2013). A comparative study of complaints in Vietnamese by native and nonnative speakers. In C. Roever & H. t. Nguyen (Eds.), *Pragmatics of Vietnamese as native and target language* (pp. 111–153) Honolulu: University of Hawai'i, National Foreign Language Resource Center.

Du Bois, J.W., Schuetze-Coburn, S., Cummings, S., & Paolonio, D. (1993). Outline of discourse transcription. In J.A. Edwards & M.D. Lampert (Eds.), *Talking data: Transcription and coding in discourse research* (pp.45–90). Hillsdale, NJ: Erlbaum.

Fraser, B. (1981). On apologizing. In F. Coulmas (Ed.), *Conversational routine: Explorations in standardized communication situations and prepatterned speech* (pp. 273–288). The Hague: Mouton de Gruyter.

Hatfield, H., & Hahn, J. (2011). What Korean apologies require of politeness theory. *Journal of Pragmatics, 43*(5), 1303–1317.

Holmes, J. (1989). Sex differences and apologies: One aspect of communicative competence. *Applied Linguistics, 10*(2), 196–213.

Huth, T. (2010). Can talk be inconsequential? Social and interactional aspects of elicited second language interaction. *Modern Language Journal, 94*(4), 537–553.

Jung, E.H. (2004). Interlanguage pragmatics: Apology speech acts. In C.L. Moder & A. Martinovic-Zic (Eds.), *Discourse across languages and cultures* (pp. 99–116). Amsterdam: Benjamins.

Kasper, G. (2006). Speech acts in interaction: Towards discursive pragmatics. In K. Bardovi-Harlig, J.C. Felix-Brasdefer, & A.S. Omar (Eds.), *Pragmatics and Language Learning (Vol. 11*, pp. 281–314). Honolulu: University of Hawai'i, National Foreign Language Resource Center.

Kasper, G. (2008). Data collection in pragmatics research. In H. Spencer-Oatey (Ed.), *Culturally speaking* (2nd ed., pp. 279–303). London: Continuum.

Kasper, G., & Rose, K.R. (1999). Pragmatics and second language acquisition. *Annual Review of Applied Linguistics, 19,* 81–104.

Kasper, G., & Rose, K.R. (2002). *Pragmatic development in a second language.* Malden, MA: Blackwell.

Kasper, G., & Schmidt, R. (1996). Developmental issues in interlanguage pragmatics. *Studies in Second Language Acquisition, 18,* 149–169.

Kiều T.H.V. (2000). *Apologies in English and Vietnamese.* (Unpublished master's thesis). Vietnam National University, Hanoi.

Kim, H. (2008). The semantic and pragmatic analysis of South Korean and Australian English apologetic speech acts. *Journal of Pragmatics, 40*(2), 257–278.

Kondo, S. (2010). Apologies: Raising learners' crosscultural awareness. In A. Martínez-Flor & E. Usó-Juan (Eds.), *Speech-act performance* (pp. 145–162). Amsterdam: Benjamins.

Kuha, M. (2003). Perceived seriousness of offense: The ignored extraneous variable. *Journal of Pragmatics, 35,* 1803–1821.

Lee, H.E., & Park, H.S. (2011). Why Koreans are more likely to favor 'apology,' while Americans are more likely to favor 'thank you'. *Human Communication Research, 37*(1), 125–146.

Long, C. (2010). Apology in Japanese gratitude situations: The negotiation of interlocutor role-relations. *Journal of Pragmatics, 42*(4), 1060–1075.

Maeshiba, N., Yoshinaga, N., Kasper, G., & Ross, S. (1996). Transfer and proficiency in interlanguage apologizing. In S.M. Gass & J. Neu (Eds.), *Speech acts across cultures: Challenges to communication in a second language* (pp. 155–187). Berlin: Mouton de Gruyter.

Meier, A.J. (1998). Apologies: What do we know? *International Journal of Applied Linguistics, 8,* 215–231.

Nguyễn Q. (1998). *Lời khen trong tiếng Việt và tiếng Anh [Compliments in English and in Vietnamese].* (Unpublished thesis). Đại học Khoa học Xã hội và Nhân văn, Hà Nội, Việt Nam.

Nguyễn V.T. (1999). *Complaints in English and Vietnamese in terms of what has been done and what has not been done.* Ha Noi: Vietnam National University.

Okada, Y. (2010). Role-play in oral proficiency interviews: Interactive footing and interactional competencies. *Journal of Pragmatics, 42*(6), 1647–1668.

Olshtain, E. (1989). Apologies across languages. In S. Blum-Kulka, J. House, & G. Kasper (Eds.), *Cross-cultural pragmatics: Requests and apologies* (pp. 155–173). Norwood, NJ: Ablex.

Olshtain, E., & Cohen, A. (1983). Apology: A speech-act set. In N. Wolfson & E. Judd (Eds.), *Sociolinguistics and second language acquisition* (pp.18–35). Rowley, MA: Newbury House.

Olshtain, E., & Blum-Kulka, S. (1985). Degree of approximation: Nonnative reaction to native speech-act behavior. In S. Gass & C.G. Madden (Eds.), *Input in second language acquisition* (pp. 303–325). Rowley, MA: Newbury House.

Phạm T.T. (1995). *Nghi thức lời nói tiếng Việt hiện đại qua các phát ngôn chào, cảm ơn, xin lỗi [Speech routines in contemporary Vietnamese through the speech acts of greeting, thanking, and apologizing].* (Unpublished doctoral dissertation). Đại học Khoa học Xã hội và Nhân văn, Hà Nội, Việt Nam.

Reiter, M.R. (2000). *Linguistic politeness in Britain and Uruguay: A contrastive study of requests and apologies.* Amsterdam: Benjamins.

Robinson, J.D. (2004). The sequential organization of "explicit" apologies in naturally occurring English. *Research on Language and Social Interaction, 37,* 291–330.

Rose, K.R. (2000). An exploratory cross-sectional study of interlanguage pragmatic development. *Studies in Second Language Acquisition, 22,* 27–67.

Siegal, M. (1996). The role of learner subjectivity in second language sociolinguistic competency: Western women learning Japanese. *Applied Linguistics, 17,* 356-382.

Tanaka, N. (1991). An investigation of apology: Japanese in comparison with Australian. *Meikai Daigaku Gaikokugo Gakubu Ronshu, 4,* 35–53.

Tanaka, N., Spencer-Oatey, H., & Cray, E. (2008). Apologies in Japanese and English. In H. Spencer-Oatey (Ed.), *Culturally speaking* (2nd ed., pp. 73–94). London: Continuum.

Trần Ngọc Thêm (1995). *Cơ sở văn hóa Việt Nam [Vietnamese cultural basics].* Hà Nội: Đại Học Quốc Gia Hà Nội.

Trosborg, A. (1986). Apology strategies in native and nonnative speakers of English. In A.Trosborg (Ed.), *Communicative competence in foreign language learning and teaching* (pp. 44–64). Aarhus: University of Aarhus.

Trosborg, A. (1995). *Interlanguage pragmatics: Requests, complaints, apologies.* Berlin: Mouton de Gruyter.

Vollmer, H.J., & Olshtain, E. (1989). The language of apologies in German. In S. Blum-Kulka, J. House, & G. Kasper (Eds.), *Cross-cultural pragmatics: Requests and apologies* (pp. 197–218). Norwood, NJ: Ablex.

Wagatsuma, H., & Rosett, A. (1986). The implications of apology: Law and culture in Japan and the United States. *Law & Society Review, 20,* 461–498.

Wolfson, N. (1989). *Perspectives: Sociolinguistics and TESOL.* Rowley, MA: Newbury House.

Wofson, N., Marmor, T., & Jones, S. (1989). Problems in the comparison of speech acts across cultures. In S. Blum-Kulka, J. House, & G. Kasper (Eds.), *Cross-cultural pragmatics: Requests and apologies* (pp. 174–96). Norwood, NJ: Ablex.

Wouk, F. (2006). The language of apologizing in Lombok, Indonesia. *Journal of Pragmatics, 38*(9), 1457 – 1486.

Yang, T. (2002). A study of Korean EFL learners' apology speech acts: Strategy and pragmatic transfer influenced by sociolinguistic variations. *Journal of the Pan-Pacific Association of Applied Linguistics, 6*(2), 225–243.

Yuan, Y. (2001). An inquiry into empirical pragmatics data-gathering methods: Written DCTs, oral DCTs, field notes, and natural conversations. *Journal of Pragmatics, 33*(2), 271–292.

Appendix A: Role-play scenarios

English version

Instruction:

You will be asked to read six situations in which you are required to have a conversation with another person. Try to respond as naturally as you would in a real situation. Before you respond to each situation you will be given a minute to think out your response. You response will be tape-recorded. Please indicate when you have finished reading.

Situation 1 Returning an assignment late (P+ D–)

Role card 1 (Participant): You are a teacher. You promised to return an assignment to your student but you forgot to read it. It's the end of the semester. Your student needs that assignment back to prepare for his/her final exam. You know that exam is coming but you have been busy and have forgotten about it.

Role card 2 (Researcher): You are a student. You are preparing for an exam. You came to your teacher's office to collect your assignment as you wanted to know his comments to better prepare for your exam. When you met him in his office, you said to him: "Hello."

Situation 2 Late for an interview (P+ D+)

Role card 1 (Participant): You are a Human Resources officer. You kept an applicant waiting for an hour for a job interview because you were busy attending a meeting.

Role card 2 (Researcher): You are an applicant for a job at Company X. You had an appointment for a job interview with a Human Resources officer. You waited for an hour but the officer did not turn up. When you saw him/her you said: "Hello. My name is...."

Situation 3 Breaking a valuable dish (P– D–)

Role card 1 (Participant): You were invited to your friend's parents' house for dinner. During the meal you accidentally broke a valuable bowl, which your friend's mum really likes.

Role card 2 (Researcher): Your daughter's friend came over for dinner. She accidentally broke a bowl, which is a souvenir from your parents, and you like it very much.

Situation 4 Spilling water over document (P – D+)

Role card 1 (Participant): You are a new employee at a company. When you were talking to your new office manager in his/her office, you accidentally spilled some water from a glass over his/her document on the table.

Role card 2 (Researcher): You are an office manager. You were talking to a new staff member when he/she spilled some water over your document. The document is a report that you need to submit tomorrow.

Situation 5 Breaking a CD player (P= D–)

Role card 1 (Participant): You borrowed a CD player from your close friend for a party. Before returning it to him/her, you found out that it did not work properly anymore.

Role card 2 (Researcher): You lent a CD player to your close friend. You expected to get it back today. When seeing your friend, you would say: "Do you have my CD player with you now?"

Situation 6 Motorbike scratch (P= D+)

Role card 1 (Participant): You were on your way to work. At a t-junction, on turning right, you accidentally crashed into someone else (similar to your age) and caused some scratches on his/her motorbike.

Role card 2 (Researcher): You were suddenly crashed into by someone from behind. You were all right but some scratches were caused to your motorbike. You said: "Oh my gosh. Can't you look where you are going?"

Vietnamese version

Hướng dẫn:

Các tình huống sau được dùng để nghiên cứu " Nghi thức lời nói tiếng Việt hiện đại". Mỗi tình huống là một cuộc hội thoại. Anh/chị hãy đọc kỹ mỗi tình huống và cố gắng ứng xử tự nhiên như các tình huống thật xảy ra trong cuộc sống.

Tình huống 1

Anh/chị là giáo viên. Hôm nay anh/chị đã hứa trả bài cho một sinh viên nhưng lại quên chưa chấm. Bây giờ đã gần cuối học kỳ rồi. Học sinh của anh /chị cần nhận lại bài để ôn thi. Anh/chị biết là kỳ thi học kỳ đang đến gần nhưng đợt này anh chi bận quá nên quên bẵng về bài này.

Tình huống 2

Anh/chị là trưởng phòng quản lý nhân sự của công ty X. Anh/chị đã bắt một người xin việc chờ cả tiếng đồng hồ cho một cuộc phỏng vấn vì anh/chị bận tham gia một cuộc họp đột xuất.

Tình huống 3
Bố mẹ một người bạn thân mời anh/chị đến nhà ăn tối. Trong bữa ăn anh /chị đã sơ ý làm vỡ một cái bát quý mà mẹ của bạn anh/chị giữ gìn rất cẩn thận (nghe nói đó là quà kỷ niệm của ông bà của bạn anh/chị).

Tình huống 4
Anh/chị đang nói chuyện với trưởng phòng của công ty mà anh/chị vừa mới chuyển về làm việc. Anh/chị sơ ý làm đổ cốc nước lên một số giấy tờ quan trọng cuả người trưởng phòng.

Tình huống 5
Anh/chị đã mượn người bạn thân một cái đài đĩa CD. Trước khi mang trả anh/chị phát hiện ra là cái đài đĩa đã bị hỏng.

Tình huống 6
Anh/chị đang đi trên đường đến cơ quan. Đi đến chỗ ngã ba thì anh/chị va phải một người lạ (trạc tuổi mình) và đã làm xây xước xe máy của người này

Appendix B: Questionnaire

Please answer the following questions about yourself.

1. What is your name?
2. How old are you?
3. What is your profession?
4. What is your gender?
5. What is your nationality?
6. What is your native language?
7. What language(s) do you speak apart from your native language?
8. When did you start learning Vietnamese? How long have you learnt it?
9. What class are you in now? Can you please self-rate your Vietnamese proficiency?
10. Have you ever been to Vietnam? If yes, how many times? For how long?
11. How often do you speak Vietnamese? With whom do you speak it?

Appendix C: Examples of open role plays

Example 1: NS12, Scenario 2

R: Dạ em chào anh ạ
PolM younger sibling greet older brother PolM
Hello

em là Lê ạ
younger sibling be Lê PolM
I am Lê

NS12: Ừ chào Lê...uhm.. à anh anh
Yes greet Lê...uhm.. oh older brother older brother
Yes hello Lê uhm I I

vừa đi họp về em vào
just go meeting return younger sibling enter
just came back from a meeting please come

phòng đi ngồi uống nước.
room ImpM sit drink water
in have a seat, have something to drink

R: Vâng ạ
Yes PolM
Yes

NS12: Em uống gì
Younger sibling drink what
What would you like to drink

em uống cà phê nhé
younger sibling drink coffee AlignM
Would you like some coffee

R: Dạ vâng
PolM yes
Yes please

NS12: Anh thành thật xin lỗi em
Older brother sincere sorry younger sibling
I am really sorry

về việc anh đã đến muộn hôm nay
about matter older brother Past. come late today
for the fact that I came late today

vì nói thật với em là
because tell true with younger sibling that
because to tell you the truth

trong thời gian vừa qua bọn anh
in time recent PluM older brother
recently we

có nhiều cuộc họp quá... hôm vừa rồi thì
have many Class. meeting so... day recent TopM
have had so many meetings... on that day

giám đốc có triệu tập cuộc họp đột xuất
manager have summons Class. meeting urgent
my manager called for an urgent meeting

em ạ.
younger sibling PolM
you know

R: Vâng vâng ạ
Yes yes PolM
Yes I know

NS12: À vì thế cho nên anh biết là
Ah because so therefore older brother know that
uh because of that, I know that

em phải chờ một tiếng đồng hồ
younger sibling must wait one hour
you had to wait for one hour

thì đó là rất là quý
so that be very be valuable
I really appreciate that

nói thật việc này đó là việc bất khả kháng
tell true thing this that be thing not able resist
to tell the truth this was beyond my control

cho nên em thông cảm
therefore younger sibling sympathize
so please sympathize

cho anh nhá
for older brother AlignM
with me

Example 2: NS2, Scenario 6

R: Trời ơi đi đứng thế à
Sky vocative go stand that QuesM
Oh gosh don't you see where you are going

NS2: Ôi: xin lỗi chị em.. đang
Oh sorry older sister younger sibling Prog.
Oh I am sorry I am

vội chị có làm sao không ạ
hurry older sister have matter no PolM
in a hurry are you okay

R: Chân tay thì không sao
leg hand EmM no why
I am not hurt

nhưng mà nhìn cái xe này
but look Class. bike this
but look at my bike

NS2: Uhm...uhm... à.. chị ơi thế:
uhm uhm ah older sister vocative so
Oh, how about

chị em mình xem có chỗ nào
older sister younger sibling us see have place which
we check whether there is any place

gần đây sửa xe đem vào để họ..
near here repair bike bring into for they
nearby that repairs bikes so they can

sửa lại cho chị được không ạ
fix again for older sister possible no PolM
fix your bike. Is that okay?

R: Ừ... nhưng mà... lần sau đi đứng nhớ
Yeah... but... time after go stand remember
Ok but next time remember

cẩn thận đấy nhá
careful AffM AlignM
to be careful

NS2: Vâng xin lỗi chị em đang
yes sorry older sister younger sibling Prog.
Yes I am sorry I am

phải vội đến cơ quan
must hurry arrive office
in a hurry to go to work

hôm nay có cuộc họp sớm... hay là bây giờ
today have Class. meeting early or be now
today I have an early meeting... how about now

hai chị em mình đi đến
two older sister younger sister us go to
we go to

hiệu sửa xe đằng kia chị nhá.
shop repair bike over there older sister AlignM
the bike repair shop over there?

Example 3: NNS2 Scenario 3

NNS2: Trời ơi cháu xin lỗi bác ạ cháu mới bể
Sky vocative nephew sorry aunt PolM nephew new break
Oh my gosh I am sorry I have just broken

ký... một ký.. chén hay đĩa gì của bác ạ...
Class. one Class. bowl or dish what of aunt PolM
the... one of your bowls or dishes

cháu xin lỗi bác nghe... cháu
nephew sorry aunt AlignM nephew
I am so sorry aunt... I

R: Thôi không sao đâu nó vỡ rồi mà
DisM no matter StaM it break already StaM
Oh no problem it's already broken

cháu...đừng lo
niece....don't worry
don't worry about it

NNS2: Cái đĩa này có có quý quá hông
Class. dish this have have valuable too no
Is this dish very valuable

có đắt lắm không
have expensive very no
is it very expensive

R: À cái đĩa này là quà kỷ niệm...bác trai
Ah Class. dish this be souvenir uncle
Ah this dish is a souvenir… my husband

NNS2: ôi dzậy à
oh really QuesM
Oh really

R: rất là thích nhưng mà thôi không sao đâu
very EmM like but DisM no matter StaM
really liked it but it's OK, no problem

cháu yên tâm đi
nephew peace heart ImpM
don't worry about it

NNS2: Ôi... dzậy mà... cháu thiệt thiệt là xin lỗi..
Oh… so… StaM nephew really really EmM sorry
Oh really I am really really sorry

cháu dzô tình thôi .. cháu quậy với bạn
nephew unintentional only .. nephew play with friend
I didn't mean it I was playing with friend

với với con của bác á rồi à cháu xin lỗi
with with child of aunt AffM then uh nephew sorry
with with your son and then uh I am sorry

Example 4: NNS5, Scenario 5

R: Fred ơi hôm nay anh
Fred vocative today older brother
Hey Fred today

có mang cái đài đĩa đi cho Lê không
have bring Class. player CD go for Lê no
Have you brought the CD player for me

NNS5: Có nhưng mà có một vấn đề vấn đề là
yes but have one problem problem be
Yes, but there's a problem, the problem is

hôm qua anh đã phát hiện ra rằng
yesterday older brother Past find out that
yesterday I found out that

đĩa cái đài đĩa của em bị hỏng
disc Class. CD player of younger sibling NegM break
your CD player was broken

anh đã mua một
older brother Past buy one
I have bought a

cái mới cho em.
Class. new for younger sibling
new one for you.

R: À thế ạ
Ah so QuesM
Oh really

NNS5: Vì .. không biết vì sao nhưng mà hôm qua
Because not know why but yesterday
Because… don't know why but yesterday

phát hiện ra là bị hỏng rồi
find out that NegM broken already
I found out that it was broken

đây là cái mới của em anh
this be Class. new of younger sibling older brother
This is the new one I

đã mua rồi
Past buy already
bought for you.

Appendix D: Coding scheme

1. ***IFIDs*** **(Illocutionary force indicating devices)**

1.1. Expression of apology

Realized by different structures of the verb *xin lỗi*

1.2. Expression of regret

Realized by the words *tiếc, lấy làm tiếc*

1.3. Request for sympathy

Realized by such words as *thông cảm*

1.4. Request for forgiveness

Realized by such words as *thứ lỗi, tha lỗi*

2. Acknowledgement of responsibility

2.1. Expression of self-deficiency

ex: Cháu sơ ý quá! (How careless I am!)

2.2. Lack of intent

ex: Em không chủ định đâu. (I did not mean to.)

2.3. Expression of embarrassment

ex: Em áy náy quá. (I feel so bad about it.)

2.4. Explicit acceptance of the blame or self-blame

ex: Lỗi tại mình mà. (That's my fault.)

2.5. Explicit acknowledgement of responsibility

ex: Cháu làm vỡ cái bát của bác mất rồi.
(I have just broken your bowl.)

2.6. Implicit acknowledgement of responsibility

ex: Vỡ mất rồi (It is broken.)

3. Explanation or account

3.1. Implicit explanation or account

ex: Cháu không hiểu là hôm nay cháu bị làm sao nữa.
(I don't know what has happened to me today.)

3.2. Explicit explanation or account

ex: Đợt này tôi bận nhiều việc qúa nên quên mất.
(I have had so much work recently that I forgot.)

3.3. Admission of facts

ex: Không hiểu sao hôm qua vẫn nghe được còn sáng nay thì nó lại tịt mít.
(I don't know why it was still working properly yesterday but this morning it did not work at all.)

4. Distracting from the offense

4.1. Minimizing the degree of the offense

ex: Em thấy nó có sao mấy đâu nhỉ.
(I don't think it matters much.)

4.2. Querying preconditions

ex: Đi giữa đường đông thế này chắc là va vào nhau cũng là chuyện bình thường.
(In such crowded streets having a bike crash is a usual thing.)

4.3. Pretending not to notice the offense

ex: Có chuyện gì vậy?
(What's the matter?)

4.4. Appeaser

ex: Em uống cà phê nhé!
(Would you like some coffee?)

5. Deflecting blame

5.1. Explicit denial of responsibility

ex: Thực ra không hẳn là lỗi của tôi.
(Actually, it's not all my fault.)

5.2. Implicit denial of responsibility

ex: talking about something else

5.3. Explicitly blame the hearer

ex: Nhưng mà cô đi sai.
(But you were in the wrong way.)

5.4. *Blame someone else*

ex: Thằng em tao nó làm hỏng mất.
(My brother broke it.)

5.5. Implicitly blame the hearer

ex: Giấy tờ quan trọng thế này sao lại để gần ly nước dzậy ta?
(Why was such an important document placed near a glass of water?)

6. Expressing concern for the hearer

Bạn đợi lâu chưa? (Have you been waiting for long?)
Bạn có sao không? (Are you ok?)

7. Promise of forbearance

8. Repair

8.1. Implicit offer of repair

ex: Không biết cái bát này có thể mua được ở chỗ nào không bác?
(Do you know whether this bowl can be bought at any place?)

8.2. Explicit offer of repair

ex: Tôi sẽ đưa cho chị một ít tiền để chị sửa xe.
(I will give you some money to fix the bike.)

8.3. Request for repair suggestion

ex: Bây giờ làm thế nào ạ?
(What can be done now?)

8.4. Request for the hearer's help

ex: Chị ơi chị làm ơn giúp em với nhé!
(Can you please help me, sister?)

9. Intensifiers of the apology

9.1. IFID internal intensifying adverbs

ex: rất (very), thành thực (truly)

9.2. Emotional expressions/exclamations

ex: Ôi trời ơi/ôi chết rồi (oh my gosh)

3 Complaints in Vietnamese by Native and Nonnative Speakers

Hà Thị Thanh Đỗ (Ha Do)
ULIS, Vietnam National University

Introduction

This study investigates the speech act of complaining in Vietnamese. It looks at both native speakers' (NSs) and nonnative speakers' (NNSs) offline knowledge to gauge the differences between native and nonnative knowledge of this speech act. The motivation for this study stems from the lack of pragmatic and interlanguage pragmatic research on complaints in Vietnamese. In addition, the increase in the number of learners of Vietnamese as a second language makes it important to investigate their interlanguage pragmatic knowledge, as this provides a baseline for pedagogy (Boxer, 2010).

In a broad sense, a complaint is an expression of discontent about a state of affairs and an attribution of responsibility (Heinemann, 2009; Heinemann & Traverso, 2009). Through complaints, speakers express a moral judgment about others' conduct and thereby construct it as a transgression (Drew, 1998). Following Olshtain and Weinbach (1987), a speaker carries out the speech act of complaining to express annoyance or displeasure as a reaction to a past or ongoing event, the result of which affects the speaker in an unfavourable way. The speaker would have expected a favourable event to take place or an unfavourable event to be prevented; however, an action previously carried out by the hearer or a third party violates this expectation as it does

Pragmatics of Vietnamese as a native and target language, pp. 111–133
Carsten Roever & Hạnh thị Nguyễn (Eds.), 2013
Honolulu, HI: University of Hawai'i, National Foreign Language Resource Center

not enable the favourable event to happen, or it fails to prevent the unfavourable event from happening.

Complaints can be described as direct if they are about a co-present recipient, or indirect if they are targeted at a third party not present in the context (Boxer, 1993; Dersley & Wootton, 2000; Drew & Holt, 1988). The latter type has also been called "gripes" (DuFon, 1995) or "whinges" (Clyne, 1994). In addition to this distinction, the acceptance of complaints also depends on who complains, about what, and to whom. For example, health professionals are found to be open to complaints about clients, yet often reject those about their colleagues (Heinemann, 2009; Laforest, 2009; Ruusuvuori & Lindfors, 2009). In the workplace, complaints are most common among European men with higher status while Southeast Asian women seldom whinge or complain (Clyne, 1994).

According to Olshtain and Weinbach's seminal study (1987), there are two aspects that the speaker has to consider when deciding to carry out the speech act of complaint and choosing its realization pattern. The first aspect is related to the situational context: Is there still any possibility for repair? If there is still room for repair, the speaker may soften his/her complaint. The second aspect is the face of the hearer and the speaker. According to Brown and Levinson (1987), complaining is a face-threatening act, which is costly to the hearer's face. Thus, the speaker can choose from the most to the least severe complaint realization. The consideration of face might be affected by the social parameters of the speaker-hearer relationship such as their social status and the social distance between them or by situational factors such as the *contract* between the speaker and the hearer. This concept is defined by Olshtain & Weinbach (1987) as "the degree to which H is expected to prevent the A (the act directly prompting the complaint)" (p. 205). Contract refers to the mutual commitment between the speaker and the hearer, including explicit commitments such as laws and written rules as well as implicit ones such as unstated ties between the speaker and the hearer.

The speech act of complaining has received some attention in cross-cultural or interlanguage pragmatic research but by far not as much as speech acts like request or apology (Martinez-Flor & Uso-Juan, 2010). Complaint studies show discrepancies between NSs and NNSs in terms of (1) the components of the complaints (Murphy & Neu, 1996; Trosborg, 1995) and (2) the use and preference of complaint strategies with regard to contextual factors (Moon, 2002; Olshtain & Weinbach, 1987). The discrepancies are believed to be grounded in different directness levels in the mother tongue and the target language. House & Kasper (1981) did a cross-cultural study on the politeness markers of German and English requests and complaints. With regard to complaints, they found that Germans tend to prefer higher directness levels and tend to intensify the speech act in conflict situations. In contrast, English speakers do not have a preference for high levels of directness, especially the highest ones. Olshtain and Weinbach's study (1987) is among the few on complaints by learners of languages other than English. It investigates the performance of complaints in Hebrew among NSs and NNSs and found that both populations seemed to make use of the same strategies in the speech-act set: (1) *Below level of reproach*, (2) *Disapproval and annoyance*, (3) *Explicit complaint*, (4) *Warning*, and (5) *Threat*. These strategies, listed in order of increasing severity, can be a word, a phrase, or a sentence that meets a particular semantic criterion and that can be used to perform the act However, both populations were found to be 'clustered' around the centre of the scale; they preferred *Disapproval and annoyance* and *Explicit complaint* to the strategies at the two extremes of the scale. One difference between the two groups was that the learners overall preferred the gentler end of the scale whereas the NSs were more severe in their complaints.

Social status was found to have an impact on how NSs of Hebrew employed strategies. When the speaker is of higher status than the hearer, the strategies of *Explicit complaint* and *Warning* were preferred. In contrast, when the speaker was of lower status, softer strategies were employed. The social distance factor was found not to have an impact on the distribution of strategies used by Hebrew speakers. The study also pointed out that the contract between the speaker and the hearer seemed to influence strategy selection of NSs of Hebrew. The distribution of strategies significantly varied according to whether the contract was explicit, implicit, or nonexistent. When the contract was explicit, more severe strategies were employed, but when the contract was implicit or nonexistent, softer strategies were preferred.

Though teaching and learning Vietnamese as a second language is undertaken widely in Vietnam as well as in countries with large Vietnamese communities like the United States, Australia, and Canada, Vietnamese interlanguage pragmatics is still largely unexplored. Many of the pragmatic studies on Vietnamese, which remain limited in number, tend to be cross-cultural and only focus on a narrow range of speech acts such as requests (e.g., Vũ, 1995), compliments (e.g., Q.Nguyễn, 1999), and greetings and apologies (e.g., Phạm, 1995). The only study on complaints is that of T. Nguyễn (1998). He focused on the linguistic form of complaints in Vietnamese and English and showed that the common form of complaints in Vietnamese consists of a statement followed by a question, an exclamatory sentence, or an imperative sentence with modal particles. His data revealed that when complaining, Vietnamese speakers expect hearers to show sympathy or to make a change to the situation. A shortcoming of T. Nguyễn's study is that it focused more on the linguistic forms than the pragmatic aspects of complaints. Even the particles, whose meanings are highly context sensitive, are only listed as linguistic forms with no discussion of their pragmatic meanings. Moreover, T. Nguyễn's study did not deal with how NNSs of Vietnamese produce this speech act.

The present study is the first to investigate complaints in Vietnamese according to the speech-act set framework first proposed by Olshtain and

Weinbach (1987) and still widely in use (e.g., in a recent contrastive study by Chen, Chen, & Chang, 2011). By describing the complaint strategies in L1 Vietnamese and comparing these with strategies used by learners of L2 Vietnamese, this study contributes to a fuller description of Vietnamese pragmatics, as well as highlighting areas of difference between native speakers and second language learners of Vietnamese.

Research questions

This study has a double purpose: to describe complaint patterns by NSs of Vietnamese and to compare NNSs' knowledge about this speech act with that of NSs. Specifically, I will answer the following two research questions:

1. What does the speech-act set of complaints consist of in Vietnamese? How do complaint strategies vary according to social and situational variables?
2. Do learners of Vietnamese tend to use the NSs' speech-act set of complaints, and does their knowledge of complaints differ from that of NSs?

Methodology

The study involved 19 male and 15 female native Vietnamese speakers (aged from 18 to 37) from Hanoi. These participants speak the Hanoi dialect, the standard variety of the Vietnamese language (Hoàng, 2002). They are from different occupational backgrounds, ranging from blue-collar workers to financial consultants.

The NNSs of Vietnamese participating in this study included 24 university students (9 males, 15 females) of Chinese language backgrounds studying Vietnamese at the College of Foreign Languages (former name of the University of Languages and International Studies), Vietnam National University. At the time of data collection, these students had been in Vietnam for three months, and they were at the upper-intermediate level as reported by the teacher who had marked their latest assessment.

A written discourse completion task (DCT) with open-ended elicitations was employed as the main instrument for collecting both NSs and NNSs data. A Chinese teacher was present to help NNSs with understanding the DCT in Vietnamese. The DCT consisted of nine scenarios, collected from real-life observations of NSs' complaints. Each item provided the participants with a detailed description of the scenario, indicating the three independent variables influencing speech-act production.

The scenarios were:

Scenario 1	S has to work late and complains to the boss.
Scenario 2	S does not receive an apology after a crash caused by another traffic user and complains to that person.
Scenario 3	S has to wait a long time when coming to an appointment with the boss of a partner company and complains to the boss.
Scenario 4	S's calculator is returned broken and he or she complains to the borrower.
Scenario 5	S complains to a close friend about not coming to his or her birthday party.
Scenario 6	S is a teacher and complains to a student about always coming late.
Scenario 7	S's child breaks a bowl during a meal and S complains to the child about carelessness.
Scenario 8	S catches a group of teenagers who always ring the doorbell for fun and complains to them about their behavior.
Scenario 9	S complains to a younger sibling for coming home late the night before.

A Vietnamese and an English version of the instrument are presented in the Appendix.

Findings

Seven strategies were identified as making up the speech-act set of complaint in the NSs data, with the use of these strategies affected by social distance, social power, and the contract between the speaker and the hearer. Though learners of Vietnamese have the same repertoire of strategies available, they employ the strategies differently from NSs. This indicates that at the upper-intermediate level, learners are still developing the sociopragmatic knowledge for this speech act, that is, the knowledge of how to say it appropriately in different situations.

Native speakers' complaints

Speech act set

The following is the speech-act set consisting of the seven major strategies of complaint found in the NSs data and the semantic descriptions, starting from the least severe.

Below level of reproach

In this strategy, the speaker (S) attempts to minimize the face threat to the hearer (H), and S avoids explicit mention of the offensive event. The linguistic features include complete avoidance of direct reference to the event and the use of solidarity address terms such as anh-em [older brother – younger sibling] (kinship terms used as address terms).

Disapproval or annoyance

In this strategy, S expresses annoyance and *Disapproval and annoyance* of the offensive event but avoids direct reference to H as the 'causer'; Instead, S can bias her or his annoyance to a third party. In this situation, there is still the possibility to avoid an open face threat. The linguistic features include avoidance of explicit reference to H or the act, but there is a very obvious hint that some offensive event has occurred.

Example 3

Context: H overtook S's motorbike and nearly knocked him/her down

```
Sao có      người     bất lịch sự     thế     nhỉ?
Why have    person    impolite        so     AlignM
How can there be such an impolite person?
```

Example 4

Context: H repeatedly rang S's doorbell for fun

```
Như   thế  sẽ     làm  cho   người  khác  khó chịu.
Like  so   will   make for   people other annoyed
Doing that can annoy other people.
```

Explicit complaint

This is an open face-threatening act towards H, but no sanctions are instigated. The strategy involves explicit reference to the event or H or both. The linguistic features in this case include reference to either H or the event or both, and the use of formal address terms to show distance: *anh – tôi* [brother – I], *ông – tôi* [grandfather – I].

Example 5

Context: H broke S's calculator

```
Hình như  anh             vừa    làm
Seem      older brother   just   make
It seems that you have just

hỏng   máy tính   của   tôi.
damage calculator  of   me.
broke my calculator.
```

Example 6

Context: H is late for a business appointment

```
Ông          làm   tôi  khó chịu  quá.
grandfather make  me   annoyed   very.
You really irritated me.
```

Warning

This strategy is an open face-threatening act, and it implies potential sanctions for the hearer. It contains explicit reference to S's future act, which will incriminate H or will be unfavourable for H, and there is often reference to H and the event. The linguistic features include expressions of the future (*sẽ*); S as agent of the future act or H as the affected subject in the sentence; and the use of informal equal nonkinship address terms: *tao – mày* [I – you (casual)], *tao – chúng mày* [I – plural you (casual)].

Example 7

Context: H (S's child) broke a bowl during the meal

```
Mẹ          sẽ     phạt      đấy.
Mother      will   punish    AffM.
I'll definitely punish you.
```

Example 8

Context: H forgot S's birthday

```
Tao           cũng  sẽ   quên
I (casual)    also  will forget
I will   also forget

sinh nhật  của   mày  luôn.
birthday   of    you  immediately.
your birthday from this day forward.
```

Mocking

This is also an open face-threatening act, however, it is done in an indirect way. There is no direct reference to the act, and the utterance implicates an *Insult*. The linguistic features are use of a full sentence and formal address terms such as *anh – tôi* [brother – I].

Example 9

Context: H broke S's calculator

```
Anh có  thường  dùng được     cái gì lâu  không?
You yes usually use  possible what   long no?
Usually, do you manage to have anything last for a while?
```

Example 10

Context: H is late for class

```
Tất cả các   thiên tài
All    PluM  genius
All geniuses

đều  đi học   muộn,
also go study late
come late to school,

tôi hi vọng    anh  cũng  là  một  thiên tài.
I   hope       you  also  be  one  genius.
I hope you're also a genius.
```

Insult

When choosing this strategy, S does a very open face-threatening act although she or he does not imply potential sanctions to H. The act is characterized by direct reference to H's virtue in a disrespectful way. The linguistic features include omission of the subjects and words with negative connotations.

Example 11

Context: H repeatedly rang S's doorbell for fun

```
Đồ      mất     dạy!
Type    lost     education.
You uneducated thing!
```

Example 12

Context: H overtook S's motorbike and nearly knock him/her down

```
Không    có     mắt à?
Not      have   eye QuesM.
Are you blind?
```

These insulting utterances draw their force from cultural norms. In Vietnamese culture, being considered uneducated is shameful as it implies that the addressee belongs to the lowest stratum of society. Similarly, when being asked *không có mắt à?* [Are you blind?], H is accused of lacking even basic sense (Trần, 1995).

Threat

When S chooses this realization pattern, she or he openly threatens H's face by making explicit or implicit reference to S's action, usually unfavourable, and using expressions of the current time. The linguistic features include subject omission and the use of expressions for present time.

Example 13

Context: H repeatedly rang S's doorbell for fun

```
Cút              ngay     ông           đánh
Leave (vulgar) at once grandfather beat
Get lost or I'll beat

bỏ    mẹ          bây giờ.
leave mother     now.
the hell out of you right now.
```

The seven major strategies (*Below level of reproach, Disapproval and annoyance, Explicit complaint, Warning, Mocking, Insult,* and *Threat*) relate to S's position towards H's face. However, the utilization of these strategies varies in the corpus of NS's complaints. The following section presents the overall tendency of strategy distribution among the respondents and the distribution of strategies according to social parameters.

Distribution of strategies

Figure 1 shows the general trend of how NSs use complaint strategies.

Overall distribution: Respondents tend to favour the less severe strategies, particularly *Disapproval and annoyance* (29.3%). *Explicit complaint* is also frequently used by the native respondents. The use of complaint strategies is influenced by social relations, social power, and the contract between S and H, as shown in Figures 2, 3, and 4 respectively.

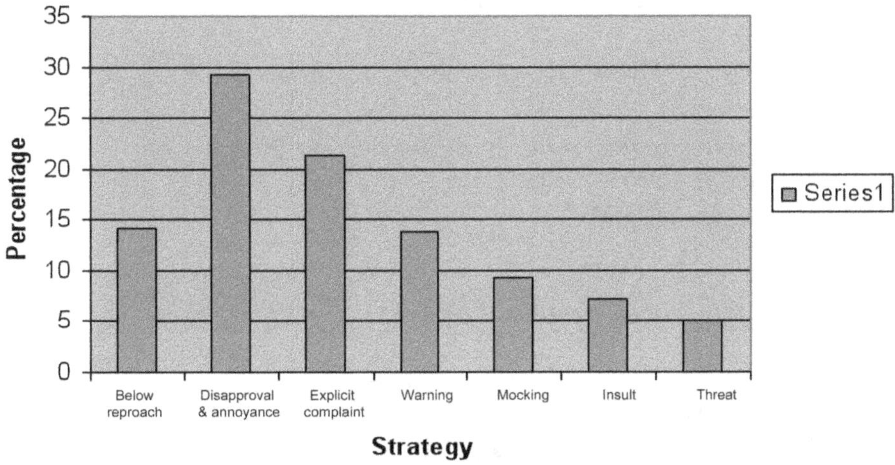

Figure 1. Overall strategy distribution among NSs.

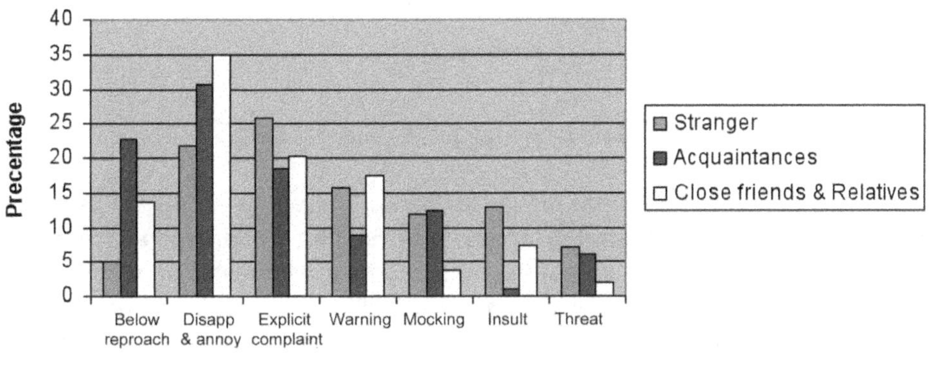

Figure 2. Distribution of strategies by social distance among NSs.

Distribution by social distance: It is clear from Figure 2 that *Disapproval and annoyance* is the most common choice in the "close friend and relative" and "acquaintances" dimensions (34.9% and 30.7%, respectively). However, in the "strangers" dimension, the most preferred strategy is *Explicit complaint* (25.7%), followed by *Below level of reproach* (21.8%). One interesting feature is that the *Warning* strategy is used more when the speaker is at the highest degree of familiarity (i.e., with close friends or relatives). In contrast, the strategies of *Insult* and *Threat* are employed more when S deals with strangers (12.8% and 7%) than with acquaintances or close friends/relatives.

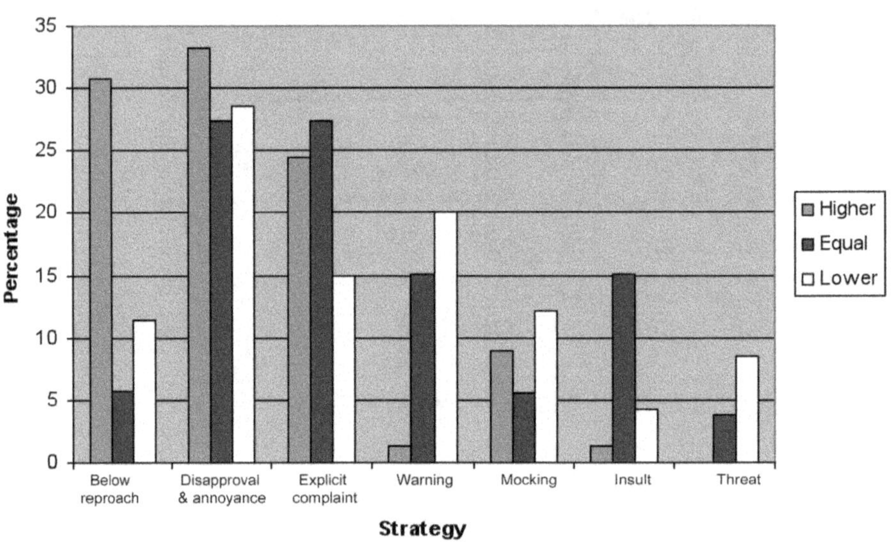

Figure 3. Strategy distribution by social power among NSs.

Distribution by social power: Figure 3 shows how the social status of the interlocutors affects the strategy choices. The first observation is that the participants have a preference for the most tactful strategies when the hearer is in a higher position (*Below level of reproach*: 30.8%; *Disapproval and annoyance*: 33.3%). There seems to be a move down the tactfulness scale when the hearer is of equal position. In this case, Strategies 2 and 3 (*Disapproval and annoyance* and *Explicit complaint*) are used with the same frequency, followed by *Warning* and *Insult* with 15.1% each. When the hearer has a lower position, *Warning* and *Threat* become more pronounced than in the other two settings (20% and 8.5% compared to 1.3% and 0%; 15.1% and 3.8%).

Distribution by contract (Figure 4): This factor is specific to the speech act of complaining; the contract indicates the degree to which the hearer is expected to prevent the act or abstain from it. Vietnamese speakers prefer the less severe realization patterns when the contract is nonexistent or implicit (i.e., the *Warning* strategy is used more). Explicit contracts among the interlocutors seem to trigger more frequent use of severe strategies than the other type of contracts (*Warning*: 21.2%; *Mocking*: 13.9%; *Insult*: 11.7%; and *Threat*: 9.5%).

Distribution of strategies by contract-NS

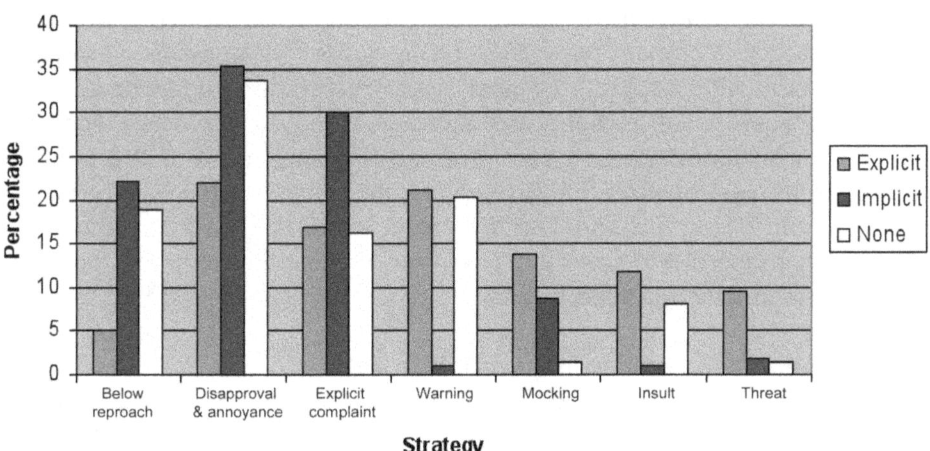

Figure 4. Strategy distribution by contract among NSs.

Combination of strategies

It is also apparent in the data that a number of native complaints include two strategies. In other words, the speaker combines more than one semantic formula in the realization of the speech act. Complaints containing double strategies were a minority, and they account for only 12% in the NS corpus. The most common combination was between *Explicit complaint* and *Below level of reproach*, which alone accounted for 39% of all combinations, and is exemplified in Example 14.

Example 14

Context: H is late for a business appointment

Tôi chờ ông anh mãi.
I wait grandfather older brother forever.
I've been waiting for you forever. (Strategy 3)

Chắc ông anh bận quá,
Certain grandfather older brother busy too much,
You must be very busy,

thôi chúng ta vào việc luôn nhé.
alright we enter work immediately AlignM.
but anyway, let's get right to business, OK? (Strategy 1)

Summary

Overall, there are seven strategies available for the realization of complaints in Vietnamese, and the speaker can choose the strategies according to the position he or she takes with respect to the hearer's face. However, on the whole, the Vietnamese NSs in the data tend to prefer softer strategies to more face-threatening strategies. When complaining to people of greater social distance, the NSs tend to opt for more severe strategies in comparison with people of lesser social distance. Social power also affects strategy choice in that softer strategies occur more often when the hearer is in a higher position compared to the speaker, and the strategy preference moves towards the stronger strategies when the hearer is in a lower position. The native speakers also tend to choose strategies according to the explicitness of the contract. The more explicit the contract, the more severe strategies they tended to employ.

NNSs' complaints in comparison with NSs data

All seven NSs' complaint strategies can be found in the NNSs corpus. However, the distribution, both in total and by variables, differs from that of the NSs.

Overall distribution

Table 1 illustrates the differences in the distribution of these strategies among NSs and NNSs.

Table 1. Distribution of seven strategies between NSs and NNSs

strategy	NSs (N=289)		NNSs (N-189)	
	raw frequency	percentage	raw frequency	percentage
Below level of reproach	46	14.2%	30	14.6%
Disapproval and annoyance	95	29.3%	59	28.6%
Explicit complaint	69	21.3%	29	14.1%
Warning	45	13.9	38	18.4%
Mocking	30	9.2%	32	15.5%
Insult	23	7.1%	6	3%
Threat	16	5%	12	6%

The general distributions of strategies among NSs and NNSs is broadly similar. Nevertheless, a close look at each strategy reveals that NNSs differ from NSs mostly in *Explicit complaint* (14.1% vs. 21.3%), followed by *Mocking* (15.5% vs. 9.2%) and *Warning* (18.4% vs. 13.9%). This can be seen as well in Figure 5.

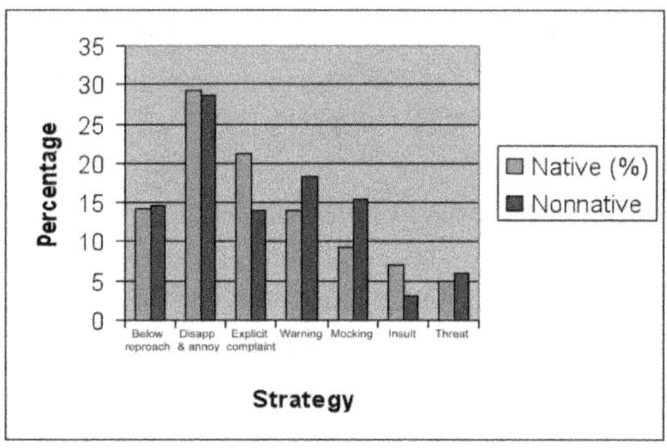

Figure 5. The distribution of strategies between NSs and NNSs.

Strategy distribution by social distance

Table 2. Distribution of strategies by social distance

strategies	strangers		acquaintances		close friends and relatives	
	NSs (n=101)	NNSs (n=70)	NSs (n=114)	NNSs (n=71)	NSs (n=109)	NNSs (n=65)
Below level of reproach	5%	1.4%	22.8%	17%	13.7%	26%
Disapproval and annoyance	21.8%	28.5%	30.7%	24%	34.9%	33.8%
Explicit complaint	25.7%	18.5%	18.4%	18.3%	20.2%	4.6%
Warning	15.8%	12.8%	8.8%	21%	17.4%	21.5%
Mocking	11.9%	20.3%	12.3%	14%	3.7%	13.8%
Insult	12.8%	8.5%	1%	0%	7.3%	0%
Threat	7%	11.4%	6.1%	5.6%	2%	0%
total	**100%**	**100%**	**100%**	**100%**	**100%**	**100%**

NNSs tend to prefer softer strategies (*Disapproval and annoyance*) when complaining to a stranger, whereas this is the second most preferred choice of NSs. However, strategies at the end of the continuum are employed by NNSs in a greater proportion compared to NSs (*Mockery*: 20.3% vs. 11.9%; *Threat*: 11.4% vs. 7%).

When the interlocutors are acquaintances, NNSs have the same preference for *Disapproval and annoyance* as NSs, however, they also seem to prefer severe strategies more than NSs (*Warning*: 21% vs. 8.8%; *Insult*: 14% vs. 12.3%).

NNSs also differ in complaints to close friends and relatives. Besides the preference for Strategies 1 and 2, NNSs tend to use direct strategies more than NSs (e.g., *Warning*: 21.5% vs. 17.4%; *Insult*: 13.8% vs. 3.7%).

Strategy distribution by power relation

Table 3. Distribution of strategies by power relationship

strategies	higher (H>S)		equal (H=S)		lower (H<S)	
	NSs (n=78)	NNSs (n=46)	NSs (n=106)	NNSs (n=66)	NSs (n=140)	NNSs (n=94)
Below level of reproach	30.8%	21.7%	5.7%	6%	11.4%	17%
Disapproval and annoyance	33.3%	30.4%	27.4%	33.3%	28.6%	24.5%
Explicit complaint	24.4%	17.3%	27.4%	18%	15%	9.5%
Warning	1.3%	10.8%	15.1%	10.6%	20%	27.6%
Mocking	9%	15.2%	5.6%	13.6%	12.1%	17%
Insult	1.3%	0%	15.1%	7.5%	4.3%	1%
Threat	0%	4.3%	3.8%	10.5%	8.5%	3.1%
total	**100%**	**100%**	**100%**	**100%**	**100%**	**100%**

Table 3 shows that NNSs' complaints are affected by power relations somewhat differently than NSs. When complaining to people of higher position, NNSs tend to employ the more severe strategies at higher rates than NSs (*Warning*: 10.8%; *Insult*: 15.2%). This preference remains similar in the *Equal* dimension. However, where NSs have the tendency to move towards the more severe strategies when dealing with people of lower position, NNSs tend to move to the opposite end, using more tactful strategies.

Strategy distribution by contract

Table 4. Distribution of strategies by contract

strategies	higher (H>S)		equal (H=S)		lower (H<S)	
	NSs (n=137)	NNSs (n=100)	NSs (n=113)	NNSs (n=65)	NSs (n=74)	NNSs (n=41)
Below level of reproach	5.1%	2%	22.1%	17%	18.9%	41.5%
Disapproval and annoyance	21.9%	27%	35.4%	38.5%	33.8%	17%

Explicit complaint	16.8%	18%	30.1%	13.8%	16.2%	4.8%
Warning	21.2%	22%	1%	9.2%	20.3%	24.4%
Mocking	13.9%	**18%**	8.8%	**13.8%**	1.4%	**12%**
Insult	11.7%	5%	1%	1.5%	8.1%	0%
Threat	9.5%	8%	1.8%	6.1%	1.4%	0%
total	**100%**	**100%**	**100%**	**100%**	**100%**	**100%**

The strategy usage patterns of NNSs in explicit and implicit contract settings are relatively similar to those of NSs except for higher rates of *Mocking*. A notable difference exists, however, in the nonexistent contract setting. Although both populations tend to use the polite end of the continuum more, NNSs employ *Below level of reproach* at a surprisingly high rate of 41.5%, compared to just 18.9% by NSs.

Strategy combination

The NNSs combine strategies less frequently than the NSs. Only 8.9% of the nonnative responses contain two strategies, and the NNSs did not combine *Explicit complaint* with *Below level of reproach*, which was the most common combination for the NSs.

Summary

The NNSs' complaint repertoires show the same strategies as NSs'. However, the NNSs tend to have greater preference for Strategies 3, 4, and 5 than the NSs. They also seem to have the ability to combine strategies in a complaint, though these combinations differ from NSs' patterns.

The NNSs' strategy use on a large scale is similar to that of the NSs. However, a close look at the distribution by variables reveals some discrepancies. Differences are most evident in strategy distribution by social power, where the NSs show the opposite tendency from the NNSs.

Discussion

The findings allow some conclusions about the speech-act set of complaints in Vietnamese and the factors affecting strategy selection for NSs of Vietnamese and Chinese learners of Vietnamese.

Complaint speech-act set and Vietnamese cultural values

The data show that the strategies of the complaining speech act in Vietnamese are generally similar to that in Hebrew as described in Olshtain and Weinbach (1987) and other languages (Chen, Chen, & Chang, 2011; Murphy &

Neu, 1996). However, there are some patterns specific to Vietnamese culture, such as mockery and insult, as discussed above.

Another feature specific to the Vietnamese complaints in the data involves the notion of politeness. When using the first of the seven strategies (*Below level of reproach*, accounting for 14.2% of the data), the speaker can minimize the cost for the hearer, who undoubtedly feels uncomfortable when being faced with an *Explicit complaint*, which is in line with the Tact Maxim (Leech, 1983) or off-the-record strategies discussed by Brown and Levinson (1987). The choice of this strategy also implies that the speaker maximizes the cost for herself or himself (Leech, 1983) as she or he could not express full annoyance in the complaint. However, in the more severe strategies in the speech-act set, except for the use of the solidarity address pair, there was little evidence of redressive techniques to tone down the severity of the face-threatening act (Brown & Levinson, 1987). Only '*anh – em*' [older brother – younger sibling] are used to reduce the severity of complaints.

Although having a wide range of strategies at their disposal, Vietnamese speakers show a general preference for *Disapproval and annoyance* (29.3%) but less inclination to use other more face-threatening strategies. This approach demonstrates a desire to reconcile the speaker's own interest with the need to maintain the relationship with the hearer. The tradition of community-oriented solidarity prevalent in Vietnamese society (Vũ, 1995) seems to underlie this behaviour. This tradition emphasizes conciliatory conduct, equilibrium and relations-based settlement of conflicts and disputes, and a social responsibility to defend face and to please each other (Trần, 1997). Thus, in order to be successful in communicating within the community, Vietnamese speakers need to cultivate tactful, delicate, and gentle speaking habits. This cultural tendency might explain participants' preferences for strategies that allow them to express their annoyance but also save the hearer's face.

The findings show that both social and pragmatic factors affect the strategy selection of Vietnamese speakers. However, the distribution of strategies by social power best reflects an important ideological factor of Vietnamese society: the Confucian rule of "lễ" (rites). "Lễ" is used to reinforce the existing hierarchy in community, lineages, families, and master-student relationships. Thus, "lễ" is a behavioural principle, requiring people to behave in conformity with their position in the social hierarchy. This explains why the participants have a preference for the most tactful strategies when the hearer is in a higher position and move down the tactfulness scale when the hearer is of equal and lower position.

Pragmatic competence of Chinese learners of Vietnamese

As would be expected, the NNSs have access to the same speech-act set of complaints as the NSs although their preference for particular strategies with respect to social and situational parameters deviates from that of the NSs.

The finding that the NNSs employ the same seven complaining strategies can be explained by the claim that strategies for linguistic action are universal, which has been evident in cross-cultural complaint studies comparing American English and Chinese (Chen, Chen, & Chang, 2target011) as well as Korean (Murphy & Neu, 1996); studies of apologies in English, French, German, Hebrew, and Thai (Olshtain, 1989); as well as in studies of requests in different varieties of English, French, Hebrew, Spanish, and Danish (Blum-Kulka, 1989). In addition, Vietnamese and Chinese cultures share some similarities (Trần, 1997), which may facilitate positive transfer of strategies.

At the same time, the learners' complaints were far from nativelike despite the learners being at the upper-intermediate level and sharing some cultural background with the Vietnamese NSs. This was especially apparent in the NNSs' insensitivity to social power. The tendency to employ more severe strategies when complaining to a person of higher position may lead to communication failure in Vietnamese. The NNSs may be judged as not having "lễ" or as being too aggressive by native hearers, and their expression of annoyance may be considered worthless as it is perceived to be spoken by a person without "lễ" or by a person in a bad temper. In contrast, the use of 'soft' strategies when dealing with children may not be effective as they might think the speaker has no power or does not take their offending act seriously. Learners may lack nativelike understanding of the impact of certain strategies, or their analysis of the social situation may be nontargetlike. This may be due to the fact that by the time of data collection, they had been in Vietnam for only three months, and this length of exposure to the target speech community may be insufficient for acquiring such a challenging speech act as complaints.

Further research

There are several areas where future research can contribute to a fuller understanding of Vietnamese pragmatics. One important aspect not covered in this study is language users' online performance. This can be investigated through role plays (Félix-Brasdefer, 2010) or preferably collection of natural data.

Another area of research is contrastive-developmental. How do learners of Vietnamese with different native languages differ in their complaint realizations at different stages of development? And what is the relative contribution of exposure and proficiency to the development of complaints in Vietnamese? Given the rapid growth of Vietnam's international ties and the increasing need for teaching of Vietnamese as a second or foreign language, such investigations are urgently needed.

Conclusion

In conclusion, we find a speech-act set of complaint in Vietnamese which is similar to that in Hebrew and English. Together with the speech-act sets found in apologies, requests, and compliments, this would indicate the universality of the speech-act set across different speech acts and languages. However, the distribution of strategies in the speech-act set according to social and situational factors is different and thus culture-specific.

New issues for both speech-act realizations in Vietnamese and interlanguage pragmatic research have also emerged from this study. Further speech-act studies of complaints in Vietnamese should look into how complaints are realized in online performance as part of extended discourse, and what social and situational variables influence strategy choice. More developmental research, especially relating learners' general linguistic development to their pragmatic performance, would also be welcome.

References

Blum-Kulka, S. (1989). Playing it safe: The role of conventionality in indirect requests. In S. Blum-Kulka, J. House, & G. Kasper (Eds.), *Cross-cultural pragmatics* (pp. 37–70). Norwood, NJ: Ablex.

Boxer, D. (1993). Complaints as positive strategies. *TESOL Quarterly, 27*(2), 277–301.

Boxer, D. (2010). Complaints: How to gripe and establish rapport. In A. Martinez-Flor & E. Uso-Juan (Eds.), *Speech act performance: Theoretical, empirical and methodological issues* (pp. 163–178). Amsterdam: Benjamins.

Brown, G., & Levinson, S. (1987). *Politeness: Some universals in language use.* Cambridge: Cambridge University Press.

Clyne, M. (1994). *Inter-cultural communication at work: Cultural values in discourse.* Cambridge: Cambridge University Press.

Chen, Y.S., Chen, C.Y.D., & Chang, M.S. (2011). American and Chinese complaints: Strategy use from a cross-cultural perspective. *Intercultural Pragmatics, 8*(2), 253–275.

Dersley, I., & Wootton, A. (2000). Complaint sequences within antagonistic argument. *Research on Language & Social Interaction, 33*(4), 375–406.

Drew, P., & Holt, E. (1988). Complainable matters: The use of idiomatic expressions in making complaints. *Social Problems, 35*(4), 398–417.

Heinemann, T. (2009). Participation and exclusion in third party complaints. *Journal of Pragmatics, 41*(12), 2435–2451.

Heinemann, T., & Traverso, V. (2009). Complaining in interaction. *Journal of Pragmatics, 41*(12), 2381–2384.

Hoàng Văn Hành (2002). *Canh huong va chinh sach ngon ngu o Viet nam [Language situation and policies in Vietnam].* Ha Noi: Nha xuat ban khoa hoc xa hoi.

House, J., & Kasper, G. (1981). Politeness markers in English and German. In F. Coulmas (Ed.), *Conversational routine: Explorations in standardized communication situations and prepatterned speech* (pp. 157–185). The Hague: Mouton de Gruyter.

Laforest, M. (2009). Complaining in front of a witness: Aspects of blaming others for their behaviour in multi-party family interactions. *Journal of Pragmatics, 41*(12), 2452–2464.

Leech, G.N. (1983). *Principles of pragmatics*. London: Longman.

Martinez-Flor, A., & Uso-Juan, E. (2010). Pragmatics and speech-act performance. In A. Martinez-Flor & E. Uso-Juan (Eds.), *Speech act performance: Theoretical, empirical and methodological issues* (pp. 3–22).

Moon, K. (2002). *Speech act study: Differences between native and nonnative speaker complaint strategies*. Retrieved March 1, 2013 from http://aladinrc.wrlc.org/handle/1961/5225

Murphy, B., & Neu, J. (1996). My grade is too low: The speech-act set of complaint. In S.M. Gass & J. Neu (Eds.), *Speech acts across cultures: Challenges to communication in a second language* (pp. 191–216). Berlin: Mouton de Gruyter.

Nguyễn Quang (1999). *Compliments in English and Vietnamese: A cross-cultural study.* Hanoi: College of Social Sciences, Dai hoc Quoc Gia Hànôi.

Nguyễn Văn Thuận (1998). *Complaints in English and Vietnamese in terms of what has been done and what has not been done.* Hanoi: Vietnam National University.

Olshtain, E. (1989). Apologies across languages. In S. Blum-Kulka, J. House, & G. Kasper (Eds.), *Cross-cultural pragmatics* (pp. 155–173). New York, NY: Ablex.

Olshtain, E., & Weinbach, L. (1987). Complaints: A study of speech-act behavior among native and nonnative speakers of Hebrew. In J. Verschueren & M. Bertuccelli-Papi (Eds.), *The pragmatic perspective*. Amsterdam: Benjamins.

Phạm Thị Thanh (1995). *Nghi thuc loi noi Tieng Viet hien dai qua cac phat ngon chao, cam on, xin loi [Contemporary Vietnamese speech routines through the speech acts of greeting, thanking, and apologizing].* Hanoi: Dai Hoc Khoa hoc Xa hoi va Nhan van.

Ruusuvuori, J., & Lindfors, P. (2009). Complaining about previous treatment in health care settings. *Journal of Pragmatics, 41*(12), 2415–2434.

Trần Quốc Vượng (1997). *Dai cuong van hoa Viet Nam [Overview of Vietnamese culture].* Ha Noi: Nha Xuat Ban Khoa hoc Xa hoi va Nhan Van.

Trosborg, A. (1995). *Interlanguage pragmatics: Requests, complaints, and apologies*. Berlin: Mouton de Gruyter.

Vũ Thị Thanh Hương (1998). *Politeness in modern Vietnamese: A sociolinguistic study of a Hanoi speech community* (Unpublished doctoral dissertation). University of Toronto, Toronto, Canada.

Appendix: Survey questionnaire

Câu hỏi điều tra

II. Thông tin cá nhân:

Xin bạn cho biết môt số thông tin về bản thân . Chúng tôi đảm bảo thông tin của bạn đươc giữ bí mât và chỉ dùng cho mục đích nghiên cứu của chúng tôi. Bạn chỉ viêc viết câu trả lời vào sau mỗi câu hỏi.

1. Giới tính: Nam/nữ
2. Độ tuổi:
3. Quốc tịch:
4. Bạn đã học Tiếng Việt được bao lâu?

II. Câu hỏi tình huống:

1. Bạn vừa đươc nhận vào làm việc ở một công ty, hôm qua, Sếp giao cho bạn rất nhiều việc, bạn phải ở lại văn phòng một mình tới tận 10 giờ đêm. Hôm nay gặp Sếp, bạn sẽ nói như thế nào?
   ……………………………………………………………………………………………
   ……………………………………………………………………………………………
2. Đang đi xe trên đường, bạn bị một người khác lách lên, va vào bạn làm bạn suýt ngã. Người ấy không xin lỗi bạn, bạn sẽ nói như thế nào với người ấy?
   ……………………………………………………………………………………………
   ……………………………………………………………………………………………
3. Bạn là nhân viên của một công ty, hôm nay bạn có hẹn làm việc với Sếp một công ty khác. Bạn đến và chờ mãi nhưng không thấy ông ta đâu. Bạn định đi về thì ông ta mới xuất hiện và làm như không có chuyện gì xảy ra hết. Bạn sẽ nói như thế nào với ông ta?
   ……………………………………………………………………………………………
   ……………………………………………………………………………………………
4. Trong một kì thi, một người ngồi cùng bàn (bạn không quen người này) mượn của bạn máy tính và làm rơi xuống đất. Người ấy trả nhưng máy không hoạt động. Bạn nói với cô/anh ta như thế nào?
   ……………………………………………………………………………………………
   ……………………………………………………………………………………………
5. Vừa rồi là sinh nhật bạn nhưng bạn thân của bạn bân không đến đươc và cũng không có quà. Hôm nay gặp người bạn đó, bạn sẽ nói như thế nào?
   ……………………………………………………………………………………………
   ……………………………………………………………………………………………
6. Bạn là giáo viên dạy trong một lớp học. Có một học sinh luôn đến muộn. Hôm nay học sinh ấy đến muôn 15 phút. Bạn nói với anh ta/cô ta như thế nào?
   ……………………………………………………………………………………………
   ……………………………………………………………………………………………

7. Trong lúc ăn, con bạn làm vỡ môt chiếc bát. Bạn nói với con như thế nào?
   …………………………………………………………………………………………
   …………………………………………………………………………………………
8. Có một nhóm trẻ con hay nghịch bấm chuông cửa nhà bạn. Lần này bạn bắt gặp chúng đang định bấm chuông cửa. Bạn nói như thế nào với chúng?
   …………………………………………………………………………………………
   …………………………………………………………………………………………
9. Hôm qua em bạn đã không nghe lời bạn đi chơi tới khuya mới về. Hôm nay bạn nói với em như thế nào?
   …………………………………………………………………………………………
   …………………………………………………………………………………………

Xin cám ơn bạn!

English survey questionnaire

Could you please provide your personal details and responses to the situations? All of your personal details and the responses are confidential and only used for the purpose of our research.

Personal details:

1. Sex:
2. Age:
3. Occupation:

Situations:

1. You have just got a job in a company. Yesterday, the boss assigned you a lot of work and you had to stay alone in the office until 10 P.M to finish it. Today, you see him; what would you tell him?

   ……………………………………………………………………………………………

   ……………………………………………………………………………………………

2. You were riding a motorcycle on the road, a person overtook you and nearly knocked you down, but s/he did not apologize you. What would you say to her/him?

   ……………………………………………………………………………………………

   ……………………………………………………………………………………………

3. You are an officer in a company; today you had an appointment with the boss of another company. You had been waiting for a long time and just when you were about to leave, he turned up. What would you say to the boss?

   ……………………………………………………………………………………………

   ……………………………………………………………………………………………

4. In an exam, the candidate sitting next to you (previously unknown to you) borrowed your calculator. When he returned it, you realized that it did not work any more. What would you say to him?

   ……………………………………………………………………………………………

   ……………………………………………………………………………………………

5. Yesterday was your birthday but your close friend did not come to the party and neither did s/he send a present to you. Today you meet her/him; what would you tell her/him?

   ……………………………………………………………………………………………

   ……………………………………………………………………………………………

6. You are a teacher in a class. There's a student who is always late; today s/he is 15 minutes late. What would you tell her/him?

   ……………………………………………………………………………………

   ……………………………………………………………………………………

7. You son/daughter broke a bowl during a meal. What would you tell her/him?

   ……………………………………………………………………………………

   ……………………………………………………………………………………

8. There is a group of teenagers who keep ringing your doorbell (for fun). Today, you caught them in action. What would you say to them?

   ……………………………………………………………………………………………

   ……………………………………………………………………………………………

9. Yesterday, your younger brother/sister did not take your advice but went out late. What would you say to him/her today?

   ……………………………………………………………………………………………

   ……………………………………………………………………………………………

Thank you very much!

4 Address Forms in Vietnamese: Learners' Sociolinguistic Competence

Vân Thị Thanh Trần
The University of Melbourne

Introduction

Systematic research on address terms began with Brown and Gilman's (1960) seminal paper on the *tu/vous* distinction in other-address to negotiate power and solidarity between interlocutors. Since then a multitude of studies have investigated address terms in several languages and found Brown and Gilman's dichotomous analysis overly simplistic. In reality, address systems vary across languages and can be highly complex in the range of choices they offer as well as the practices used in everyday communication (Djenar, 2006; Wardhaugh, 2002; Warren, 2006; Williams-van Klinken & Hajek, 2006), and this complexity causes difficulties for language learners (Barron, 2006). While closely related languages may have similar address term options but differ in their practices of address term use and the social context factors that impact that use (e.g., German and Swedish; Clyne, Kretzenbacher, Norrby, & Schüpbach, 2006), the range of address term choices and the types of factors that influence address term selection can vary greatly between more distant languages. One criticism of Brown and Gilman's original work was its focus on Indo-European languages (Braun, 1988), which consequently results in a need to document address terms in other languages. The present study will investigate the address system of a non-European language, Vietnamese,

Pragmatics of Vietnamese as a native and target language, pp. 135–176
Carsten Roever & Hạnh thị Nguyễn (Eds.), 2013
Honolulu, HI: University of Hawai'i, National Foreign Language Resource Center

and take a variationist sociolinguistic perspective, focusing on the effects of the variables age, gender, and social distance, to probe native and nonnative speakers' beliefs about the Vietnamese address system.

In the sections below, I will first provide a description of address forms in Vietnamese, a review of studies on the proficiency and exposure effects in second language acquisition, and a review of studies on the acquisition of address forms. Then I will present an empirical study on how learners of Vietnamese use address forms in various contexts.

Address forms in Vietnamese

The address system in Vietnamese has been investigated by several descriptive linguists (e.g., Lương, 1990; C. V. Nguyễn, 1993, 2004; Đ. T. Nguyễn, 1996; Q. Nguyễn, 2002; Thompson, 1965). However, unlike the present study, their works are nonempirical, relying on authors' intuitions, observations, and quotations from literary works. These researchers agree that the Vietnamese address system, like that of many Asian languages, is complex, with the extension of kinship terms to nongenealogically related interlocutors. Generally, the address system in Vietnamese consists of three grammatical categories: personal pronouns, kinship terms, and proper nouns.

Personal pronouns

In Vietnamese, personal pronouns used to address someone can be classified according to person as shown in Table 1 (adapted from C. V. Nguyễn, 2004 and Đ. T. Nguyễn, 1996).

Table 1. Personal pronouns used as address forms in Vietnamese

number	first person	second person	third person
singular	*tao, ta, tôi, mình, tớ, người ta*	*mày, cậu, đằng ấy*	*nó, hắn, con đó, thằng đó*
plural	*tụi tao, chúng ta, chúng mình, tụi tôi, chúng tớ*	*chúng mày, tụi mày, bọn mày*	*chúng nó, tụi nó, bọn đó, bọn ấy, họ*

These pronouns are often used as complementary pairs in addressing (i.e., the use of the first person form influences the use of the second person form). For example, when an interlocutor refers to himself or herself as *người ta* [myself], the other interlocutor will be addressed as *đằng ấy* [that-side, you] (see Table 4 for the symmetrical pairs of these forms).

Kinship terms

The most complicated address forms in Vietnamese are kinship terms because they reflect and construct personal relationships in Vietnamese society. Dương (2002) claims that Vietnamese has 89 kinship terms describing three generations either below or above oneself. These terms include the words denoting the members of the nuclear family as well as the extended family, including in-law relationships. Moreover, kinship terms in Vietnamese emphasize age and gender; for example, Vietnamese speakers use *anh* [older brother] to address an older male and *chị* [older sister] to address an older female. In the extended family, this system also distinguishes relatives by using different words for one's paternal side or one's maternal side. For instance, Vietnamese speakers use *chú* [paternal uncle] to address one's father's younger brother, and *cậu* [maternal uncle] to address one's mother's younger brother. To make the matter more complex, kinship terms vary across the three major dialects of Vietnamese: Northern, Central, and Southern Vietnamese. For example, in the Northern dialect, one's father's younger sister is addressed as *cô* [aunt - younger than one's father], but in the Central dialect this relative is addressed as *o*.

While a striking feature of Vietnamese address forms is that the Vietnamese tend to use kinship terms frequently in everyday conversations between nongenealogically related interlocutors (Đ. T. Nguyễn, 1996; Trương, 1999), they do not use all the kinship terms for addressing others in social interactions. The most commonly used forms are *ông* [grandfather], *bà* [grandmother], *bác* [uncle/aunt – older than one's father/mother], *chú* [uncle – younger than one's father], *cô* [aunt – younger than one's father], *cháu* [grandchild/nephew/niece], *anh* [older brother], *chị* [older sister], and *em* [younger sibling].

Proper nouns

In Vietnamese, speakers may use first names in addressing, but they do not use last names as English speakers do. Instead, in spoken interaction, Vietnamese speakers both refer to themselves and address their interlocutors by first name if the interlocutors are of roughly the same age. In some cases, young people address their friends who belong to the same age group by their first names and refer to themselves as *tôi* [servant I], *tớ* [servant I], *mình* (literally means body) [intimate I].

Particularly in the South of Vietnam, in addressing, speakers use the formulation of *title + order of birth* of the addressee in his or her family. For example, the addressee can be called *ông Ba* [Mr. Third], *bà Tám* [Mrs. Eighth], *anh Hai* [Brother Second].

Given the limited scope of this exploratory study, I will focus on address forms commonly used in everyday social interactions. The following table (Table 2, based on T. N. Vũ, 1996) presents some common forms and their usage.

Table 2. The use of common address forms in Vietnamese

address form	translation	usage
cụ	great-grandfather	to address an old man in formal situations or a man who is as old as addressor's great-grandfather
ông	grandfather	to address a man in formal situations or a man who is as old as addressor's grandfather
bà	grandmother	to address a woman in formal situations or a woman who is as old as addressor's grandmother
bác	uncle/aunt–older than one's father/ mother	to address a person, regardless of gender, who is older than the parent of the addressor
cô	aunt – younger than one's mother	to address a woman younger than the addressor's mother
chú	uncle – younger than one's father	to address a man younger than the addressor's father
thầy (giáo)	male teacher	to address a male teacher
cô (giáo)	female teacher	to address a female teacher
anh	older brother	to address a man of the same generation who is older than the addressor
chị	older sister	to address a woman of the same generation who is older than the addressor
em	younger sibling	to address a person of the same generation, regardless of gender, who is younger than the addressor
các em	younger brothers/sisters (plural form)	to address people of the same generation, regardless of gender, who are younger than the addressor
cậu	uncle – younger than one's mother	to address a friend in an intimate way; sometimes to address a man who is much younger than the addressor, for example from a teacher to a male student
mày	you (informal)	to address a friend in a colloquial way

bạn	friend	to address a friend in a friendly way
bọn mày/ chúng mày	you (plural; informal)	to address a group of people younger than addressor in a colloquial way
cháu/	grandchild/niece/nephew	to address a person who is (one generation) younger than the addressor
các cháu	grandchildren (plural)	to address people who are (one generation) younger than the addressor

Self-reference forms in Vietnamese

A salient feature of the Vietnamese address system is that an address form is normally accompanied by a corresponding selfreference form. Each pair is normally of the same category of address term. For instance, a personal pronoun co-occurs with another personal pronoun, and a kinship term also co-occurs with another kinship term.

While the addressing and selfreferencing functions of personal pronouns are normally unchanging according to person, kinship terms are used interchangeably as address forms or selfreference forms. That is, if a kinship term is used as an address form, its complementary kinship term is used as a selfreference form and vice versa. For instance, if X addresses Y as *ông* [grandfather] and refers to himself/herself as *cháu* [grandchild/nephew/niece], Y then addresses X as *cháu* [grandchild/nephew/niece] and refers to himself as *ông* [grandfather].

The co-occurrence of address forms and selfreference forms is presented in the lists below (see Table 2 above for translation of the forms).

Table 3. Corresponding pairs of kinship terms (following Q. Nguyễn, 2002, p. 162)

first person	second person
cụ	*cháu*
ông	*cháu*
bà	*cháu*
bác	*cháu*
chú	*cháu*
cô	*cháu*
anh	*em*
chị	*em*

Table 4. Corresponding pairs of pronouns (adapted from Q. Nguyễn, 2002)

first person	second person
mình [intimate I]	*người ta* [intimate you]
tớ [servant I]	*đằng ấy* [other side–you]
tớ [servant I]	*mình* [intimate you]
tên riêng (first name)	tên riêng (first name)
tớ [servant I]	tên riêng (first name)
tớ [servant I]	*ấy* [intimate you]
tớ [servant I]	*cậu* [uncle–casual you]
mình [intimate I]	*cậu* [uncle–casual you]
tôi [servant I]	*cậu* [uncle–casual you]
tao [informal I]	*mày* [informal you]

Practices of addressing in Vietnamese

In addition to the wide range of address forms, the Vietnamese address system is complex because the addressor's choice of address forms is determined by social factors, the speaker's positioning toward the recipient, and the activity at hand. First, in social interactions, the interlocutors must take into consideration sociolinguistic factors such as relative age, social status, gender, profession, degree of acquaintance, and respect in choosing the right address terms (Lê, 1999; Lương, 1990; Đ. T. Nguyễn, 1996). Due to the Confucian reverence for age, respect for elderly people is frequently encoded in social interactions. For example, when a doctor is much younger than a patient, she or he should refer to herself or himself as *cháu* [grandchild] and the patient as *cụ* [great grandfather/grandmother] or *bác* [uncle – older than one's father/mother], depending on the age of the patient.

Moreover, the basic rule for addressing in Vietnamese is "*Xưng là phải khiêm, hô là phải tôn*" [Humble yourself when selfreferring, elevate others when addressing] (Lê, 1999; C. V. Nguyễn, 2004; H. T. T. Vũ, 1997) which means that addressors should show modesty when referring to themselves and respect when addressing their interlocutors. For example, when conversing with a stranger, a speaker may call himself or herself *em* [younger sibling] and call the stranger *anh* [older brother] or *chị* [older sister] even when the speaker is older than the stranger.

Second, the choice of address forms in conversations also varies according to the context and the affective stance that the conversational participants want to convey (C. V. Nguyễn, 2004). For example, the pair *mày* [you] and *tao* [I] is normally used in informal situations between interlocutors of the same age and social status, or between close friends. However, a parent may use these forms to refer to herself or himself and to address her or his child when angry with the child. As another example, when a man changes the address form toward his female colleague from *tôi - cô* (an almost neutral address between strangers of the same age range) to *anh - em* (a closer/intimate address, normally used between lovers or spouses), it can be understood that the man is attempting to shift their relationship toward a more intimate level, and in certain conditions, this change might be understood as an explicit love proposal (Cao, 2001). The sensitivity of address terms to the action being performed is also demonstrated in H. Nguyễn's (2009) study on recommendation sequences in family discourse. She found that the father used the address terms *ba – con* and *ba – [child's name]* when he initiated a recommendation sequence, but omitted the subject in subsequent turns in the same recommendation sequence.

The appropriate use of address forms can be expected to be challenging for cultural novices, such as children and nonnative speakers. In order to master the Vietnamese address system, learners need to acquire both pragmalinguistic knowledge of address forms and sociopragmatic norms for determining the use of address forms in everyday social interactions.

Research into learners' acquisition of pragmatic knowledge indicates that the two most influential factors that affect interlanguage pragmatic (ILP) development (including that of address terms) include general proficiency and exposure to the target language environment, to which we will now turn.

Acquisition of address forms

Researchers in interlanguage pragmatics have investigated the influence of individual difference factors such as amount of language input, proficiency, and learning environment, on students' acquisition of address systems. In a study looking at a study-abroad environment, Kinginger (2008) investigated American learners of French in their sojourn in France, and found that the learners' communicative competence (including general academic language proficiency, pragmatic competence, and language awareness) developed through their interaction with native speakers. In particular, the learners' ability to use address forms significantly developed toward the native norms. The students were able to move from the overuse of formal *vous* to the use of appropriate forms thanks to their experience of interaction in a broad array of social interactive settings during their study-abroad period. In an earlier report of the same project, Kinginger and Farrell (2006) focused on learners' awareness of the use of address forms *tu* and *vous* in different social interactions. They concluded that studying abroad has a significant effect on learners' addressivity development no matter how high their metapragmatic awareness is.

Also, in an investigation into the acquisition of address forms by learners of Indonesian in a study-abroad environment, DuFon (1999) suggested that the input provided by native speakers did not always promote learners' appropriate use of address forms because native speakers might change their choice of address forms unnaturally in foreigner talk. In this longitudinal study, DuFon compared the pragmatic competence development of two groups of learners of Indonesian: a group at the beginner level and a group at the intermediate level. She found that learners' acquisition of address forms did not depend on their proficiency but on their awareness of the use of address forms in social contexts. A beginner learner, after a four-month course in Indonesia, used the address forms far more appropriately than two intermediate learners because she focused her attention on the use of address forms by native Indonesians. She thought that address forms were an important aspect of language, so she developed strategies to learn these forms. Similarly, an intermediate learner was able to use targetlike address forms because he paid attention to acquiring the use of address forms. However, some learners opted to preserve their personal values, which limited the amount of effort they spent on the acquisition of address forms.

In another study on pragmatic performance by learners of Indonesian, Hassall (2008) examined Bialystok's (1993) two-dimensional model of knowledge versus control by using retrospective verbal reports. He confirmed that high-proficiency learners with study-abroad experience excelled and paid more attention to pragmatic norms than their low-proficiency counterparts without study-abroad experience. The contribution of his research in address form usage is in identifying the difference between knowledge and performance: despite their knowledge of both the form and the social rule governing the use of the address form, some learners did not use the correct form.

Focusing on the effects of telecollaboration outside of the language classroom, Belz and Kinginger (2003) examined the development of pragmatic competence by a group of learners of German through networked collaboration with native peers. The group of English learners of German enjoyed interaction with German learners of English via email. The language used in the emails was German, and native German speakers corrected the English learners' use of the second-person pronouns *du* (familiar) and *Sie* (formal). The researchers found that most learners developed their pragmatic competence regarding the appropriate use of address forms in this social context through telecollaboration with native German peers over a two-month period. They concluded that learners' participation in different contexts promotes their sociopragmatic competence regarding the use of address forms.

Similarly, González-Lloret (2008) reported a case study of American learners of Spanish in computer-mediated collaboration with native speakers. She argued that the Spanish address system is especially difficult for learners because Spanish is a pro-drop language in which subject pronouns can be omitted, and because address forms in Spanish are complex and vary according to geographical regions, dialects and speakers' sociocultural and economic circumstances. She hypothesized that learners would develop targetlike address behavior via online collaboration with their Spanish peers because of the native speakers' correction, and she confirmed the hypothesis in her study. The findings suggested that synchronous computer-mediated communication is an excellent supplementary environment to the language classroom to develop learners' sociolinguistic competence, as long as instructors engage learners in appropriate tasks for sufficient periods of time.

In sum, the learning environment and L2 speakers' opportunities for interaction with native speakers of the target language play a significant role in the acquisition of L2 address forms. Learners' language proficiency as well as their awareness and attention also impact their learning of L2 address. However, there are no published studies of the acquisition of address forms by L2 learners of Vietnamese, despite numerous descriptions of the Vietnamese address system (e.g., Dương, 2002; C. V. Nguyễn, 1992, 2004; Đ. T. Nguyễn, 1996; Lương, 1990; Trương, 2002; H. T. T. Vũ, 1997). The current study sets out to contribute to filling that gap.

Research questions

This study addresses the following three questions:

1. What do L2 learners of Vietnamese know about the use of address forms in social contexts? How does their knowledge coincide with or differ from native speaker norms?
2. Does exposure to Vietnamese-speaking environments promote learners' knowledge of Vietnamese address forms?
3. Does the learners' language proficiency affect the accuracy in their knowledge about address forms?

Methodology

Study design

This study employs a comparative model. It describes the use of address forms by learners of Vietnamese and then compares their use with that of native Vietnamese speakers. Through a cross-sectional design, this study also explores the relationship between exposure, language proficiency, and learners' accuracy in using the Vietnamese address forms. A cross-sectional design allows the researcher to control extraneous variables affecting the learners' performance, thus making it feasible to administer the study given the limited time frame.

Furthermore, a cross-sectional study can identify issues in learners' pragmatic development, thus laying the basis that will inform the research hypotheses for subsequent longitudinal studies (Bardovi-Harlig & Hartford, 1993).

Participants

Given the scarcity of learners of Vietnamese, participants in the research were selected through the researcher's personal contacts. Fifty-nine learners of Vietnamese and 46 native speakers of Vietnamese took part in the study.

Twenty male and 39 female university students, aged from 19 to 25, learning Vietnamese in two institutions in Hanoi participated in the study. They were grouped according to their length of stay in Vietnam at the time of data collection and their proficiency level. The first group consisted of 21 Chinese students who had been living in Vietnam for one month, and they were placed in a preintermediate level by their institution. The second group consisted of 38 Chinese students who had been in Vietnam for at least five months. This group of students had been previously majoring in Vietnamese in China, and they were continuing their studies at an institution in Hanoi. Their proficiency level was considered advanced according to their institution.

Nine male and 36 female native Vietnamese speakers from Hanoi, aged from 20 to 43, participated in the study. They all spoke the Hanoi dialect, the same variety of Vietnamese learned by the nonnative participants (this dialect is also the official variety of the Vietnamese language; Hoàng, 2002). The NS participants differed in their occupations, including students, teachers, nurses, and blue-collar workers.

A summary of participant characteristics is presented in Table 5 below.

Table 5. Summary of participants' characteristics

group	number of participants	age range	gender distribution
preintermediate (PI)	21	21–23	6 males 15 females
advanced (AD)	38	19–25	14 males 24 females
native speakers (NS)	46	20–43	9 males 36 females

Instruments

Discourse completion task

The written discourse completion task (DCT) utilized in the study included 12 scenarios which had been selected from previous observations of native speakers' interactions in everyday life (Appendices A and B). Each scenario in the DCT consisted of a detailed description, including the variables prevalent in the choice of address forms by NS Vietnamese: age, gender, and social status. Table 6 shows a brief summary of the twelve scenarios.

Table 6. DCT scenarios

number	scenario
1	Ask a female teacher a question.
2	Greet a female neighbor who is younger than your mother.
3	Talk to a patient who is much older than you are. [you are the doctor]
4	Borrow a document from your male boss who is older than your father.
5	Say sorry to a stranger of the opposite gender and at your age who you bumped into in the street.
6	Ask your close friend's younger sister to buy a book for you.
7	Say sorry to a colleague of the same gender and at your age after you left a book at home that you promised to lend him/her.
8	Give comments on a coat that your close friend tried on and intends to buy.
9	Ask for a signature on a document from the dean of the faculty, who you have never met.
10	Talk to a male student who makes noise in class. [you are the teacher]
11	Talk to the housemaid who broke the vase that you liked.
12	Talk to a group of teenagers who keep teasing your dog.

DCTs were considered suitable research instruments for this study because they facilitate a high degree of standardization and comparability between cohorts, in this case native and nonnative speakers of Vietnamese. They also allow elicitation of respondents' knowledge and beliefs about address terms, which is the focus of this study.

The authenticity of the scenarios was initially based on the researcher's intuition as a cultural member and post hoc confirmed with the native speakers in the study. All of them indicated that most of the scenarios were highly authentic, noting that they had encountered most of these scenarios in their everyday spoken interactions. However, five out of ten interviewees found the scenario between the doctor and the old patient difficult as it is profession specific, and they had not previously encountered it. More importantly, they all commented that the description of scenarios with variables such as age, gender, profession, and generation were informative and useful for them to decide which address forms to use. Notably, three informants stated that they were not sure whether in actual conversation they would address their conversationalists as they did in the questionnaire because in real-life interaction, responses from their interlocutors may influence their choice of address terms. This point reflects the reflexive nature of address terms in social interaction and a common limitation of the use of DCTs.

Interviews

Retrospective interviews were conducted with ten NSs in the study to obtain in-depth understanding of the native respondents' use of address forms. In addition, the interviews were used to confirm the authenticity of the scenarios in the DCT as mentioned above. The interviews were semistructured with an interview guide (see Appendix C). The interview guide provided the researcher with a clear focus when interviewing participants, thus ensuring that predetermined topics were covered. Furthermore, the flexibility of the semistructured interviews enabled the researcher to pursue emerging topics that had not been articulated in advance (Caspecken, 1996) or topics that provided a comprehensive understanding of the interviewee's use of address forms.

Due to logistical constraints, it was not possible to conduct interviews with the learners of Vietnamese. In order to gain a deeper understanding of the informants' knowledge of the use of the Vietnamese address forms, two open-ended questions were included following the DCT portion of the questionnaire. The first question asked which of the 12 scenarios the participants found to be most difficult and for what reasons. The second question asked why they selected the chosen address form(s).

Data collection procedure

The students completed the DCT as an exercise during their class time. The class teachers gave oral explanations, first in Vietnamese and then in Chinese, if there were comprehension problems. The students were also advised not to discuss their answers with each other while completing the DCT.

The DCT was administered to Vietnamese native speakers either in person or electronically. Ten NS participants were selected to be interviewed individually upon completion of the DCT to investigate their perceptions of the scenarios as well as their use of address forms in everyday social interactions.

Analytical procedure

Data from the DCT

First, the address forms used by the learners in each scenario were extracted and counted. Although selfreference forms were not the focus of this study, given the complementary nature of address and selfreference forms in Vietnamese, the use of selfreference forms by learners was also analyzed. Then the NS data was analyzed in the same way, and these address forms and selfreference forms then served as the benchmark against which the students' use of address forms was compared. All cases where learners did not provide any answers, or used forms without any addressing function, or used several address forms in a response, were omitted. Finally, the NNS data was compared between the two learner groups to examine the relationship between accuracy of use and exposure and proficiency.

Data from the interviews

The interviews were coded according to three main issues: (a) the authenticity of the scenarios in the DCT, (b) the variables influencing the choice of address forms in social interactions, and (c) the most difficult scenario and the reason why they selected the address form(s) for that scenario. Similarly, the students' responses to the additional questions in the DCT were coded according to (a) the reasons why they found the scenario difficult, and (b) the variable(s) affecting their choice of address form in that scenario.

Results

Results from the DCT

Use of address forms by learners of Vietnamese

Although each scenario in the DCT was designed to elicit the use of a particular address form, the findings from the DCT responses will be presented according to each group of scenarios (classified by their sociopragmatic features) in the section below. As discussed in the literature review, address forms in Vietnamese are normally accompanied by the complementary selfreference for the addressors. As a result, the use of selfreference by the native speakers and the two groups of learners will also be presented following the address forms in each group of scenarios. However, due to the large variation in the use of selfreference forms among the three groups, only the forms that account for 5% or more are reported in the sections below.

Teacher-related scenarios

Table 7. Use of address forms in teacher-related scenarios

address form	scenario								
	1			9			10		
	NS	AD	PI	NS	AD	PI	NS	AD	PI
cô	100%	89%	90%						
thầy	0%	0%	5%	96%	92%	90%			
giáo sư				4%	0%	0%			
no address form				0%	5%	0%			
*thầy...ông**				0%	0%	5%			
*ông ... thầy**				0%	0%	5%			

continued...

Table 7. Use of address forms in teacher-related scenarios *(cont.)*

address form	scenario								
	1			9			10		
	NS	AD	PI	NS	AD	PI	NS	AD	PI
cậu							13%	0%	0%
no address form							13%	0%	19%
first name							9%	0%	0%
các em							4%	0%	0%
em + first name							2%	3%	0%
bạn							2%	5%	5%

Note: NS=native speakers; AD=advanced learners; PI=preintermediate learners
* the respondent changes the forms from sentence to sentence

As Table 7 shows, both groups of advanced and preintermediate learners used the same form as native speakers with relatively similar frequency (e.g., 89% and 90%, compared to 100% of NS) in this group of scenarios. They even used honorifics to indicate respect to teachers as native speakers do, as illustrated in Examples 1–3.

Example 1: NS -S1

```
Thưa         cô,               cô               có thể
(Honorific) female teacher, female teacher possible
Teacher, could you please

giảng   lại   phần này  được      không ạ?
explain again part this possible  not   PolM
explain this part again?
```

Example 2: AD-S1

```
Thưa         cô,               em
(Honorific) female teacher, younger sibling (student)
Teacher, I

không  hiểu        lắm   bài    này,
not    understand much  lesson this
don't understand this lesson very much,

xin cô              giảng   lại   một lần nữa.
beg female teacher explain again one time more
Could you explain it once more?
```

Example 3: PI-S9

```
Thưa          thầy,          xin lỗi,
(Honorific) male teacher, sorry,
Excuse me, teacher,

em                          xin    ông
younger sibbling (student) beg    grandfather
could I have

chữ ký     ở  đây,   được không?
signature in here, possible no
mister's signature here, please?
```

In Scenario 10, in which a teacher addresses a male student (see Appendix B for details), the two groups of learners also produced the form *em,* which was similar to native speakers. However, both of the advanced and preintermediate learner groups employed this form even more frequently than native speakers, exceeding native speaker use by 20% (84% and 71%). While 19% of preintermediate learners opted to avoid using any address forms, as did a minority of native speakers, none of their advanced peers avoided address. Neither of the learner groups chose to address their interlocutor as *cậu* [uncle – mother's younger brother to mean "you"], although some native speakers did. Native speakers probably use this form to convey a certain degree of intimacy between the speaker and the hearer. Learners may know this form but may not have experienced it in teacher-learner interactions, which accounts for the absence of the form in their answers.

Table 8. Use of selfreference forms in teacher-related scenarios

address form	self-reference form	scenario 1			9			10		
		NS	AD	PI	NS	AD	PI	NS	AD	PI
cô	*em*	98%	87%	86%						
thầy	*em*				93%	79%	81%			
	no self-reference				2%	11%	5%			
	cháu				0%	0%	5%			
em	no self-reference							35%	61%	57%
	cô							20%	13%	5%
	thầy							0%	8%	5%
	chị							0%	0%	5%
no address form	no self-reference							4%	0%	19%

Similarly, there is almost no difference among the three groups in their use of selfreference forms, except for those in Scenario 10, as shown in Table 8. In the classroom context, the selfreference form *em* [younger sibling (student)] is always used in conjunction with the address form *cô* [female teacher] (Lê, 1999).

In Scenario 1, while the preintermediate group was closer to the native speakers in the use of this selfreference form than their advanced counterparts (81% and 79%, respectively), a learner of this group deviated from the native speakers by using the form *cháu* [nephew/niece] to refer to herself in Example 4.

Example 4: PI-S10

```
Chào  thầy          ạ,    cháu
Greet male teacher PolM, grandchild/nephew/niece
Good morning, teacher. I

là sinh viên của lớp X,
be student   of  class X,
am a student of class X,

cháu                    muốn thầy         chữ ký
grandchild/nephew/niece want male teacher signature
I would like you to sign

giúp cháu                    ở  đây, có thể   không?
help grandchild/nephew/niece in here, possible not?
here for me, is that ok?
```

In Scenario 10, the advanced learners provided no selfreference form almost twice as frequently as native speakers (61% and 35%, respectively) when *em* is used as the address form, and 57% of the preintermediate learners employed the same strategy. In conjunction with the address form *em*, approximately the same percentage of native speakers and advanced learners (20% and 13%, respectively) referred to themselves as *cô,* as in Examples 5 and 6, compared with 5% of the preintermediate group. Surprisingly, 19% of preintermediate learners chose to use neither address forms nor selfreference forms at all, compared with only 4% of native speakers and 0% of advanced learners.

Example 5: NS-S10

```
(Tên học sinh),   em                         đang
(Student's name), younger sibling (student) Prog.
(Student's name), you

làm phiền cô             và  các    bạn     đấy!
disturb   female teacher and plural friends AffM!
are disturbing me and your friends!
```

Example 6: PI-S10

```
Bây giờ cô             cảm thấy không hài lòng.
Now     female teacher feel     not    satisfied
I am not pleased with you right now.

Xin em                        không được
Beg younger sibling (student) not   possible
Please don't

đùa nghịch  trong lớp học!
fool around in     class!
fool around in class!
```

It appears that native speakers' and learners' use of the address forms and self reference in this group of scenarios is fairly clear and homogeneous because these are teacher-specific scenarios. However, their usage differed and became more dispersed when the addressee roles changed to other common roles in social interactions, to which now we turn.

Scenarios in which the addressee is older than the addressor

Table 9. Use of address forms in scenarios in which the addressee is older than the addressor

address form	scenario								
	2			3			4		
	NS	AD	PI	NS	AD	PI	NS	AD	PI
cô	93%	87%	62%	0%	0%	10%			
chị	0%	3%	19%						
bác	0%	5%	5%	87%	63%	19%	78%	26%	10%
bà	0%	0%	5%	0%	5%	0%	0%	0%	5%
em	0%	0%	10%						
*ông/bà**				2%	0%	5%			
chú				0%	8%	5%	13%	5%	0%
ông				0%	5%	38%	0%	55%	81%
*bác/ông**				0%	0%	5%			
*bác/chú/ anh/chị**				0%	0%	5%			
xếp							7%	8%	0%

Note: * slash (/) indicates that respondent uses several different address forms

As shown in Table 9, both groups of learners used the forms as most native speakers did in this group of scenarios, but the learners selected more varied address forms than the native speakers, and some forms were not chosen by any native speakers. However, the advanced learners produced the forms preferred by NSs with much higher frequency than the preintermediate learners (e.g., 87% vs. 62% in Scenario 2), as seen in Examples 7 and 8.

Example 7: NS-S2

```
Cháu          chào   cô!  Cô    đi làm ạ?
Nephew/niece  greet aunt! Aunt go work PolM?
Good morning, auntie! Are young going to work?
```

Example 8: AD-S2

```
Cháu         chào   cô!  Cô   có   khoẻ không?
Nephew/niece greet  aunt! Aunt yes well  no?
Good morning, auntie! How are you?
```

In Scenario 2, a large number of preintermediate learners (19%) employed the form *chị* [older sister] (see Example 9), which was not used by any native speakers. This form is used to address a woman who is in the same generation as the addressor; therefore, it is inappropriate to use it to address a woman who is in the generation above the addressor. Similarly, the form *em* [younger sister] was not used by any native speakers in this scenario.

Example 9: PI-S2

```
Chào  chị          ạ!   Ăn sáng        chưa ạ!
Greet older sister PolM! Eat breakfast PolM!
Good morning, sister! Have you had breakfast?

Chị          đi đâu   đấy?
Older sister go where AffM?
Where are you going?
```

In Scenario 3, the preintermediate learners tended to prefer the form *ông* [grandfather], which was not selected by many of the native speakers. The same percentage of preintermediate learners (19%) employed the form *cụ* [great-grandfather] and *bác* [uncle], and 10% of the preintermediate learners even addressed the patient as *cô* [aunt], which was not used by the native speakers as it is only used when the addressee is younger than the addressor's mother.

Example 10: AD-S3

```
Bác   ơi,       bác   cảm thấy thế nào ạ?
Uncle vocative, uncle feel     how     PolM?
How do you feel, uncle?
```

In Scenario 4, the native speakers used the form *xếp,* which literally means "boss" and tends to convey a closeness to addressees. Only the advanced learners used this form, and the preintermediate group did not. Yet, both groups of learners provided the form *ông* [grandfather/sir], with the preintermediate learners using this form more frequently than the advanced learners (81% and 55%, respectively), as shown in Example 12. This form was utilized by none of the native speakers, who strongly preferred *bác* [uncle] as the advanced learner also did in Example 11.

Example 11: AD-S4

```
Bác   ơi,        xin cho  cháu          mượn
Uncle vocative, beg give nephew/niece borrow
Uncle, I'd like to borrow

một số  tài liệu ạ.
several document PolM
some documents please.
```

Example 12: PI-S4

```
Cháu         chào   ông         ạ!
Grand child greet grandfather PolM!
Good morning, sir.

Cháu        mới xin được  một  công việc mới.
Grandchild new beg PosM  one  job        new.
I have just been accepted to a new job.

Cháu        muốn mượn   một số  tài liệu
Grandchild want borrow several document
I would like to borrow several documents

với  ông          có  được    không ạ?
with grandfather yes posible no PolM
with you, is that OK?
```

Table 10. Use of selfreference forms in scenarios in which the addressee is older than the addressor

address form	self-reference form	scenario								
		2			3			4		
		NS	AD	PI	NS	AD	PI	NS	AD	PI
	cháu	93%	79%	5%						
	no self-reference	0%	8%	48%						
cô	*em*	0%	3%	10%						
cô	*cháu*									

continued...

Table 10. Use of selfreference forms in scenarios in which the addressee is older than the addressor *(cont.)*

address form	self-reference form	scenario								
		2			3			4		
		NS	AD	PI	NS	AD	PI	NS	AD	PI
bác	*cháu*				0%	50%	0%	80%	26%	5%
	no self-reference				0%	13%	0%			
	em							0%	0%	5%
chú	*cháu*							13%	3%	0%
	cháu							0%	55%	14%
ông	*em*							0%	11%	52%
	no self-reference							0%	0%	10%

Table 10 indicates that despite minor differences, the advanced learners used selfreference forms with fairly equal frequency to the native speakers, whereas the preintermediate learners differed significantly from the native speakers. For example, in Scenario 2, 79% of the advanced learners used the selfreference form *cháu* [grandchild] as did 93% of the native speakers. In contrast, approximately half of the preintermediate learners (48%) chose no selfreference form. Ten percent of these preintermediate learners even utilized the nontargetlike forms *cô* – *em* [female teacher – younger sibling (student)] as in Example 13.

Example 13: PI-S2

```
Em               chào  cô   ạ!    Cô   có  khoẻ không?
Younger sibbling greet aunt PolM! Aunt yes well no?
Good morning, auntie! How are you?
```

In this scenario, the expected address form pair is *cô* [aunt (younger than one's father)] – *cháu* [nephew/niece], not *cô* [female teacher] – *em* [younger sibling (student)] as in Scenario 1, which takes place in a classroom context. The differentiation between the two pairs is realized only through the choice of selfreference forms, and this seemed to have confused some learners, as shown in Example 13.

In Scenario 4, there were differences from native speakers in both groups of learners. While 80% of the native speakers chose the pair *bác* – *cháu* [uncle (older than parents) – nephew/niece], only 13% of them utilized the pair *chú* – *cháu* [uncle (younger than parents) – nephew/niece]. More than half of the advanced learners (55%) opted for the pair *ông* – *cháu* [grandfather – grandchild], whereas approximately half of their preintermediate peers (52%) opted for the nontargetlike pair *ông – em* [grandfather – younger sibling] as in Example 14.

Example 14: PI-S4

```
Ông          ạ!     Em               muốn mượn
Grandfather PolM! Younger sibling want borrow
Sir, I would like to borrow

một số     tài liệu   không được     ạ!
several    document   not   possible PolM!
some documents, couldn't I?
```

Scenarios in which the addressee is the same age as the addressor

Table 11. Use of address forms in scenarios in which the addressee is the same age as the addressor

address form	scenario								
	5			7			8		
	NS	AD	PI	NS	AD	PI	NS	AD	PI
no address form	35%	16%	24%	39%	3%	10%	35%	11%	10%
anh	20%	34%	19%	0%	11%	10%	2%	8%	5%
*anh/chị***	4%	0%	5%						
chị	4%	13%	0%	2%	5%	14%	0%	3%	24%
bạn	0%	21%	38%	11%	45%	43%	11%	37%	33%
em	0%	11%	5%						
cậu	0%	0%	5%	13%	26%	10%	15%	26%	14%
ông	0%	0%	5%						
mày				13%	8%	0%	24%	16%	5%
first name				7%	0%	0%			
mình				0%	0%	5%	0%	0%	5%
tôi				0%	0%	5%			

Note: * the respondent changes the forms from sentence to sentence
**a slash (/) indicates that respondent uses several different address forms

It is immediately apparent from Table 11 that in this group of scenarios, there was a broad range of address forms used by learners. Although overall, the native speakers avoided using address forms altogether, the learner groups preferred to use them.

For example, in Scenario 5, while the advanced learners produced the form *anh* [older brother] more often (34%), the preintermediate learners utilized the form *bạn* [friend] more frequently (38%), as in Examples 15 and 16 below. This form is acceptable in this scenario, but it is less polite than the form *anh/chị* [older brother/sister] (Lê, 1999).

Example 15: AD-S5

```
Xin lỗi, anh           có  sao    không?
Sorry,   older brother yes matter no?
I am sorry. Are you hurt?
```

Example 16: PI-S5

```
Xin lỗi, tôi vô ý     quá.
Sorry,   I   careless too much.
I am sorry. I was not careful enough.

Bạn    có  việc gì không?
Friend yes matter  no?
Are you all right?
```

In Scenario 7, the form *bạn* [friend] appears to be the most favored form among both advanced and preintermediate learners with a fairly equal percentage of 45% and 43%, respectively (see Example 17). The number of advanced learners who produced the form *cậu* is approximately three times as much as that of the preintermediate learners.

Example 17: AD-S7

```
Thật không may, mình         quên   quyển  sách đó
Unfortunately, (intimate) I forget Class. book that
Unfortunately, I forgot the book

ở nhà,   chiều     nay  mình
at home, afternoon this (intimate) I
at home. This afternoon I

nhất định  mang  cho  bạn.
definitely bring give friend.
will definitely bring it to you.
```

In Scenario 8, most learners chose the more polite forms *bạn* and *cậu,* as in Example 18 below. Although the two groups of learners tended to utilize the form *bạn* most frequently for this scenario, they differed markedly in the use of the form *cậu* (26% vs. 14%); see Example 18). Yet, 24% of the preintermediate group opted for the form *chị* as shown in Example 19 below. This form, however, is not used by native speakers because it is normally inappropriate to address a close friend in this way.

Example 18: AD-S8

```
Cậu            ơi,          mình          thấy áo khoác này
(casual) you vocative, (intimate) I see  coat     this
Hey you, I think this coat

không thích hợp với  cậu           ạ.
not   suit      with (casual) you PolM.
does not really suit you.
```

Example 19: PI-S8

```
Chị          thích chiếc  áo   ấy   à?
Older sister like  Class. coat that QuesM?
Do you like that coat?

Mình         cảm thấy không hay,
(intimate) I feel     not   interesting,
I think it's not interesting,

không vừa chị.
not   fit older sister.
it does not suit you.

Chị          phải xem mấy     chiếc.
Older sister must see several ones.
You should try on several ones.
```

Table 12. Use of selfreference forms in scenarios in which the addressee is the same age as the addressor

address form	self-reference form	scenario 5 NS	5 AD	5 PI	7 NS	7 AD	7 PI	8 NS	8 AD	8 PI
	no self-reference	35%	0%	0%				9%	0%	5%
	tôi	0%	11%	19%				0%	0%	5%
	em	0%	3%	5%						
no address form	*tao*							15%	3%	0%
	tớ							9%	3%	0%
*anh/chị***	*tôi*	28%	0%	0%						
anh	*em*	0%	34%	5%						
	no self-reference	0%	0%	10%						
	no self-reference							0%	18%	0%

continued...

Table 12. Use of selfreference forms in scenarios in which the addressee is the same age as the addressor *(cont.)*

address form	self-reference form	scenario								
		5			7			8		
		NS	AD	PI	NS	AD	PI	NS	AD	PI
	tôi	24%	13%	33%				0%	0%	10%
	mình	11%	2%	5%				0%	16%	10%
bạn	*em*				0%	0%	5%			
	mình				17%	3%	0%			
no address form	*tao*				9%	0%	0%			
	tớ				9%	0%	10%			
cậu	*mình*				13%	11%	0%	13%	16%	5%
	tớ				4%	11%	0%	9%	11%	10%
mày	*tao*				13%	0%	0%	17%	16%	5%
	mình				0%	21%	24%			
	tôi				0%	8%	5%			
	bạn				0%	5%	0%			
	tớ				0%	5%	5%			
	no self-reference				0%	5%	0%			
chị	*mình*							0%	0%	10%
	chúng ta							0%	0%	5%
	em							0%	0%	5%
	tôi							0%	0%	5%

As shown in Table 12, both learners and native speakers used a variety of selfreference forms. For example, in Scenario 5, learners showed a preference for particular selfreference forms such as *em*, *tôi*, and *mình*. The advanced group opted for the more polite address form *anh*, resulting in 34% using the selfreference form *em* as shown in Example 20. Similarly, 33% of the preintermediate group chose to refer to themselves as *tôi* when addressing their interlocutors as *bạn*.

Example 20: AD-S5

```
Em                xin lỗi anh           nhé!
Younger sibling sorry   older brother AlignM.
I am sorry, brother.

Em                không   để ý.
Younger sibling not     take notice.
I wasn't paying attention.
```

On the other hand, in Scenario 7, both groups of learners selected the polite pair *bạn –mình* [friend – self], with a slightly higher percentage by the preintermediate group (24% vs. 21%; see Example 21).

Example 21: PI-S7

```
Xin lỗi bạn,      mình          quên   mang
Sorry   friend, (intimate) I forget bring
I am sorry, my friend.

quyển  sách đó   đến đây.
Class. book that to  here.
I forgot to bring the book with me.

Mình          không cố ý,        mong bạn    thông cảm.
I (intimate) not   deliberate, hope friend sympathize.
It wasn't intentional, I hope you'll understand.
```

In Scenario 8, each group showed a wide range of selfreference forms with fairly equal frequency of usage. Because this is a conversation between close friends, the native group employed the informal pair *mày – tao* [(informal) you – (informal) I] most frequently (17%). Thirteen percent of the native speakers opted for the intimate pair *cậu – mình* [uncle (casual "you") – self], which was also chosen by 16% of advanced learners. The most common form among the advanced group was no selfreference form while addressing the interlocutor as *bạn*. The other two pairs selected by 16% of the learners in this group are *cậu – mình* and *bạn – mình*. The preintermediate group showed a preference for polite pairs such as *cậu – tớ*, *bạn – mình,* and *bạn – tôi* with a frequency of 10% for each pair. However, another 10% of the preintermediate learners utilized the pair *chị – mình*, which was not selected by any native speakers.

Scenarios in which the addressee(s) is younger than the addressor

Table 13. Use of address forms in scenarios in which the addressee is younger than the addressor

address form	scenario								
	6			11			12		
	NS	AD	PI	NS	AD	PI	NS	AD	PI
em	83%	71%	19%	61%	76%	33%	2%	16%	5%
cô	2%	8%	10%	4%	3%	5%			
first name	2%	13%	0%						
cô giáo	2%	21%	0%						
cậu	0%	8%	10%						
chị	0%	5%	29%	2%	0%	5%			

continued...

Table 13. Use of address forms in scenarios in which the addressee is younger than the addressor *(cont.)*

address form	scenario								
	6			11			12		
	NS	AD	PI	NS	AD	PI	NS	AD	PI
bạn	0%	0%	24%	0%	5%	14%			
*em/cậu**	0%	0%	5%						
no address form				26%	8%	24%	9%	0%	14%
mày				2%	5%	0%			
anh				0%	0%	10%			
các cháu							33%	5%	10%
các em							24%	34%	43%
mấy đứa							13%	13%	0%
chúng mày							11%	0%	0%
các trẻ con							0%	3%	10%
cháu							0%	8%	0%
các anh							0%	0%	5%

Note: * slash (/) indicates that respondent uses several different address forms

As Table 13 indicates, learners used a range of forms in this scenario, although only a small number were employed with fairly high frequency. For example, in Scenario 6, while 71% of the advanced learners employed the form *em* as most native speakers did, only 19% of the preintermediate learners utilized this form (see Example 22). The second most utilized form among the advanced learners was *cô giáo* [female teacher], whereas the second among the preintermediate learners was *chị* [older sister] (see Example 23). The form *chị* is inappropriate in this scenario because the addressee is supposed to be younger than the addressor.

Example 22: AD-S6

```
Em             ơi,        em             có thể
Younger sister vocative, younger sister possible
Sister, could you

mua hộ  chị          một cuốn  sách tiếng Anh
buy help older sister one Class. book English
help me buy an English book

được không à?
not QuesM?
please?
```

Example 23: PI-S6

```
Tôi muốn học   tiếng Anh.
I   want learn English.
I want to learn English.

Chị          giúp tôi mua quyển  sách được     không?
Older sister help I   buy Class. book possible not?
Could you help me buy a book?
```

The form *bạn* [friend] was the next most utilized form among preintermediate learners, but it was utilized by none of the native speakers.

In Scenario 11, 76% of the advanced learners produced the form *em* as most native speakers did (see Example 24), but only 33% of their preintermediate peers chose this form. Also, the degree of address avoidance among the preintermediate group was nearly the same as for the native speakers (24% and 26%, respectively; see Example 25), while only 8% of the advanced learners avoided address.

Example 24: AD-S11

```
Lần  sau  em              làm việc phải cẩn thận nhé!
Time next younger sibling do  work must careful  AlignM!
Please do be careful next time!
```

Example 25: PI-S11

```
Không sao,  nhưng lần  sau  làm cẩn thận nhé.
No problem, but   time next do  careful AlignM.
No problem, but do be careful next time.
```

In Scenario 12, both groups of learners chose the form *các em* [plural younger sibling] (see Example 26), with the preintermediate learners using this form more often than the advanced learners (43% and 34%, respectively). Although the advanced learners utilized the form *mấy đứa* [some (casual) children] with the same frequency as the native speakers (13%), they also used forms such as *em* [younger sibling] and *cháu* [grandchild], which are singular nouns not appropriate in this scenario and which require the use of a plural address form. Fourteen percent of the preintermediate learners, on the other hand, opted to avoid using any forms, as did 9% of the native speakers (see Example 27). Although 10% of these preintermediate learners used plural forms such as *các cháu* [plural grandchildren] and *các trẻ con* [plural children], the latter was used by none of the native speakers.

Example 26: AD-S12

```
Các    em               à,         không được
Class. younger sibling vocative, not   possible
Hey guys, don't

trêu chọc con    chó, rất  nguy hiểm.
tease     Class. dog, very dangerous.
tease the dog. It is very dangerous.
```

Example 27: PI-S12

```
Đừng  làm như  thế,
Don't do  like that,
Don't do that

động vật là bạn    của loài    người.
animals  be friend of  species human.
animals are human beings' friends.
```

Table 14. Use of selfreference forms in scenarios in which the addressee is younger than the addressor

address form	self-reference form	scenario 6			scenario 11			scenario 12		
		NS	AD	PI	NS	AD	PI	NS	AD	PI
	chị	57%	29%	14%	15%	5%	0%			
	anh	26%	29%	0%						
	tôi	0%	5%	0%	0%	5%	0%			
	mình	0%	3%	5%						
em	no self-reference				41%	66%	29%	0%	16%	0%
	em				0%	0%	5%			
	em	0%	0%	14%						
chị	*mình*	0%	0%	5%						
cậu	*mình*	0%	0%	10%						
	no self-reference				22%	5%	19%	4%	0%	14%
	người ta				2%	0%	0%			
no address form	*tôi*				2%	0%	5%			
bạn	no self-reference				0%	0%	10%			
	mình				0%	0%	5%			

các cháu	no self-reference			28%	5%	10%
	no self-reference			22%	34%	33%
các em	*chị*			2%	0%	10%
mấy đứa	no self-reference			11%	11%	0%
chúng mày	no self-reference			9%	0%	0%
các trẻ con	no self-reference			0%	0%	10%

As shown in Table 14, similar to the use of address forms, certain selfreference forms are used with high frequency. For example, in Scenario 6, there was an equal percentage of advanced learners (29%) employing the two forms *anh* [older brother] and *chị* [older sister], the latter being the most preferred form among native speakers (57%; Example 28). The preintermediate learners were also able to produce the targetlike pair *chị* – *em* [older sister – younger sibling] with a small percentage of 14% (see Example 29). Ten percent of these learners chose the intimate pair *cậu* – *mình* [uncle (casual "you") – self], which was not used by the other two groups.

Example 28: NS-S6

```
Em              mua giúp chị
Younger sibling buy help older sister
Can you please help me buy

quyển  sách đó   nhé!
Class. book that AlignM
that book?
```

Example 29: PI-S6

```
Em              ơi,       mua hộ   chị
Younger sibling vocative, buy help older sister
Hey sister, can you help me buy

một cuốn    sách tiếng Anh, được      không.
one Class. book English,   possible  no
an English textbook?

Em              biết được  hơn  chị          nhiều.
Younger sibling know PosM  more older sister much.
You know more about them than I do.
```

In Scenario 11, both groups of learners opted for the same strategy of using the address form *em* [younger sibling] and giving no selfreference form, similar to native speakers. Nevertheless, while 19% of the preintermediate learners avoided using either address forms or selfreference forms as 22% of the native speakers did, only 5% of the advanced learners employed this avoidance. Ten percent of the preintermediate learners chose the intimate address form *bạn* and used no forms to refer to themselves (as in Example 30), the strategy chosen by neither the native nor the advanced group.

Example 30: PI-S11

```
Ôi trời  ơi.        Bạn     làm việc nên    cẩn thận
Oh sky   vocative. Friend do   work should careful
Oh my god. You should be careful

và chăm chỉ.    Lần  sau  phải chú ý.
and  diligent.  Time next must pay attention
and diligent. Pay more attention next time.
```

In Scenario 12, a fairly equal percentage of the advanced and the preintermediate learners produced no selfreference forms with the address form *các em* [plural younger sibling], compared to the slightly lower percentage of native speakers. Apart from this strategy, 16% of the advanced learners chose the address form *em* [younger sibling] with no selfreference form, which none of the native speakers opted for. Yet, 14% of the preintermediate learners avoided using either address or selfreference forms as did some native speakers.

Summary

The data from the DCT show that most of the advanced learners and preintermediate learners were able to use the address forms that were most frequently used by the native speakers in all the scenarios despite some nontargetlike forms. The advanced group tended to be closer to the native speakers in their use of address forms than their preintermediate counterparts. The two groups of learners, however, still showed differences from native speakers such as using some address forms which were never utilized by native speakers in the scenarios.

The learners also demonstrated their ability to use selfreference forms similarly to the native speakers. In teacher-specific scenarios, both the advanced and preintermediate learner groups used the pair *thầy/cô* and *em*. In other scenarios, learners were able to produce the complementary pairs of address forms and selfreference forms as native speakers did: for example, *bác – cháu*, *chú – cháu*, *chị – em*, *bạn – mình*, and *mày – tao*.

Nevertheless, there were some minor differences found in the use of selfreference forms by the two groups of learners. They both used the kinship term *ông* as the address form and *em* as the selfreference form in Scenario 4. This pair never co-occurs in the native speakers' data because the form *em* is used with address forms such as *anh* or *chị* to refer to people of the same generation, or with *thầy* [male teacher]/*cô* [female teacher] in teacher-specific scenarios. Similarly, the two groups supplied the pair *cô–em* in Scenario 2 where the required pair is *cô–cháu*.

Results from the questionnaire

The two open-ended questions at the end of the questionnaire focus on the respondent perceptions of the most difficult scenario and the reason why they selected the specific address form(s) for that scenario. The results from these two questions will be presented in the section below.

Advanced learners

Most of the advanced learners wrote that no scenario was difficult for them. They reported selecting the address forms in the scenarios based on (a) their habits of language use, (b) the addressee's age, (c) imitation of their Vietnamese friends, and (d) their knowledge of the Vietnamese language. Some students in this group, however, noted that the scenario between the new employee and the boss was the most difficult because they had never experienced that scenario. Therefore they had to guess which address form to use.

Preintermediate learners

Most of the preintermediate learners also found the scenario between the new employee and the boss the most difficult. Some of them stated that all of the scenarios were difficult. They reported that they based their choices of address forms on (a) teachers' instruction; (b) factors such as age, generation, relationship, politeness and gender; and (c) Vietnamese customs.

Results from the interviews with native speakers

The following list is based on the native interviewees' opinions of the factors influencing their choice of address forms. The most important factors were (a) age, (b) social distance, (c) gender, (d) social status, and (e) profession. Five informants emphasized that age is the most decisive factor for them in choosing an address form. The second most important factor was social distance. According to these five interviewees, the level of intimacy between the interlocutors is important in choosing the form for the addressees, especially when they are friends of the same age. For example, if the participants are ordinary colleagues, they normally use the pair *bạn – mình* [friend – self] or *cậu – tớ* [uncle (casual "you") – (casual) I]. However, if they are colleagues who are also close friends, they normally employ the colloquial pair *mày – tao* [(colloquial) you – (colloquial) I]. Three informants noted that social status influences the choice of address forms when the interlocutors are younger than them but hold a higher rank or position in the work environment. On the other hand, three participants thought that profession decides the choice of formal or informal address forms. For instance, they would choose formal address forms to address doctors or teachers, and informal forms for people with humbler professions such as laborers.

Discussion

The findings from the study enable tentative explanations for learners' L2 repertoires and selection of address forms.

Development of address forms by L2 speakers of Vietnamese

The results show that proficiency level and length of stay have an influence on how the L2 speakers selected address forms in Vietnamese. Overall, the advanced group showed a closer tendency towards native speaker norms in the use of address forms than the preintermediate group.

Repertoire of address forms

In most cases, the learners' overall repertoire of address forms was similar to that of the native speakers. Sociolinguistic practices in the learners' first language (Chinese) might have had a positive transfer effect on their knowledge of Vietnamese address forms because kinship terms are a component of the Chinese address system as well (Chao, 1976; Gu, 1990). For example, Gu (1990) reported that Chinese people use kinship terms such as *yéye* [grandpa], *năinai* [grandma], *shūshu* [uncle], and *a'yi* [aunt] "to address people who have no familial relation whatsoever with the addresser" (p. 250).

There are, however, some differences between the learners' and the native speakers' use of address forms. For example, in the scenario between the new employee and the boss, both groups of learners provided the form *ông*, which was used by none of the native speakers. Interestingly, the frequency of the preintermediate group utilizing this form was approximately 1.5 times higher than that of the advanced group (see Table 3). There may be several reasons for the L2 speakers' usage. First, this form might be transferred from the learners' native language as the word *lao ban* (the boss) exists in Chinese (T. Yang, personal communication, June 20, 2005). Second, Phạm (2004) states that in the work context, Chinese people tend to use a noun referring to the boss's position and a variation of the address form *nín* (formal "you"). The lack of the equivalent form in the learners' linguistic repertoire might have resulted in their politeness-biased form *ông* (grandfather). Probably learners did not understand the word *xếp*, which is a colloquial word for *boss*, and chose the formal form *ông,* which they may have thought was appropriate in this scenario.

The evidence indicates that in almost every scenario, advanced learners showed a better command of address forms than their preintermediate peers. For instance, the advanced learners could use the form *cô* [aunt (younger than one's parents)] to address a neighbor who is a generation older than the addressor but younger than the addressor's mother, whereas the preintermediate learners used both, *cô* and *chị* [older sister], although the latter is commonly used to address a woman who is older than the addressor but of the same generation.

Similarly, in the scenario where the addressor wants his or her close friend's younger sister to buy an English book, a majority of the advanced learners produced the address form *em* [younger sibling], as did most native speakers. Also, the advanced group's second and third most common forms were first name and *cô giáo*, and these forms also appeared in native speakers' choices of address forms. The most common forms used by the preintermediate learners were *chị*, *bạn* [friend], and *cậu* [uncle (younger than one's mother)], which are normally not appropriate for an interlocutor who is younger than or of the same generation as the addressor.

The difference between the two proficiency levels is even clearer in the use of selfreference forms. The number of advanced learners using correct pairs of complementary address and selfreference forms was generally higher than that of the preintermediate learners across scenarios. Of course, both groups of learners still showed some differences from the NS group, such as the use of *ông – em* [grandfather – younger sibling] in the scenario involving addressing the boss, but the advanced learners used this pair much less frequently than the preintermediate learners. The preintermediate group, on the other hand, produced several mismatched pairs such as *chị – mình*, *chị – tớ*, *bạn – em*, *thầy – cháu*, which did not appear in the advanced group's data at all.

Context-sensitive selections of address forms

The strong command of the use of address forms by the Chinese learners in the data might be explained by the fact that Vietnamese and Chinese cultures share some similarities (Trần, 1997) in their judgments of context variables, which enables sociolinguistic transfer from the learners' native language into Vietnamese. In an investigation into the address practices of Chinese people, Phạm (2004) found that Chinese speakers also consider age to be the most important factor governing the choice of address forms. Thus, it might be argued that Chinese learners are able to draw on their culture-specific sociolinguistic knowledge when they learn how to address people in Vietnamese.

There are two sources of evidence taken from the present study to support this argument. First, the Chinese learners in the study employed omission of address forms in a similar way as the native speakers. That is, they either produced imperatives (see Example 25 and Example 27) or produced answers that included the selfreference forms only (see Example 21). Second, both groups of learners in this study were able to use politeness forms *anh*/*chị* [older bother/sister] to address a stranger as did most native speakers. According to Gu (1990) and Phạm (2004), Chinese people apply the rule "elevate others – humble yourself" in social interactions. This similarity to the Vietnamese norm may have facilitated the use of correct address forms by Chinese learners of Vietnamese. In their responses to the questionnaire, some learners noted that they selected the address forms according to the interlocutor's age. Other learners also stated that they chose the address forms by habit, which suggests that their sociolinguistic knowledge of address form selection is already proceduralized to some degree.

Apart from the positive transfer from their native language, there were some differences in the use of address forms by both groups of learners. A source for these differences could be lack of input in specific language use settings in Vietnamese. For example, many learners chose the nonnativelike pair *ông* [grandfather] – *em* [younger sibling] in talking with the boss, and many learners also reported that this scenario was the most difficult for them because they had never experienced such a scenario. Although mentioned earlier, it should be noted that the participants learned Vietnamese for business purposes. Because their goal of learning Vietnamese is for business, this explanation reveals a gap in the curriculum and emphasizes the importance of the availability of input (Bardovi-Harlig & Hartford, 1996).

The learners also opted for formal forms when they were not appropriate. In the request to a close friend's younger sister to buy a book, the preintermediate learners produced the form *chị* [older sister] rather than the correct form *em* [younger sibling]. Their choice of the more respectful form in this case does not fit, as the use of *chị* [older sister] to address a younger woman may only occur between strangers in formal contexts. Again, lack of contact with Vietnamese speakers may be to blame.

In summary, based on the cross-sectional evidence reported above, significant development can be inferred in the learners' competence with respect to the use of address terms. As expected, higher level learners outperformed their lower level peers in using address forms and selfreference forms. Learners were all likely to be aware of the importance of age when selecting the forms to address their interlocutors. The similarities between Vietnamese and Chinese address forms and cultural values might have exerted a positive influence on learners' acquisition of sociolinguistic norms governing the use of address forms in Vietnamese. However, some negative transfer of address forms from Chinese was also found in the learners' data.

Future research can take investigations of address terms further by analyzing different types of data and varying learner background variables more systematically. With regard to data, extended interaction would be a highly desirable data source as it can show learners' online performance. In addition, naturally occurring data is likely to reflect dynamic changes in address forms in the course of an interaction with interactants changing address forms according to their interlocutors' changing wants and actions.

As to learner background variables, it would be interesting to investigate the learning of address forms by learners from a cultural background that is more remote from Vietnamese (e.g., learners from Europe or North America). Given the important role of age and gender in Vietnamese address, systematically varying learners and interlocutors along those dimensions would also be interesting.

The study also suggests some implications for Vietnamese instruction. First, address forms should be presented in connection with selfreference forms so that learners have a clearer understanding of which forms to pair with each other. Second, the factors governing the choice of address forms, such as age, social distance, gender, should be emphasized in teaching Vietnamese. Also, the rule "elevate others – humble yourself" (in formal contexts) should be included in instruction to direct learners to appropriate use of address forms. Finally, learners need targeted input that suits their learning purposes; for example, learners of Vietnamese for business purposes like the ones in this study should be instructed how a superior is to be addressed in a business setting. Role plays and awareness-raising activities can go a long way towards this goal.

References

Bardovi-Harlig, K. (1999). Exploring the interlanguage of interlanguage pragmatics: A research agenda for acquisitional pragmatics. *Language Learning, 49,* 677–713.

Bardovi-Harlig, K., & Hartford, B.S. (1993). Learning the rules of academic talk: A longitudinal study of pragmatic development. *Studies in Second Language Acquisition, 15,* 279–304.

Bardovi-Harlig, K., & Hartford, B.S. (1996). Input in an institutional setting. *Studies in Second Language Acquisition, 18,* 171–188.

Belz, J.A., & Kinginger, C. (2003). Discourse options and the development of pragmatic competence by classroom learners of German: The case of address forms. *Language Learning, 53*(4), 591–647.

Bialystok, E. (1993). Symbolic representation and attentional control in pragmatic competence. In G. Kasper & S. Blum-Kulka (Eds.), *Interlanguage pragmatics* (pp. 43–59). New York, NY: Oxford University Press.

Braun, F. (1988). *Terms of address: Problems of patterns and usage in various languages and cultures.* Berlin: Mouton de Gruyter.

Brown, R., & Ford, M. (1961). Address in American English. *Journal of Abnormal and Social Psychology, 62,* 375–385.

Carspecken, P.F. (1996). *Critical ethnography in educational research.* New York, NY: Routledge.

Cao Xuân Hạo (2001). Mấy vấn đề về văn hóa trong cách xưng hô của người Việt [Some issues of culture in addressivity by Vietnamese people]. In Xuân Hạo Cao (Ed.), *Văn Việt – tiếng Việt – người Việt [Vietnamese literature – Vietnamese language – Vietnamese personality],* (pp. 297–304). Sài Gòn: Nhà xuất bản Trẻ.

Chao, Y.R. (1976). *Aspects of Chinese sociolinguistics.* Stanford, CA: Stanford University Press.

Clyne, M., Kretzenbacher, H.L., Norrby, C., & Schüpbach, D. (2006). Perceptions of variation and change in German and Swedish address. *Journal of Sociolinguistics, 10*(3), 287–319.

Djenar, D.N. (2006). Patterns and variation of address terms in colloquial Indonesian. *Australian Review of Applied Linguistics, 29*(2), 22.1–22.16.

DuFon, M.A. (1999). The acquisition of linguistic politeness in Indonesian as a second language by sojourners in a naturalistic context. *Dissertation Abstracts International, 60,* 3985.

Dương Thị Nụ (2002). Từ chỉ quan hệ thân tộc trong tri nhận của người Anh và người Việt [Kinship terms in cognition of Anglo and Vietnamese people]. *Ngôn ngữ, 12,* 67–78.

Fasold, R. (1990). *The sociolinguistics of language.* Cambridge: Basil Blackwell.

Fink, A. (1995). *How to ask survey questions.* Thousand Oaks, CA: Sage.

Fontana, A., & Frey, J.H. (2000). The interview: From structured questions to negotiated text. In N.K. Denzin & Y.S. Lincoln (Eds.), *The handbook of qualitative research* (pp. 654–672). Thousand Oaks, CA: Sage.

González-Lloret, M. (2008). Computer-mediated learning of L2 pragmatics. In E. Alcón Soler & A. Martínez-Flor (Eds.), *Investigating Pragmatics in Foreign Language Learning, Teaching and Testing* (pp. 114—132). Bristol: Multilingual Matters.

Gu, Y. (1990). Politeness phenomena in modern Chinese. *Journal of Pragmatics, 14*(2), 237–257.

Hassall, T.J. (1997). *Requests by Australian learners of Indonesian.* (Unpublished doctoral dissertation). Australian National University, Canberra, Australia.

Hassall, T.J. (2008). Pragmatic performance: What are learners thinking? In E. Alcón Soler and A. Martínez-Flor (Eds.), *Investigating Pragmatics in Foreign Language Learning, Teaching and Testing* (pp. 72—93). Bristol: Multilingual Matters.

Hoàng Văn Hành (2002). *Cảnh huống và chính sách ngôn ngữ ở Việt Nam [The context and language policy in Vietnam].* Hà Nội: Nhà xuất bản Khoa học Xã hội.

Kasper, G., & Rose, K. (2002). *Pragmatic development in a second language.* Malden, MA: Blackwell.

Kinginger, C. (2008). Language learning in study abroad: Case studies of Americans in France. *Modern Language Journal Winter 2008 Supplement,* 92, 1—124.

Kinginger, C., & Farrell, K. (2004). Assessing development of meta-pragmatic awareness in study abroad. *Frontiers: The Interdisciplinary Journal of Study Abroad 10*, 19—42. Retrieved from http://www.frontiersjournal.com/issues/vol10/index.htm

Lê Biên (1999). *Từ loại tiếng Việt hiện đại.* [Word class in modern Vietnamese] Hà Nội: Nhà xuất bản Giáo dục.

Lương Văn Hy (1990). *Discursive practices and linguistic meanings.* Amsterdam: Benjamins.

Lynch, B. (1996). *Language program evaluation.* Cambridge: Cambridge University Press.

Martiny, T. (1996). Forms of address in French and Dutch: A sociopragmatic approach. *Language Sciences, 18*(3–4), 765–775.

Mojica-Diaz, C.C. (1992). The use of address pronouns in Bogota: A comparative study of two stages of acquisition by nonnative speakers. *Dissertation Abstracts International, 53(*1): 140-A.

Nguyễn Văn Chiến (1992). *Ngôn ngữ học đối chiếu và đối chiếu các ngôn ngữ Đông Nam Á [Contrastive linguistics and comparison of Southeast Asian languages].* Hà Nội: Trường Đại học Sư phạm Ngoại ngữ.

Nguyễn Văn Chiến (2004). *Tiến tới xác lập vốn từ vựng văn hóa Việt [Toward building vocabulary of Vietnamese culture].* Hà Nội: Nhà xuất bản Khoa học Xã hội.

Nguyễn Thị Đẹp (1996). *An investigation into the Vietnamese system of person reference.* (Unpublished master's thesis). The University of Melbourne, Melbourne, Australia.

Nguyễn Quang (2002). *Giao tiếp và giao tiếp giao văn hóa [Communication and crosscultural communication].* Hà Nội: Nhà xuất bản Đại học Quốc gia Hà Nội.

Phạm Ngọc Hàm (2004). *Đặc điểm và cách sử dụng của lớp từ ngữ xưng hô tiếng Hán [Characteristics and usage of address forms in Chinese].* (Unpublished doctoral dissertation). Luận án Tiến sĩ Ngữ văn, Trường Đại học Khoa học Xã hội và Nhân văn, Đại học Quốc gia Hà Nội, Hà Nội.

Regan, V. (1995). The acquisition of sociolinguistic native speech norms: Effects of a year abroad on second language learners of French. In B.F. Freed (Ed.), *Second language acquisition in a study abroad context* (pp. 245–267). Amsterdam: Benjamins.

Rendle-Short, J. (2010). 'Mate' as a term of address in ordinary interaction. *Journal of Pragmatics, 42,* 1201–1218.

Richards, J., Platt, J., & Platt, H. (1992). *Longman dictionary of language teaching and applied linguistics.* Essex: Longman Group UK Limited.

Sheatsley, P. (1983). Questionnaire construction and item writing. In P. Rossi, J. Wright, & A. Anderson (Eds.), *Handbook of survey research* (pp. 195–230). New York, NY: Academic Press.

Thomas, J. (1983). Cross-cultural pragmatic failure. *Applied Linguistics, 4,* 91–112.

Thompson, L.C. (1987). *A Vietnamese reference grammar.* Honolulu: University of Hawai'i Press.

Trần Quốc Vượng (1997). *Đại cương văn hóa Việt Nam [Generalities of Vietnamese culture].* Hà Nội: Nhà xuất bản Khoa học Xã hội và Nhân văn.

Trương, Thị Diễm (1999). Nghĩa và sự chi phối cách sử dụng các danh từ thân tộc: Kỵ, chắt, chút, vợ, chồng, dâu, rể [Meaning and its influence on the use of kinship terms: Great-great grandfather, great-great grandchild, great-great-great grandchild, wife, husband, daughter-in-law, son-in-law]. *Ngôn ngữ, 6,* 63–72.

Vũ Thị Thanh Hương (1997). *Politeness in modern Vietnamese: A sociolinguistic study of a Hanoi speech community.* (Unpublished doctoral dissertation). University of Toronto, Toronto, Canada.

Vũ Ngọc Tú (1996). *Tiếng Việt cơ sở[Fundamentals of Vietnamese]*. Hà Nội: Nhà xuất bản Khoa học Xã hội.

Wardhaugh, R. (2002). *An introduction to sociolinguistics*. Malden, MA: Blackwell.

Warren, J. (2006). Address pronouns in French. *Australian Review of Applied Linguistics, 29*(2), 16.1–16.17.

Williams-van Klinken, C., & Hajek, J. (2006). Patterns of address in Dili Tetum, East Timor. *Australian Review of Applied Linguistics, 29*(2), 21.1–21.18.

Appendix A: Discourse completion test (Vietnamese version)

Câu hỏi điều tra

Bản câu hỏi điều tra này nhằm mục đích nghiên cứu về cách sử dụng từ xưng hô trong tiếng Việt. Nếu bạn đồng ý tham dự nghiên cứu này và cho phép chúng tôi sử dụng dữ liệu mà bạn cung cấp, đề nghị bạn hãy điền câu trả lời vào chỗ trống dưới những câu hỏi sau đây. Những thông tin mà bạn cung cấp sẽ được giữ bí mật tuyệt đối. Xin cảm ơn bạn đã hợp tác với chúng tôi.

Thông tin cá nhân:

1. Tuổi: ____________________
2. Giới tính: ____________________
3. Nghề nghiệp: ____________________
4. Tiếng mẹ đẻ của bạn là tiếng gì? ____________________
5. Bạn đã học tiếng Việt được bao lâu? ____________________
6. Bạn đã ở Việt Nam bao lâu? ____________________

Tình huống:

1. Trong lớp học, bạn muốn hỏi cô giáo về một điều mà bạn không hiểu. Bạn nói như thế nào với cô giáo?

   ____
2. Buổi sáng khi ra khỏi nhà bạn gặp người hàng xóm (nữ, ít tuổi hơn mẹ bạn nhưng thuộc thế hệ trước bạn). Bạn nói với người đó thế nào?

   ____
3. Bạn là bác sĩ. Hôm nay bạn có hẹn khám cho một bệnh nhân nhiều tuổi hơn bạn rất nhiều (thuộc thế hệ trước bạn). Bạn hỏi người đó về các triệu chứng như thế nào?

   ____
4. Bạn vừa xin được một công việc mới. Bạn cần mượn xếp (nam, nhiều tuổi hơn bố của bạn) một số tài liệu. Bạn sẽ nói với ông ấy thế nào?

   ____
5. Bạn va phải một người lạ (giới tính khác bạn, cùng độ tuổi với bạn) trong khi đi bộ trên đường. Bạn sẽ nói với người đó thế nào?

   ____
6. Bạn muốn nhờ em gái của bạn thân của bạn mua hộ một cuốn sách học tiếng Anh. Cô ấy là giáo viên tiếng Anh. Bạn đã biết cô ấy lâu rồi. Bạn sẽ nói với cô ấy thế nào?

   ____
7. Bạn đã hứa mang cho một đồng nghiệp của bạn (cùng giới tính với bạn, cùng độ tuổi với bạn) một quyển sách nhưng bạn lại để quên ở nhà. Hôm nay đến cơ quan, gặp người đó bạn sẽ nói thế nào?

   ____

8. Bạn và bạn thân của bạn cùng đi mua áo khoác. Anh/Cô ấy mặc thử một chiếc áo khoác và định mua nhưng bạn không thích chiếc áo ấy. Bạn sẽ nói với bạn của bạn thế nào?

   ____

9. Bạn là sinh viên. Bạn đến gặp thầy Chủ nhiệm khoa để xin chữ ký. Thầy là Giáo sư và trung tuổi. Bạn chưa gặp thầy bao giờ. Bạn sẽ nói với thầy như thế nào?

   ____

10. Bạn là giáo viên. Trong lớp có một học sinh nam (ít tuổi hơn và thuộc thế hệ sau bạn) đùa nghịch và bạn cảm thấy không hài lòng. Bạn sẽ nói với học sinh đó như thế nào?

    ____

11. Người giúp việc trong nhà bạn (ít tuổi hơn bạn) lỡ tay làm vỡ lọ hoa mà bạn rất thích. Bạn sẽ nói với người đó thế nào?

    ____

12. Một nhóm trẻ con hay trêu chọc con chó nhà bạn. Hôm nay bạn bắt gặp chúng đang làm như vậy. Bạn sẽ nói với chúng như thế nào?

    ____

Câu hỏi phụ:

1. Trong các tình huống trên, bạn thấy tình huống nào là khó trả lời nhất? Tại sao?

   ____

2. Tại sao bạn lại chọn từ xưng hô như vậy cho tình huống đó?

   ____

Appendix B: Discourse completion test (English version)

Questionnaire

This questionnaire is for the study of the use of address forms in Vietnamese. If you agree to participate in the research, please fill in the questionnaire. The confidentiality of your personal information and the answers you provide will be completely protected.

Personal information:

1. Age:
2. Gender:
3. Occupation:
4. What is your first language?
5. How long have you been learning Vietnamese?
6. How long have you been living in Vietnam?

Scenarios:

1. In a class, you want to ask your female teacher about a point that you do not understand.
   You say: ______________________________
2. When you get out of your house in the morning, you see your neighbor (a woman who is younger than your mother but a generation older than you).
   You say: ______________________________
3. You are a doctor. Today you see a patient who is much older than you (older than your parents). You want to ask him/her about his/her symptoms.
   You say: ______________________________
4. You have just got a new job. You need to borrow some documents from your boss (a man who is older than your father).
   You say: ______________________________
5. You bumped against a stranger (opposite gender, same age) while you were running in the street.
   You say: ______________________________
6. You want to ask your close friend's younger sister, who you have known for a long time, to buy an English textbook for you. She is a teacher of English.
   You say: ______________________________
7. You promised to lend a book to your colleague (same gender, same age), but you left it at home. You see your colleague in the office today.
   You say: ______________________________
8. You and your close friend go shopping together. She wants to buy a new coat. She tries a coat on and you do not think the coat looks good on her.
   You say: ______________________________
9. You are a student. You want to see the dean of your faculty to have him sign a document. He is a professor and middle-aged. You have never seen him before.
   You say: ______________________________

10. You are a teacher. A male student (a generation younger than you) makes a lot of loud noises in the class.
    You say: ____________________
11. The maid (younger than you) in your house accidentally broke a vase you like very much.
    You say: ____________________
12. There is a group of teenagers who keep teasing your dog. Today you caught them in the act.
    You say: ____________________

Additional questions:

1. Of the scenarios above, which one is the most difficult to you? Why?
   ____
2. Why do you choose the address form(s) you selected in that scenario?
   ____

Appendix C: Interview guide

1. Have you experienced the scenarios in real life?
2. What are the factors governing your choice of address forms in everyday interactions?
3. Which scenario(s) do you find the most difficult to answer?
4. Why do you find it difficult?

5 Inviting in Vietnamese, With Comparison to Some English Patterns

Hạnh thị Nguyễn
Hawai'i Pacific University

Speech act of inviting

Inviting is a complex social action. In inviting, the speaker expresses his or her desire to have the company of the recipient in a certain activity (i.e., to offer some form of 'social good' to the recipient in order to receive a similar 'social good' from the recipient). Edmondson and House (1981) characterized the speech act of inviting as when "A wishes B to know that he is in favor of a future action to be performed by B, which he [A] believes may involve costs to himself and benefits to B. He also believes however that the costs involved will be outweighed for himself by the social benefits consequent to B's doing that future action" (pp. 131–132). An invitation, then, is both an offer and a request (see also Chu, 1995). At the same time, inviting is a double-binding act, with both a directive and a commissive illocutionary force. Hancher (1979) noted, "When I invite you to do something, I am indeed trying to direct your behavior. But more than that is involved... it [an invitation] commits the speaker to a certain course of action itself" (p. 6). Also, since the eventual occurrence of the future act depends on the invitee's response (acceptance or refusal), invitation has been classified as a 'semi-impositive' speech act (Lee, 1976). In Brown and Levinson's (1987) terms, inviting threatens the hearer's negative face (i.e., his or her desire to be left alone), while also promoting his or her positive face (i.e., his or her desire to be appreciated; see also Mao, 1992).

Pragmatics of Vietnamese as a native and target language, pp. 177–211
Carsten Roever & Hạnh thị Nguyễn (Eds.), 2013
Honolulu, HI: University of Hawai'i, National Foreign Language Resource Center

Another duality in the speech act of inviting, as noted by Mao (1992) concerning Chinese, is that invitations embody a dual politeness strategy, with the inviter and invitee attending to both a "public posture" and a "private desire." As such, how one invites and what one invites the hearer to do may also reflexively indicate one's identity, desires, and preferences.

This orientation to social relationship in invitation can be seen in the sequential organization of invitation sequences. Because in an invitation sequence, the preferred response is acceptance and the dispreferred response is rejection, the inviter may issue a *preinvitation* before the actual invitation to gauge the possibility of the invitation being accepted (Schegloff, 2007). Preinvitations are questions such as "Are you doing anything?" or "Are you free this weekend?" The invited party may respond to a preinvitation with a *go-ahead* such as "Nothing" or "Not much" to encourage the projected invitation; a *blocking* such as "Oh, I've got to finish a term paper" or "We're planning to go to the beach" to discourage the projected invitation; or a *hedging*, which may take the form of "Why?" or "Uhm, possibly" and neither encourages nor discourages the upcoming invitation but allows the invited party to give a full response depending on what the invitation will be (pp. 29–32).

In pragmatics, the structure of the invitation speech act itself (in English) has been described by Edmondson and House (1981) as containing the following elements: (1) tentative expressions or less tentative expressions, (2) grounding moves, (3) flattering the hearer, and (4) the invite (1981, pp. 132–133). Edmondson and House did not define what they mean by each term, but they illustrated them with examples (pp. 132–133). For *tentative expressions,* they suggested that they are direct or indirect questions, such as "Would you like to come to a party with me?", "How about going to a party with me?", or "I wonder if you'd like to go to a party with me." Examples of *less tentative expressions* are "John, you've got to come to my party tomorrow" or "I'm having a party tomorrow, you've got to come." *Grounding moves* are expressions that give the context for the invitation (e.g., "I'm inviting a few friends over for a party this Saturday night so I want to ask you as well, of course."). *Flattering the hearer* may take the form of "Mr. and Mrs. Smith would like to have the pleasure of (inviting Mr. and Mrs. Smith on the occasion of their son's wedding)" or "(You must come to my party,) everybody would love to have you." The *invite* is the core of the invitation and explicitly performs the act of inviting (e.g., "We would like to invite you to dinner tomorrow night.").[1]

Inviting in Vietnamese

Although invitations in English and some other languages have been well documented (e.g., Edmondson & House, 1981; Isaacs & Clark, 1990; Mao, 1992; Prokop, 1989; Szatrowski, 1987; Wolfson, 1981), studies on inviting in Vietnamese are still preliminary. Two rare papers that deal with inviting in Vietnamese (Chu, 1995; Đào, 1999) are both published only in Vietnamese with limited circulation. In the first paper, Chu (1995) defined the speech act of inviting and classified invitation types in Vietnamese based on observational data. First, in addition to what had been discussed in the English literature, Chu pointed out that the future action mentioned in an invitation is something that the speaker and hearer believe will not take place unless the speech act of inviting is performed. Chu then classified invitations based on four criteria: (a) the social context, including the inviter-invitee relationship, the invited activity's formality and financial cost, and whether the action of inviting makes up the entire encounter or is a part of a larger activity; (b) the purpose of the invitation, including true invitations (both sincere and ritual) and invitations that are meant to achieve another action, such as checking someone's attitude, or to show off an existing relationship toward a third party; (c) the effect of the invitation, including acceptance, forced acceptance, and refusal; and (d) the organization of the inviting sequence, including a single adjacency-pair organization (e.g., inviting – accepting) and a multiple adjacency-pair organization (e.g., inviting – explaining – refusing – persuading – accepting).[2] Đào discussed the similarities and differences between the speech acts of *mời* and *rủ,* two related but distinct verbs in Vietnamese which can be both translated into English as "invite." Đào pointed out that even though both speech acts involve the imposition of a future action on the listener, *mời* is often used in formal situations (sometimes in written format), everyday rituals, or when the speaker is responsible for the material cost of the action, while *rủ* is only performed among peers in informal situations in spoken format, and the future action is always to be carried out by both the speaker and listener. Thus, it seems that the different nuances of the inviter-invitee relationship in an inviting action as well as the formality of the situation are emphasized in the Vietnamese language via these two distinct lexical items.

Although they provide useful insights about inviting in Vietnamese, these authors' observations lack the support of a systematic analysis of a wider sample of discourse as it is spoken or perceived to be spoken by native speakers. Further, since they focused on categorization, they do not show us much about inviting habits and the variables that could affect the speaker's choice of different forms of invitation. The present chapter differs from these two papers in its utilization of empirical data to infer patterns of inviting and its focus on how choices of invitation forms are made. In order to highlight the distinctiveness of inviting patterns in Vietnamese and with the goal of providing information useful for second language pragmatic development, this chapter also compares inviting in Vietnamese with English. Finally, it also aims to go beyond the linguistic forms and attempts to explain these forms by referring to the speakers' larger social and cultural context.

Present study

Research questions

This study aims to answer the following three questions:

1. What are some common patterns of inviting in Vietnamese as perceived by young adults?
2. What are some distinctive features of inviting in Vietnamese in contrast to some patterns of invitation in English as perceived by native English speakers?
3. What are some social and cultural explanations for the general inviting patterns perceived by the Vietnamese speakers?

Scope of investigation

This study is an exploratory study to understand what native speakers of Vietnamese perceive to be the typical formulation of invitations. As such, it focuses on only the first pair part of the inviting adjacency pair (Sacks, Schegloff, & Jefferson, 1974), and does not deal with the second pair part, which is the response to invitations. Also, it does not answer questions about inviting in naturally occurring spoken discourse, which may involve negotiation of meaning in ostensible invitations (e.g., Isaacs & Clark, 1990), unambiguous and ambiguous invitations (e.g., Wolfson, 1981), and possibly phenomena such as verbal play (Mao, 1992). In limiting itself to the formulation of invitations, this study does not describe the invitation sequence (see review of Schegloff, 2007, above) nor does it address the question of how invitations fit in the larger sequential organization of social interaction (cf. Chu, 1995; Edmonson & House, 1981; Mao, 1992). To do so would require recording of naturally occurring talk in interaction, which, although a very worthwhile pursuit, is outside the focus of the current study. Finally, this study also focuses on Vietnamese young adults, specifically, high school students. Thus, it does not claim to generalize about Vietnamese inviting patterns by people of all ages and all educational backgrounds. By the same token, the Vietnamese inviting patterns are compared to only some inviting patterns in English used by a limited number of participants, and thus this study does not aim to generalize about inviting in English in different international varieties and by people of different gender and age.

Data and method

The instrument used was a written discourse completion task (DCT) in which the respondents were asked to write what they would say in each scenario involving inviting. They were also given the choice not to say anything. Motivated by Chu's (1995) observation that the speech act of inviting is affected by the social context and the purpose of the invitation, the original DCT included 16 inviting scenarios involving contexts familiar to high school students, ranging from informal to formal, involving both oral and written channels of communication, and from home settings to school settings. Since the scenarios were created for the Vietnamese context, the English-speaking respondents were also asked to indicate whether each scenario was "authentic" or "nonauthentic" for them. After the DCT was given, based on the number of completed responses and the representativeness of the scenarios, more than half of the scenarios were eliminated and only six will be reported here.[3] These scenarios are (a) inviting a friend for some coffee after class, (b) inviting a friend to a meal with one's family, (c) inviting a friend to join a picnic (written channel), (d) inviting a friend to a birthday party (written channel), (e) inviting a friend to a sister's wedding, and (f) inviting someone to strike up a relationship. An additional part of the survey consists of ten *yes or no* questions about the informants' inviting habits in general. Appendix A contains the questionnaire in Vietnamese and Appendix B contains the English questionnaire.

The limitations of the DCT have been discussed in the introduction to this volume. Here, I would like to highlight only one prominent problem observed in the data that was in line with prior criticism about the DCT, and it is that the written responses by the Vietnamese participants were at times wordy or bookish, and thus probably not very close to what would be heard in similar scenarios in spoken discourse (see also Hartford & Bardovi-Harlig, 1992). However, as it will be made clear in the analysis, reasons for this could be the effect of the DCT, or there could be some culturally specific factors. As a tool to get at the respondents' general perceptions, or their pragmalinguistic and sociopragmatic knowledge (Kasper & Rose, 2002, p. 96), about their own inviting patterns in a short amount of time, the DCT was found to be useful and effective.

The focal participants of this study included 90 native speakers of Vietnamese who were twelfth-graders from two high schools in Hue, central Vietnam. Sixty-four of the students were female, and 26 were male. Their ages, at the time of the test, ranged from 17 to 19 years old. The respondents answered questions from a written questionnaire in Vietnamese. For the purpose of highlighting the distinctiveness of the Vietnamese invitations collected, the same questionnaire (translated into English) was also given to a smaller group of respondents consisting of 20 English speakers: three from the United States, two from South Africa, five from Britain, and ten from Canada. Eleven of the people were female and nine were male. Their ages, at the time of this questionnaire, ranged from 16 to 53 years.[4]

The data gathered from the questionnaire were inevitably based on the respondents' subjective reflections of their own habits of inviting in everyday contexts; however, as explained above, this fit the goal of the study, which was to understand Vietnamese and English speakers' pragmalinguistic and sociopragmatic knowledge about the formulation of invitations. Data coding followed the system of terminology modified from Edmonson and House (1986) as specified above. Recognizing that coding of any kind can easily run into problems of ambiguity and ad hoc decisions (Garfinkel, 1967), I will add qualitative interpretation of specific examples as well as attempt to incorporate my membership knowledge as a native resident of the data site whenever it is possible. While this does not fully address the problems with coding, I hope that it helps to present a more detailed and in-depth picture of the data.

Findings

Coding

Based on preliminary analysis of the Vietnamese and English data collected, I reorganized and extended Edmonson and House's categorization (mentioned above) to describe the structure of invitations in this study as follows. First, an invitation contains the *invite* and optional *adjuncts.* The invite is the expression used to achieve the language function of inviting whether it explicitly contains various forms of the word "invite" or not, and the adjunct is any part of the invitation that does not serve to perform the function of inviting but accompanies it (in other words, it can be absent and the act of inviting is still performed). There are two types of invites: (a) a *tentative expression* is an inviting expression that gives the invitee the option to either accept or refuse the invitation, such as in the form of a question or a conditional, and (b) a *less tentative expression* is an inviting expression that strongly obligates the invitee to accept the invitation, such as in the form of an imperative. There are three types of adjuncts: (a) a *grounding move* includes expressions to inform the invitee of the reasons or the occasion of the invitation; (b) a *flattering-the-hearer move* is a part of the invitation in which the inviter tries to persuade and/or encourage the invitee into accepting the invitation, often (but not always) by expressing directly or indirectly some positive attributes toward the invitee; (c) a *precommitment* is the part of the invitation in which the inviter tries to engage the invitee into a "commitment" to accept the invitation before the invite is issued, thus reducing the possibility of the invitation being refused. A precommitment serves a similar function as a preinvitation (Schegloff, 2007) or preannouncement (Schegloff, 1986); however, I retain the term "precommitment" in this paper because my data do not contain naturally occurring interaction, for which "preinvitation" and "preannouncement" are used. Of these three types of adjuncts, the flattering-the-hearer move was further specified to accommodate both English and Vietnamese data, and includes expressions of some positive feelings by the inviter if the invitee accepts the invitations (e.g., *We'd be very happy if you could make it*), expressions of the inviter's interest in the invitee's acceptance of the invitation (e.g., *Mong bạn đừng từ chối [I hope that you won't refuse]*[5]), expressions of strong obligation toward the invitee (e.g., *You've gotta come*), kind threats (e.g., *Nếu mày không tới, tao sẽ giận đó. [If you don't come, I'll be angry with you]*), expressions to assure the invitee that there will be no inconvenience (e.g., *Không có ai đâu mà sợ [There's nobody to be afraid of really]*), expressions to point out the benefits to the invitee if she or he accepts the invitation (e.g., *It'd be a great chance for you to meet my friends*), and expressions to downplay the occasion (e.g., *Cơm chẳng có gì đâu [The meal is nothing really]*). The following diagram (Figure 1) summarizes this structural template of an invitation, which will be used to guide the analysis of my findings.

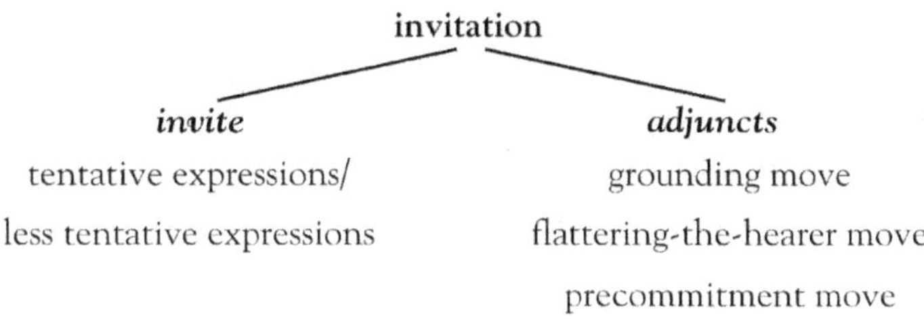

Figure 1. Formal structure of the invitation.

Results

Scenario 1: Inviting a friend out for some coffee after class

In this question, the participants were asked what they would say to a friend if they wanted to invite that friend out for a cup of coffee after class. In Chu's (1995) terms reviewed above, the inviter-invitee relationship in this scenario is close and equal; the invited activity is informal and involves minimal cost; the invitation is a part of a larger activity (attending school) and the invitation is a true invitation. Some examples of invitations reported for this context are shown in the following.

```
1.  Đi    uống  cà phê không?
    go    drink coffee no
    Want to go for a cup of coffee?

2.  Lâu  rồi      chưa    đi uống  cà phê.
    long already not yet go drink coffee.
    We haven't been out for coffee for a while.

    Đi không?
    go no
    Want to go?

3.  Sông Xanh[6] chớ?
    River Blue StanM
    Song Xanh, yes?

4.  Đi uống  cà phê đi!
    go drink coffee ImpM
    Let's go for a cup of coffee!

5.  Đi uống  cà phê với   tao         cho vui.
    go drink coffee with  I (casual) for fun
    Join me for a cup of coffee for a good time.
```

Examples (1) - (3) contain an invitation in the form of a question and thus are tentative, because the question to some extent legitimates both options to accept or reject the invitation. On the other hand, the invitations in Examples (4) and (5) are in imperative form, which implies to a stronger degree the preference for an acceptance. Invitations recorded in the survey generally fell into the two categories exemplified by (1) - (5) above: They either contained a tentative or a less tentative expression as the main part of the invitation, plus some optional grounding moves (e.g., *Lâu rồi chưa đi uống cà phê [We haven't been out for coffee for a while]*) as in (2), or flattering moves (e.g., *cho vui [for a good time]*) as in (6). These optional adjuncts occurred either before or after the inviting expression.

Quantitative data showed that most of the Vietnamese high school students indicated that they would use less tentative expressions in the form of directives (68.9%, *n*=62 out of 90) in this scenario. In contrast, the English data showed that speakers generally would use tentative expressions, often in the form of questions (85%, *n*=17 out of 20). Examples of the English invitations collected are below.

6. Let's go for a cup of coffee!
7. How about a cup of coffee after class?
8. Coffee?
9. Hey, I'm going for a coffee. You wanna come?

A closer look at the adjuncts in the invitations reported by the Vietnamese shows that most of them (73.3%) gave a grounder before the invite, some initiated the invitation with a precommitment (16.7%), and a few also included formulaic expressions to flatter the hearer (6.7%), as in Example 5 above. In this same scenario, the English-speaking respondents seemed to use fewer grounders (only 15%), fewer precommitments (5%), and none used expressions of flattering the hearer (Table 1). It is interesting to also note that the practice of making clear the question of who was going to pay at the end of the invitation was not unique to the Vietnamese group; several English respondents did the same, thus reflecting the low-cost nature and casual level of the activity (Examples 10–11).

10. Tí nữa ghé Sông Xanh không? Tao bao.
    little more stop by Song Xanh no I (casual) cover
    How about stopping by Song Xanh later? I'll pay.

11. Wanna have a cup of coffee? It's on me.

Table 1. Inviting a close friend for a coffee after class

types of adjuncts	Vietnamese (*N*=90)	English (*N*=20)
flattering	6.7% (*n*=6)	0% (*n*=0)
precommitment	16.7% (*n*=15)	5% (*n*=1)
grounder	73.3% (*n*=66)	15% (*n*=3)
no adjunct	26.7% (*n*=24)	85% (*n*=17)

It seems that overall, the Vietnamese respondents were more elaborate in their invitations than the American, British, Canadian, and South African respondents. There might be a cultural explanation for this. For these Vietnamese high school students, going to a coffee house together was a significant activity for bonding and socializing,[7] perhaps more so than it might have been for the Anglo-Saxon culture that the English-speaking respondents shared. In Hue at the time of data collection in particular, where the pace of life was calmer and more relaxed than other industrial urban centers, going to a coffee house for high school students was *the* entertainment activity, where relationships were built and maintained. It could be the special cultural meaning of this activity that prompted the Vietnamese respondents to make more elaborate invitations than the English speakers.

Scenario 2: Inviting a friend to a meal with one's family

In this question, the participants were asked what they would say to invite the friends in their study group, who had been studying at their house, to dinner with their family. They were also asked whether they would repeat the invitation a few times if the friends refused the first time. Again, in Chu's (1995) terms, the inviter-invitee relationship in this scenario is close and equal, and the invited activity is informal; however, the social cost might be high since it involves the invitee's imposition on the inviter's entire family. The invitation is, as with the first scenario, part of a larger activity (study group get-together), and the invitation is a true one. Similar to Scenario 1, the invitations in this scenario included grounding moves (Examples 12, 13) or a flattering–the-hearer move (Examples 14, 16) before or after the invite. Regarding the invite itself, examples of tentative expressions are in (12) and (13), and examples of less tentative expressions are in (14)–(16) below.

```
12.  Mình có   đề nghị     thế này:
     I    have suggestion  so  this
     I have this suggestion:

     Tất cả ở lại đây  ăn  cơm  với  nhà   mình
     all    stay  here eat rice with house I
     You all stay here and have dinner with my family

     rồi  học   tiếp.
     then study continue
     Then we'll continue studying.
```

```
13.  Đói    chưa? Ở lại ăn   cơm  cho vui.
     hungry yet? stay  eat rice for happy
     Are you hungry yet? Stay and eat for a good time.

14.  Mấy khi  có   dịp,
     few time have occasion
     Occasions like this are rare,

     thôi mời    mấy  bạn    ở lại ăn  cơm  luôn.
     DisM invite some friend stay  eat rice along
     well, please stay and have dinner with us.

15.  Ở lại  ăn  cơm  rồi  hẵng về.
     stay   eat rice then return
     Stay and eat before you leave.

16.  Bữa nay  ở lại ăn  với  nhà   tao          nghe.
     day this stay  eat with house I (casual) AlignM
     You must stay and eat with my family today.

     Không được      về       đâu   đó.
     no    possible  return   StanM AffM
     You're absolutely not allowed to leave.
```

Example (12) above was coded as "tentative" because the invitation was formulated as a suggestion, and Example (13) was because it was expressed in a question. In both cases, the inviter left an equal option for the invitee to accept or reject the invitation. In (14) - (16), the invitations were less tentative (i.e., the inviter strongly implicated the relevance of the acceptance of the invitation), via the use of imperatives (as in 15), explicit use of the word "invite" in a declarative sentence (as in 14), or the use of a stance marker and affirmative marker with an absolute (negative) imperative (as in 16).

The patterns above are also similar to what was found in the English data: The invitations either contained a tentative expression (Examples 17–19) or a less tentative expression (Examples 20–21).

```
17.  I'm starving. It's time for a break.

     Why don't you stay for dinner?

18.  Hey guys, you wanna stay for dinner?

     We're having pizza!

19.  Can you stay for dinner tonight?

20.  Let's have dinner. There's a lot to eat.

21.  Look, since you're here, you should stay for dinner.

     We've got plenty, it's no trouble.
```

However, quantitative data show that very few of the Vietnamese high school students used less tentative expressions (6.7%, *n*=6), while most of the English-speaking respondents (85%, *n*=17) used these types of expressions. This marked difference may again reflect the pragmatic conventions of each language. It seems that in Vietnamese, joining a friend's family for a meal on the spot is considered a significant imposition,[8] and thus it may be considered impolite to accept the invitation too eagerly. In fact, an invitee will often decline the invitation the first time, and only accept the invitation after the host's repeated affirmative invitations. This was indeed supported by the data from the Vietnamese high school students. More than 80% of them indicated that they would repeat the invitation if their friends refused the first time (this is in contrast with only about 50% of the English speakers who said they would do so). Thus, the reason why the Vietnamese inviter used more affirmative expressions in responding to this scenario might have been to reduce the invitee's option to refuse.

The Vietnamese respondents' perception of this speech act's high degree of imposition in this scenario can be reflected in the type of adjuncts they used. In two thirds of the invitations (66.7%, *n*=60), Vietnamese respondents included some self-effacing expressions referring to the meal (Examples 22–25), expressions to address the invitee's potential shyness (Examples 26, 27), and expressions to emphasize the relationship-building nature of the activity (Examples 28–30).

22. Chỉ là cơm thường thôi.

    only be rice normal only
    It's just a simple meal.

23. Chỉ là cơm đạm bạc thôi.
    only be rice meager only
    It's just a meager meal.

24. Chỉ cơm rau với muối thôi.
    only rice vegetable with salt only
    It's just a simple meal of vegetable and salt.

25. Cơm chẳng có gì đâu.
    rice no (emphasis) have anything StaM
    The meal has nothing really.

26. Nhà có ai đâu mà sợ.
    house have nobody StanM CondM fear
    There's nobody here to be afraid of.

27. Đừng làm khách.
    don't make guest.
    Don't be a stranger.

28. Cứ coi như nhà mày đi.
    AffM consider as house you (casual) ImpM
    Just be at home.

29. Ở lại ăn cơm cho có tình cảm.
    stay eat rice for have feelings
    Stay and eat so we can feel good about it.

```
30.  Không được      từ chối đâu    đó.
     no    possible  decline StanM AffM
     You absolutely can't refuse.

     Nếu mà      từ chối
     if  CondM   decline
     If you say no,

     thì  tau          không dám  ăn  cơm
     then I (casual)  no    dare eat rice
     I'll never eat

     nhà   mày           nữa       đâu.
     house you (casual)  any more  StaM
     at your house again.
```

The Vietnamese adjuncts are quite unique when compared to the invitations reported by the English-speaking respondents, who noted that they would highlight the abundance of the food or the positive quality of the food (Examples 31, 32), and none mentioned the invitee's potential shyness.

31. There's plenty to eat here.
32. We're having pork chops and bacon. They're both good.

First, the content of the Vietnamese invitations reflects the fact that eating at others' houses is considered crossing a group boundary and, being outside of one's familiar group (the family), the Vietnamese may be expected to feel shy (Trần, 1996). This did not seem to be an issue with the Anglo respondents. Second, the contrast between the two groups of respondents regarding their stance toward the food being offered is very interesting. While the Vietnamese speakers tried to disparage the meal, the English speakers told the invitee that there was enough food or that the food would be very good. A possible explanation for this is Vietnam's history of prolonged poverty, which may be a deep-rooted factor that manifests itself on the cultural level. Because resources are limited, one should not take food away from others. Hence, if an inviter wants to encourage the invitee to share the meal with his or her family, the inviter needs to convince the invitee that what is being taken away is of very little value. Along with this, the Vietnamese respondents appealed to the relationship-building aspect of the activity as a way to steer away from the material goods involved in sharing a meal. This is in contrast to the Anglo cultural context, in which food has been generally more available in recent times. As a result, the English-speaking respondents in the data encouraged the invitee to accept the invitation by referring to the positive quality of the food (as in Example 32).

Scenario 3: Inviting a friend to join a picnic

The given context asked respondents to leave a message (using written channel) to invite an old friend to join a picnic with a group of new friends.

Following Chu (1995), the inviter-invitee relationship is close and equal, and the invited activity is informal, but the social cost might be high because it involves the invitee joining a planned activity with a large group. The action of inviting in this case makes up the entire encounter (i.e., not part of a larger activity), and the invitation is true.

Almost all of the messages written by the Vietnamese respondents (94.4%, *n*=85) had the following structure:

Heading
Grounding moves
Invite
Grounding moves/Flattering the hearer
Closing

Example (33) illustrates this structure.

```
33. Heading
     Hà thân!
     Ha close
     Dear Ha,

     Grounding moves
     Mình không gặp  được Hà nên viết  giấy  này
     I     no    meet PosM Ha so  write paper this
     I didn't see you so I'm writing this note

     Invite
     có    nhã       ý   mời    Hà ngày … đi …
     have graceful idea invite Ha day …  go …
     to cordially invite you to go to … on …

     với  nhóm  bạn    của mình.
     with group friend of  I
     with my group of friends.

     Flattering the hearer
     Hà cố gắng đi nhé.
     Ha try     go AlignM.
     Please try to come.

     Grounding move
     Nhóm  bạn     của mình rất  dễ thương, đừng lo.
     group friend  of  I    very lovely     don't worry
     My friends are very lovely, don't worry.

     Flattering the hearer
     Mình hy vọng Hà sẽ   không từ chối.
     I    hope    Ha will  not   refuse
     I hope that you won't refuse.

     Closing
     Bạn    gái,
     friend girl
     Girl friend,

     Thi
```

While this overall structure was found in the English data as well (100%, *n*=20), the Vietnamese invitations appeared quite elaborate and 'flowery' compared to the English respondents' brief messages that were very close to spoken language (Example 34 below). Quantitatively, this is shown in the fact that a large majority (95.5%, *n*=86) of the Vietnamese respondents, but only less than half of the English (42%, *n*=8 out of 19)[9], used flattering-the-hearer moves in their invitations. The Vietnamese invitations, like those in English, had grounding moves before the invites.

```
34.   Mary,
      Picnic tomorrow at. . . . The whole gang is going.
      We're expecting you.
      Call and let me know.
      John
```

In flattering the hearer to encourage him or her to join the picnic with a group of new friends, the Vietnamese respondents not only gave positive comments about the future picnic (something that the English speakers also did), but they also went further to assure the invitees that the group of new friends is very friendly (e.g., "dễ thương" [lovely], "rất hay" [very interesting], "vui tính" [cheerful],"cởi mở" [open], "dễ quen" [easy to be friends with]), and that there was nothing to worry about. These Vietnamese young adults obviously assumed that their friends would be shy with new friends, which reflects the Vietnamese appreciation of reservedness and shyness towards strangers (Nguyễn, 1985). The English-speaking adults did not include these details in their invitation, possibly due to their older age as well as their cultural backgrounds.

Scenario 4: Inviting a friend to a birthday party

In this scenario, the respondents were asked what they would say to invite a friend to their own birthday party. They were also asked to indicate whether they would use oral invitations or written invitations for the birthday party. Again, in Chu's (1995) framework, the inviter-invitee relationship in this scenario is close and equal; the invited activity is semiformal (at least in Vietnamese culture), and its cost might be high since the invitee is being requested to join a party that is usually elaborate in modern Vietnamese culture. The action of inviting is the core of the encounter and is not part of a larger activity, and the invitation is a true one.

Most of the Vietnamese (72%, *n*=65) indicated that they preferred to use printed invitations (for a sample of a standard Vietnamese birthday invitation card, see Appendix C). This is in sharp contrast to the English data, in which only one respondent (or 5%) indicated that she would use a written invitation. This difference may reflect a social practice in central Vietnam at the time of this data collection: Blank birthday invitation cards were sold at bookstands, and it was common to use these printed cards for birthdays. This speculation is supported by data from another scenario not reported here, in which the respondents were asked to invite a friend to a party to celebrate a personal achievement. In that scenario, the subjects were also given the choice to use oral or written invitations, but 86% of the Vietnamese chose oral invitations. Thus, according to the Vietnamese respondents, using written invitations was a social practice for birthday invitations but not for all party invitations.

Examples 35–38 show examples of the oral invitations as reported by the Vietnamese respondents.

35. Mai là sinh nhật mình.
tomorrow be birthday I
Tomorrow's my birthday.

Loan có đến được không?
Loan have come possible no
Can you come, Loan?

36. Mai là sinh nhật mình.
tomorrow be birthday I
Tomorrow's my birthday.

Huong tới cho vui nghe.
Huong come for fun AlignM.
Please come for a good time, Huong.

Hai giờ chiều tại quán cà phê X.
two hour afternoon at shop coffee X
Two o'clock at X coffee house.

37. Mai mời mấy bạn tới dự
tomorrow invite pl. friend come attend
Tomorrow I'd like to invite you guys to come to

sinh nhật mình ở quán cà phê X, bốn giờ.
birthday I at shop coffee X, four hour
my birthday party at X coffee shop, four o'clock.

Nhớ đến nghe.
remember come AlignM.
Please don't forget to come!

38. Chiều nay bạn có rảnh không?
afternoon this friend yes free no
Are you free this afternoon?

Đến quán X lúc 2 giờ chiều nhé.
Come shop X at two hour afternoon AlignM
Please come to X coffee shop at two.

Sinh nhật mình đó!
birthday I AffM
It's my birthday!

As reflected in the examples, most of those who chose to invite orally (88%, *n*=22 out of 25) used less tentative expressions in the form of imperative speech (Examples 36–38) and only a few (12%, *n*=3 out of 25) used tentative expressions (Example 35). This is again in sharp contrast with the English speakers, a majority of whom (95%, *n*=18 out of 19) elected to use tentative expressions in the form of a question or conditional (Examples 39–41).

```
39.  Can you come to X coffee shop at ... tomorrow
     because it's my birthday?
40.  Hey, want to come to my birthday party?
     There's going to be a bunch of people.
     We're going over to a coffee shop.
41.  I'm having a little party at ... on...,
     if you'd be able to come.
```

With respect to the forms of adjuncts, most of the Vietnamese invitations (84%, *n*=75) have a structure quite similar to what was found in most of the English data: A precommitment or grounder was sometimes found before or after the core invite. Quantitative data showed that most invitations reported by the Vietnamese (56%, *n*=14 out of 25) contained a grounder (as in Example 42), some (28%, *n*=7 out of 25) contained a precommitment move (as in Example 43), and only a few contained no adjunct at all (16%, *n*=4 out of 25).

```
42.  Mai        là sinh nhật mình.
     tomorrow be birthday  I.
     Tomorrow's my birthday.

     Nhi tới  dự     cho vui nghe.
     Nhi come attend for fun AlignM
     Please come over for a good time, Nhi.

     Hai giờ  chiều      tại quán cà phê X.
     two hour afternoon at   shop coffee X
     It's at two at X coffee house.

43.  Chiều       nay bạn    có  rảnh không?
     afternoon this friend yes free no
     Are you free this afternoon?

     Đến  quán X lúc hai giờ  nhé.
     come shop X at  two hour AlignM
     Please come to X coffee shop at two.

     Sinh nhật mình đó.
     birthday  I    AffM
     It's my birthday.
```

This pattern is similar to the pattern found in the English data, in which most invitations (84%, *n*=16 out of 19) were found to have a grounder, some (16%, *n*=3 out of 19) had no adjunct at all, and only one (5%) had a precommitment move.

A difference between the Vietnamese birthday invitations and the English ones in the data, however, is the degree of significance each group gave to the birthday celebration. Of the 25 Vietnamese speakers who used oral invitations, 12% gave the purpose of the invitations at the end, after the invites had been made and the time and place of the party specified (as in 43). This reflects the fact that some Vietnamese tend to downplay the importance of their birthday celebration, which might stem from the habit of self-effacing, common among Vietnamese, (Vũ, 1992) and from Vietnamese tradition. Particularly, in the old days, people did not celebrate their own birthdays, and birthday celebration in modern Vietnam is an adoption of Western culture (Phan, 1990).[10] Perhaps due to these cultural and historical factors, the Vietnamese speakers in the data tended to downplay the significance of their birthday parties. This is further supported by the fact that of the 25 Vietnamese respondents, two (counting for 6%) did not want to reveal the purpose of the invitation at all. Even though there were some downplaying elements in the English invitations reported (Examples 44, 45), they were not as strong as in the Vietnamese invitations.

44. It's my birthday tomorrow and I'm having a small party at X coffee shop. Come along, won't you?

45. Are you free on Sunday? How would you like to come to my birthday party at around... .

Scenario 5: Inviting a friend to a sister's wedding

In this scenario, the respondents were asked what they would say to invite a friend to a sister's wedding. In Chu's (1995) terms, the inviter-invitee relationship is close and equal; the invited activity is formal, and the financial cost is relatively high. The action of inviting is the core of the encounter (not part of a larger activity), and the invitation is meant to be true.

More than half of the Vietnamese participants (63.4%, *n*=57) indicated that they would pass the sister's printed invitation on to the friend, a similar practice reported by most of the English respondents (55%, *n*=11). This similarity may result from the fact that in both cultures, wedding etiquette is to send printed invitations (for samples of English and Vietnamese printed invitations for weddings, see Appendices D and E).

Focusing on the printed wedding invitation in the two languages, the most noticeable difference is that in the English invitation, the invitees are requested to inform the inviter in writing if they can come to the party or not, but in the Vietnamese invitation, this is not part of the speech act. This might be traced to dining habits and social practices in the two cultures. At a wedding reception, English diners normally eat their individual helpings served on their own plates, which requires some exactness in the host's food preparation and seating arrangement. By contrast, Vietnamese dining guests at wedding receptions share the food from common dishes and bowls, allowing the total amount of the food served to be less fixed. Naturally, while it is more important for the English host to know the exact number of the guests, the Vietnamese host can be more flexible and thus can afford knowing only an approximate number of guests.[11] Furthermore, the wedding invitation activity is done differently in the two languages. While most wedding invitations in the cultures of the English-speaking respondents are sent by postal mail, most wedding invitations in Vietnamese are delivered in person or, if they have to be mailed, a phone call often follows the printed invitation. Thus, the act of inviting constitutes a more complex social activity (often requiring a visit to the home of the invitee) in which the inviter and invitee can discuss and negotiate the invitee's attendance at the wedding. For that reason, the written invitation does not include a request about the invitee's intention to attend. Thus, the structures of the written wedding invitation in Vietnamese and in English reflect the larger social and cultural context of the speech act, and while in Vietnamese, the wedding invitation needs to be done both on paper and in face-to-face interaction, the English wedding invitation can technically be done only on paper.[12]

Among those who indicated that they would invite the friend to a sister's wedding orally, a large majority of the Vietnamese respondents (97%, *n*=32 out of 33) used less tentative expressions in the form of directives (Examples 46–52) and only one (3%) used a tentative expression in the form of a wish (Example 53). While some male respondents used emphatic language to show intimacy as in Examples 49 and 50, some female respondents used rather emotional invitations, as in Examples 51 and 52. The reason why these females mentioned saying goodbye is that the party at the bride's house one day prior to the party at the groom's house (*lễ vu quy* in Vietnamese) is the farewell party for her before she joins her husband and his family. This party can be quite emotional (Phan, 1990), which is due to the traditional practice (still widely honored today) that after the wedding, the woman will "belong" to her husband's family and thus can only visit her own family occasionally.

46. Ngày mai đến dự đám cưới chị tao nghe,
tomorrow come attend wedding older sis. I AlignM
Please come to my sister's wedding tomorrow,

sáu giờ chiều.
six hour afternoon.
six o'clock.

Nhớ đến nghe!
remember come AlignM
Please don't forget to come!

47. Chiều mai đám cưới chị tao,
afternoon tomorrow wedding older sister I
Tomorrow afternoon is my sister's wedding

mày sang giúp một tay nhé.
you come over help one hand AlignM
Please come and give a hand.

48. Thứ Tư này là đám cưới chị mình
Wednesday this be wedding older sister I
Wednesday is my sister's wedding,

bạn đến dự nhé.
friend come attend AlignM
please do come.

Sáu giờ chiều.
six hour afternoon
It's at six in the afternoon.

Nhớ đến cho vui.
remember come for fun
Don't forget to come for a good time.

Tối mai đám cưới chị tao.
evening tomorrow wedding older sister I (casual)
Tomorrow evening is my sister's wedding.

Tụi mày tới đánh chén nhé!
PluM you (casual) come fight eat (casual) AlignM
You guys, come for the big feast!

49. Chuyện quan trọng bậc nhất:
affair important level first
This is a most important event:

Ngày mai đám cưới chị tao!
tomorrow wedding older sister I (casual)
Tomorrow is my sister's wedding!

Yêu cầu tất cả có mặt.
require all have face
I require that you all be present.

50. Chủ nhật này là đám cưới chị mình rồi.
Sunday this be wedding older sis. I already
This Sunday is my sister's wedding already.

Thế là chị sắp đi xa.
so be older sister be going to go far
That means she's about to go far away.

Bạn tới để chia tay nhé.
friend come in order to bid farewell AlignM
Please come to bid her farewell.

51. Thứ Ba này là chị mình "sang ngang,"
Tuesday this be older sister I cross the river
Next Tuesday my sister's going to "cross the river,"[13]

tụi mày tới tiễn chị nghe.
PluM you come see off older sister AlignM
please come to see her off, guys.

52. Chị mình bảo mình mời bạn
older sister I tell I invite friend
My sister told me to invite you

ngày mai đến dự đám cưới.
tomorrow come attend wedding
to her wedding tomorrow.

```
53.  Mong  bạn     cố gắng đến    chung vui
     wish friend   try     come   share  joy
     I really wish you'll try to come to share the joy

     cùng      gia đình mình.
     together  family   I
     with my family.

     Sáu giờ   chiều      nhé.
     six hour  afternoon  AlignM
     Please be there at six.
```

The assertiveness of the Vietnamese invitations is highlighted when one examines the English patterns. Most of the English-speaking respondents (91%, *n*=10 out of 11) wrote down tentative expressions (Examples 54–57) for what they would say in this scenario.

```
54.  My sister's getting married next week, she says I can
     invite some of my friends. Would you like to come?
55.  My sister's wedding's next Sunday. Can you come?
56.  Sylvia's getting married next week and wants you
     to come. It's gonna be great so don't miss it.
57.  My sister is getting married and she asked me to
     invite some friends. I immediately thought of you.
     It's on. . . . Can you make it?
```

With respect to the grounding moves, as can be seen in the examples above, most invitations in Vietnamese, similar to those in English, used some form of grounders to give some context to the invitations, and some form of flattering-the-hearer move (as in 47 and 53) to persuade the invitee.

Scenario 6: Inviting someone to strike up a relationship

In this context, the respondents were asked what they would say to invite a new person they just met at a party to go out for a cup of coffee. The scenario was presented as two possibilities. In the first one (which will be referred to as Scenario 6a), the invitee was of the same gender as the respondent, and in the second (which will be referred to as Scenario 6b), the invitee was of the opposite gender. In Chu's (1995) terms, the inviter-invitee relationship in this scenario is equal but not close; the invited action is informal, and the financial cost is low. The invitation is part of a larger activity (the party), and the invitation is meant to accomplish something else (to strike a relationship).

In Scenario 6a, where the person to be invited is of the same gender as the inviter, 100% of the respondents indicated that they would make the invitation. Unlike inviting a close friend (see Scenario 1), a number of the Vietnamese respondents used polite personal pronouns for themselves (*mình* [self]), the invitee (*bạn* [friend]), and for themselves and the invitee (*chúng ta* [we]), which can mark the language as semiformal and elaborate (Examples 58–61).

58. Chúng ta hãy đi uống cà phê
we let go drink coffee
Let's go for a cup of coffee
để đánh dấu tình bạn mới.
in order to mark friendship new
to mark our new friendship.

59. Mình thấy bạn hay hay.
I see friend interesting interesting
I find you very interesting.

Ta đi uống cà phê nhé?
We go drink coffee AlignM
Shall we go for a cup of coffee?

60. Gần đây có một quán cà phê dễ thương lắm.
near here have one shop coffee lovely very
There's a very lovely coffee shop near here.

Bạn có thể đi uống cà phê với mình
friend can go drink coffee with I
Can you join me for a cup of coffee

cho vui được không?
for fun possible no
for a good time?

61. Ở đây ồn ào quá,
in here noisy too much
It is so noisy here,

hay là ta đi đâu đó uống cà phê đi.
or be us go somewhere drink coffee ImpM
how about going some where for some coffee?

Quantitative data show that about half of the Vietnamese respondents (45.5%, *n*=41) reported invitations with tentative expressions via the use of questions (Examples 59–61). The Vietnamese inviting behavior in this scenario is markedly more tentative compared to the other scenarios examined. However, the Vietnamese invitations in this scenario are still quite assertive when compared to the English invitations in the data, in which a large majority (95%, *n*=19) of the invitations contain tentative expressions (Examples 62–63).

62. Too early to go home, how about a cup of coffee at the Redlight?[14]
63. How about a cup of coffee after this? We can continue talking there.

As for the type of adjuncts, it is worth noting that also unlike the scenario in which the respondents were asked to invite a close friend out for coffee (Scenario 1), most of the grounding moves in Vietnamese (60%, compared to 40% in the English data) involved excuses about the physical factors of the environment, such as noise and stuffy air (Example 61; compare with Example 62 in the English data). Plausibly, when the inviter does not know the invitee well, there is a need to seek reasons as grounding moves for the invitation. A possibly distinctive feature of the Vietnamese invitations is the use of flattering-the-hearer moves in about half of the reported invitations (55.5%, *n*=50), in contrast to a lower frequency in the English invitations (33%, *n*=6). Also, some Vietnamese respondents (8.9%, *n*=8) used a precommitment move in their invitations but none of the English invitations had this move. Finally, only a few Vietnamese respondents (24.4%, *n*=22) used a bare invitation without any adjuncts, but several English respondents (45%, *n*=9) did so.

In Scenario 6b, involving a new friend of the opposite gender, inviting is more complicated for the Vietnamese. It is important to note that with the gender shift, the distance between the inviter and invitee might increase, and the purpose of the invitation may change (to possibly strike up a romantic relationship).[15]

Most of the Vietnamese females (65.6%, *n*=42 out of 64 females) indicated that they would not make the invitation in this scenario. However, only some of the Vietnamese males (15.4%, *n*=4 out of 26 males) wrote that they would not make the invitation. This is in sharp contrast to the English-speaking respondents, who all, except for one female (9%, *n*=1 out of 11 females), reported that they would make the invitation. There seems to be two possible explanations for this. First, the English-speaking group included some older participants who might be bolder in inviting a stranger compared to the younger Vietnamese. Second, in Vietnamese culture, reservedness and shyness toward strangers of the opposite gender are recommended for young women (Nguyễn, 1985); hence, many female respondents may have felt that they should not make the invitation.

In this second scenario, the participants were also asked whether they would try to invite the new friend directly or in indirect ways. About half of the Vietnamese females who reported that they would make the invitation (55%, *n*=12 out of 22) indicated that they would invite the new friend out indirectly, but only about one third of the Vietnamese male inviters (35%, *n*=9 out of 26) selected this option. This gender-based difference in the Vietnamese data was similar to the reported behavior among the English-speaking inviters in this scenario. While most females (73%, *n*=8 out of 11) indicated that they would invite indirectly, only about half of the men (45%, *n*=4 out of 9) chose this option.

The data on direct invitations show that unlike other scenarios, most Vietnamese invitations reported for this scenario (86%, *n*=38 out of 44 inviters) involved tentative expressions in the form of a conditional (Example 66), a request to invite (Example 64), or a hedge (Example 65). Only a few (14%, *n*=6 out of 44 inviters) used a less tentative expression in this scenario (Example 67). In both types of invitations, the respondents formulated elaborate invitations, which are rarely found in other scenarios. They also tended to use fixed polite expressions (e.g., "Please allow me to invite you" as in Example 64) and polite personal references (*bạn* [friend] and *mình* [self], seen in Examples 64–67).

```
64.  Cho  phép         mình được mời    bạn
     give permission I    PosM invite friend
     Please allow me to invite you

     đi uống  cà phê và  kết  bạn    với  bạn.
     go drink coffee and bond friend with friend
     to some coffee and become friends with you.

65.  Mình không biết bạn    có  từ chối
     I    no    know friend yes refuse
     I don't know if you will refuse

     lời mời     của mình không.
     invitation  of  I    no
     my invitation or not.

     Mình muốn mời    bạn    đi uống  cà phê với  mình.
     I    want invite friend go drink coffee with I
     I would like to invite you to some coffee with me.

66.  Nếu bạn     không bận,
     if  friend  no    busy
     If you're not busy,

     mời    bạn    đi uống  cà phê với   mình
     invite friend go drink coffee with  I
     I'd like to invite you to some coffee with me.

67.  Mình rất  muốn mời    bạn    đi
     I    very want invite friend go
     I really want you to invite you

     uống  cà phê với  mình
     drink coffee with I
     to some coffee with me.

     Mong bạn     không từ chối.
     hope friend  no    refuse
     I hope you won't refuse.
```

The Vietnamese respondents' tendency to opt for tentative expressions is similar to the English data, in which all of the respondents used a tentative expression in the form of a question, a conditional, or a modal of probability (Examples 68–70).

68. How about a cup of coffee after this?
69. If you are not busy after this, maybe we can go for a cup of coffee and continue the conversation.
70. I'm gonna head out for some coffee. If you're not doing anything, I'd love some company.

Quantitatively, it is noteworthy that the frequency of tentative expressions for the Vietnamese respondents increased from inviting a close friend (Scenario 1) to inviting a new acquaintance of the same gender (Scenario 6a), to inviting a new acquaintance of the opposite gender (Scenario 6b), as shown in Table 2. This trend is apparent in the English data as well. This suggests that in both cultures, people are more tentative when inviting a stranger. A closer look at the data shows that the frequency of tentative expressions jumped remarkably with the gender change (Scenarios 6a to 6b) for the Vietnamese respondents but not for the English respondents. This seems to indicate that the Vietnamese high school students acted more differently according to gender when inviting a stranger than the English speakers did.

Table 2. Use of tentative expressions in three inviting scenarios: A comparison between Vietnamese and English Data

	scenarios	Vietnamese	English
1	Inviting a close friend	31.1%	85%
6a	Inviting a new acquaintance of the same gender	45.5%	95%
6b	Inviting a new acquaintance of the opposite gender	86%	100%

Turning now to the indirect invitations, the Vietnamese respondents described various ways to invite someone of the opposite gender out for coffee without inviting that person upfront. Many of the strategies reported involved making an invitation eventually, but this invitation was often embedded in a larger activity other than inviting. Another strategy reported by many Vietnamese male and female respondents was to ask a common friend to invite the target person out, and then the group would go together. This strategy is similar to what several English-speaking respondents said they would do. One distinctive strategy reported by many males (but none of the females) was to ask to accompany the girl to her home at the end of the party and, on the way, invite her for a cup of coffee. This is related to a common practice in Vietnam (at least at the time of this data collection), in which a young man may offer to share the bike ride home with a young woman as a way to show consideration for her safety or to show his interest in her. A young woman, however, would normally never make such an offer to a young man of the same age or older. Another strategy that may be unique to the Vietnamese group was to pass a note to the intended invitee. Also, a few females indicated that they would use some study-related excuses to invite the target person out, a strategy not found among any of the male respondents.

Some general inviting practices

As mentioned above, a brief metapragmatic survey was included at the end of the DTC, and it reveals some interesting self-reported inviting practices. First, when asked whether they usually inform the invitee of the other people also invited, only 25% of the Vietnamese respondents said that they would do so, while 90% of the English-speaking respondents indicated that they would. This suggests that compared to the English-speaking respondents, the Vietnamese respondents tended to focus more on the event of the occasion and the inviter-invitee relationship and less on the socializing opportunities that the future event offers to the invitee. Second, most Vietnamese respondents (60%) reported that they usually repeated the time and place of the invited event before saying goodbye to the invitee, a pattern similar to what most of the English respondents (70%) reported. This is consistent with findings in conversation analysis on English data, in which arrangements for future encounters are often found in preclosing and closing moves of mundane conversations (Schegloff & Sacks, 1973). This further suggests that the two languages may share some common pragmatic conventions in conversation closings. On the other hand, what people say in each language to remind the invitee may not be the same. When asked whether they usually asked the invitee to remember to come, a majority of the Vietnamese (83%) indicated that they often did, while only some (25%) of the English-speaking respondents said that they would. In a related question asking whether they would insist that the invitee come on time, half of the Vietnamese surveyed indicated that they would do so, while only a minority of the English-speaking respondents (5%) wrote that they would. This may reflect the fact that in most social events in Vietnam, people tend to come late, and people's expectations of the 'appropriate' late time may be more varied than those of the cultures of the English-speaking respondents.

Discussion and conclusion

In this chapter, I have reported on the forms of invitation made in Vietnamese, compared them with some forms of invitation in English, and discussed how social and cultural contexts may influence the linguistic shapes of the speech act. In most scenarios analyzed, the Vietnamese respondents reported more frequent use of less tentative inviting expressions compared to the English respondents (an exception to this is when the Vietnamese participants were asked to invite a stranger). This difference between the two languages has direct implications for second language learning. Because the use of questions and conditionals may sound distant and tentative to the Vietnamese, English-speaking learners of Vietnamese need to use more direct forms such as imperatives to make invitations if they want to sound committed and enthusiastic. On the other hand, Vietnamese learners of English may risk sounding too 'pushy' or imposing if they continue their first language's inviting routines (e.g., using imperatives, obligation modals, and 'kind threats') in English.

The data also show that the gender differences between the inviter and invitee can increase the social distance for both Vietnamese and English speakers; this is particularly noticeable for the former group. This supports Brown and Levinson's (1987) politeness theory in showing that greater social distance can lead to the use of more elaborate linguistic means to redress the increased level of face-threat of the speech act. It also suggests that gender should be considered as an important factor that may influence the choice of invitation forms in Vietnamese.

Perhaps not unexpectedly, the findings in this study also show that cultural, historical, and social factors played a significant role in the formulation of the invitations, particularly the adjuncts, in both languages. In every scenario examined, this larger context is engrained in the linguistic forms of the invitation. Or, seen another way, an analysis of the speech act of inviting provides a valuable window into the local culture and social practices of the target culture. Again, this offers useful implications for language teaching and learning. Learners of Vietnamese can further appreciate the layers of meaning in Vietnamese linguistic forms if they are provided with relevant cultural, social, and historical knowledge.

With respect to specific linguistic routines, there are some expressions that occurred with fairly high frequency in the Vietnamese self-reported invitations. The phrase *tới cho vui* [come for a joyous time] was used the most frequently. It occurred in 14.3% of the 1,013 oral invitations reported by the Vietnamese respondents. In written form, the equivalent phrases *chung vui* or *góp vui* or *chia vui* (varied ways to say "to share the joy") were also found with high frequency. Altogether, they appeared in 44.3% of the 149 written invitations reported. These seem to be formulaic expressions that, although not containing any words related to inviting, may co-occur with the speech act of inviting. This also bears important implications for the teaching of Vietnamese as a second or foreign language. Learners should be prepared to recognize and produce these expressions in the speech act of inviting.

As an exploratory study, this chapter prompts further questions for future research. First, the findings here show the tendency of tentative or less tentative expressions and the occurrence of certain types of adjuncts in certain inviting scenarios, but they do not show what may trigger the inviter to choose a certain linguistic form. If inviting is such a socially and culturally sensitive speech act, it should be studied when it is embedded in naturally occurring social activities. By looking at interaction as it unfolds, the analyst may then be able to see the particular actions that a given inviting turn may achieve. Second, as mentioned earlier in this chapter, invitation is only the first part of an adjacency pair. It would be extremely important to study invitations and responses to invitations, not as two separate parts, but as they occur together. This line of research, I believe, can also be accomplished by studying inviting behaviors in naturally occurring discourse. Finally, it would be useful to examine how learners of Vietnamese develop their pragmatic competence in making and responding to invitations. These are a few questions that, with the information provided in this present study, we can begin to explore towards a more thorough understanding of Vietnamese pragmatics.

Notes

1 In some languages such as Chinese, invitation sequences often also involve verbal play rituals, through which the inviter and invitee perform their identities and relationship (Mao, 1992). However, this phenomenon goes beyond this chapter's focus on the first pair part of an invitation.

2 The concept of social cost is alluded to in Chu's categorization, and future research is needed to determine more specifically what are considered low or high social cost in Vietnamese society.

3 These other scenarios include a diverse collection of contexts such as inviting a friend to visit one's home on an ordinary day and on Tet (New Year's Day), inviting a friend to join a party at one's family's house, inviting a teacher to an official meeting, inviting someone to stay the night at one's house for convenience, and inviting a friend to join a group on the way to playing some electronic games.

4 Due to limited access to English-speaking subjects at the time and location of this study, the English-speaking group is much smaller and more diverse than the Vietnamese group, and they are also of a different age range. This set of English data is, however, sufficient for the purpose of serving as the backdrop against which the distinctiveness of the Vietnamese inviting patterns may be highlighted. As stated above in "Scope of Investigation," I do not aim to generalize about inviting in English in general.

5 Functional English translations will be provided throughout the paper; however, attempts were also made to preserve the original Vietnamese meaning as much as possible.

6 Name of a popular local coffee shop.

7 This is in the context of Hue city in 1995.

8 There is a fixed expression in Vietnamese, *ăn chực,* to refer to a child's joining another family's meal on the spot without the parents' permission. It is usually considered bad behavior, and children are taught not to do so.

9 One of the English speakers indicated that he would use the phone to make the invitation and did not write an invitation in this scenario.

10 Also following Phan (1990), in precolonial times, only wealthy families could afford birthday parties.

11 The difference between the two cultures is not black and white; rather, it is a matter of degree. Of course the English host can manage if the number of actual guests is slightly different from the planned number, and the Vietnamese host would benefit greatly if s/he knew the exact number of guests in advance. In addition, the difference between the two cultures regarding this wedding invitation practice may also relate to their differences in future event planning and scheduling. Although future events are usually planned well ahead of time in many English-speaking western countries, in Vietnam, people are generally more flexible with future event scheduling, and it is not unusual that a wedding guest cancels at the last minute

without telling the host. This is thus an example of how a specific, concrete linguistic form may be linked to the much larger social and cultural context.

12 The Vietnamese wedding invitation practices described here are still true as of 2006.

13 To "cross the river" (*sang ngang*) is a Vietnamese euphemism for getting married, used only for women.

14 Name of a coffee house.

15 This is of course based on the assumption that romantic attraction only occurs between people of opposite sexes. While this assumption unfairly excludes gays and lesbians, I will use it here because it was what the Vietnamese subjects would most likely believe in, given their time and cultural context. The data on inviting patterns in this scenario also support this observation.

16 Blank spaces on commercially printed cards to be filled with the relevant information are marked with underlines in this sample.

17 The closing formula to be used in this blank space depends on the relationship between the inviter and the invitee. If it is a junior-senior relationship, the appropriate formula is *kính* [respectfully], if it is between friends, the formula is *thân* [closely].

18 A sweet party is where desserts (e.g., candies, cookies, cake) are served.

19 See endnote 17.

20 Personal references for the invitee are used in this blank. Sometimes names are also included.

References

Brown, P., & Levinson, S. (1987). *Politeness: Some universals in language usage.* Cambridge: Cambridge University Press.

Chu, Thi Thanh Tâm (1995). Hành vi mời và đoạn thoại mời [The speech act of inviting and the inviting sequence]. *Ngôn Ngữ, 1,* 47–52.

Đào Thi Thúy Nga (1999, April). *Sự tương đồng và khác biệt giữa hành vi ngôn ngữ "mời" và "rủ" trong tiếng Việt [The similarities and differences between the speech acts of "mời" and "rủ" in Vietnamese].* Paper presented at the First Pragmatics Conference, Hanoi.

Edmondson, W., & House, J. (1981). *Let's talk and talk about it: A pedagogic interactional grammar of English.* Munchen: Urban & Schwarzenberg.

Garfinkel, H. (1967). *Studies in ethnomethodology.* Englewood Cliffs, NJ: Prentice Hall.

Hancher, M. (1979). The classification of cooperative illocutionary acts. *Language in Society 8*(1), 1–14.

Hartford, B., & Bardovi-Harlig, K. (1992). Experimental and observational data in the study of interlanguage pragmatics. In L.F. Bouton & Y. Kachru (Eds.), *Pragmatics and language learning monograph* (Vol. 3, pp. 33–52). Urbana-Champaign, IL:

Division of English as an International Language, University of Illinois at Urbana-Champaign.

Isaacs, E.A., & Clark, H.H. (1990). Ostensible invitations. *Language in Society, 19*(4), 493–509.

Kasper, G., & Rose, K. (2002). *Pragmatic development in a second language*. Malden, MA: Blackwell.

Lee, P. (1976). Impositive speech acts. *Ohio State University Working Papers in Linguistics, 21,* 98–144.

Mao, L. (1992). Invitational discourse and Chinese identity. *Journal of Asian Pacific Communication, 3*(1), 79–96.

Nguyễn Đức Uy (1985). *Văn minh, lịch sự, tế nhị [Being civilized, polite, and tactful]*. Hà Nội: The Culture and Ideology Publishing House.

Phan Kế Bính (1990). *Vietnam phong tục [Vietnamese customs]*. Hanoi: Đồng Tháp Publishing House.

Prokop, I. (1989). The speech act invitation/suggestion/agreement in German and Polish. *Studia Germanica Posnaniensia, 16,* 195–207.

Sacks, H., Schegloff, E.A., & Jefferson, G. (1974). A simplest systematics for the organization of turn-taking for conversation. *Language, 50*(4), 696–735.

Schegloff, E.A. (1986). The routine as achievement. *Human Studies, 9,* 111–152.

Schegloff, E.A., & Sacks, H. (1973). Opening up closings. *Semiotica, 8,* 289–327.

Szatrowski, P. (1987). A discourse analysis of Japanese invitations. *Annual Proceedings of the Berkeley Linguistics Society, 13,* 270–284.

Trần Ngọc Thêm (1996). *Tìm về bản sắc văn hóa Việt Nam [Discovering the identity of Vietnamese culture]*. Hồ Chí Minh City: Ho Chi Minh City Publishing House.

Vũ Hạnh (1992). *Người Việt cao quý [The Noble Vietnamese]*. Hồ Chí Minh City: The Publishing House of the Ho Chi Minh City Arts and Literature Association.

Wolfson, N. (1981). Invitations, compliments and the competence of the native speaker. *International Journal of Psycholinguistics, 8*(4), 7–22.

Appendix A: Vietnamese questionnaire

Bảng Điều Tra

Bảng câu hỏi dưới đây nhằm tìm hiểu cách người Việt mời nhau. Các câu trả lời của bạn là rất quan trọng đối với sự thành công của cuộc nghiên cứu này. Các dữ liệu của việc điều tra sẽ chỉ được sử dụng cho công việc nghiên cứu, và KHÔNG vì một mục đích nào khác.

Trân trọng cám ơn sự hợp tác của bạn.

Phần A

Bạn vui long đọc kỹ câu hỏi, đặt mình vào tình huống, thong thả cân nhắc câu trả lời rồi ghi rõ bạn nói gì hoặc viết gì trong mỗi tình huống.

Với những trường hợp có sự chọn lựa giữa Viết giấy mời và Mời miệng, đề nghị bạn đánh dấu X vào ô mà bạn chọn. Ví dụ:

[ ] Viết giấy mời [ ] Mời miệng

Bạn có thể ghi ra mẫu đối thọai giữa mình và người được mời nếu thấy cần thiết. Nếu không đủ chỗ cho câu trả lời của bạn, bạn hãy viết ra mặt sau của tờ giấy.

Bạn vui long điền vào các chỗ trống sau:

Tuổi: _______ Nam _________ Nữ __________

Tình huống 1: Sau buổi học này, bạn muốn mời một người bạn thân đi uống cà phê. Bạn nói như thế nào?

Tình huống 2: Bạn và một số bạn khác học nhóm. Tới giờ ăn tối, bạn mời các bạn ở lại ăn cùng gia đình. Bạn nói như thế nào?

Nếu các bạn ấy từ chối, bạn có cố mời them đôi ba lần hay không?

____ Có ____ Không

Tình huống 3: Nhóm bạn cũ của bạn tổ chức đi chơi ngòai trời. Bạn muốn mời một người bạn mới của mình đi cùng, và giả sử bạn không gặp trực tiếp được người ấy, bạn phải viết giấy nhắn. Bạn viết những gì để mời?

Tình huống 4: Sắp tới sinh nhật của bạn, bạn sẽ tổi chức một bữa tiệc nhỏ tại quán cà phê và mời các bạn tới dự. Bạn sẽ:

[ ] Viết giấy mời [ ] Mời miệng

Nội dung mời:

Tình huống 5: Đám cưới chị gái của bạn, bạn được phép mời vài người bạn tới dự. Bạn mời như thế nào?

[ ] Viết giấy mời [ ] Mời miệng

Nội dung mời:

Tình huống 6a: Tại một buổi liên hoan, bạn quen một người cùng giới bạn rất thích. Bạn muốn mời người ấy sau buổi liên hoan đi uống cà phê. Bạn nói như thế nào?

Tình huống 6b: Cũng tại một buổi liên hoan, bạn quen một người khác giới mà bạn muốn kết thân. Bạn có mời người ấy trực tiếp không?

____ Có ____ Không

Nếu có, bạn nói như thế nào?
Nếu không, bạn có mời gián tiếp không?
____ Có ____ Không
Nếu có, bạn mời như thế nào?

Phần B

Dưới đây là một số câu hỏi dạng trắc nghiêm. Đề nghị bạn đánh dấu (+) và trước khả năng bạn muốn chọn. Ví dụ:

[ ] Có [+] Không

Bạn hãy thong thả cân nhắc rồi mới trả lời.

1. Khi mời ai, bạn có hay cho người ấy biết những ai khác cũng được mời không?
   [ ] Có [ ] Không
2. Khi mời ai, bạn có hay dặn đi dặn lại người ấy cố gắng nhớ đi hay không?
   [ ] Có [ ] Không
3. Khi mời ai, bạn có hay nhấn mạnh yêu cầu người đó đi đúng giờ hay không?
   [ ] Có [ ] Không
4. Khi mời ai xong rồi, lúc chia tay người đó, bạn có hay nhắc lại thời gian, địa điểm mời hay không?
   [ ] Có [ ] Không

Xin chân thành cảm ơn bạn.

Appendix B: English questionnaire

This survey is to find out how native English speakers make invitations in everyday scenarios. Your responses are very important to the success of this survey. The data will be used for a research project and NO other purposes. Your cooperation will be most appreciated.

Part A

Please read the questions carefully, put yourself in the given contexts, and write down what you actually say or write in each scenario.

Please also indicate if a context sounds authentic or non-authentic to you. For example:

[ ] Authentic [ ] Non-authentic

In cases when there is a choice between Written and Oral, please check the box of your choice. For example:

[ ] Written [ ] Oral

In some scenarios, you might want to write down the whole conversation between you and the one(s) invited. If you need more space for any particular item, please write on the back of the paper.

Your nationality: ______________________________

Your age: ________ Male __________ Female __________

Scenario 1: After a class, you want to invite a friend to a cup of coffee. What do you say?

[ ] Authentic [ ] Non-authentic

Scenario 2: You and some friends are working on some group work at your house and it is time for dinner. You invite your friends to join you for dinner. What do you say?

[ ] Authentic [ ] Non-authentic

If your friends refuse your invitation the first time, do you insist on inviting them?

____ Yes _______ No

Scenario 3: You and some old friends are going to have a picnic. You want to invite a new friend to join you, and suppose you can't find him/her so you want to write a message. What do you write?

[ ] Authentic [ ] Non-authentic

Scenario 4: Your birthday is coming up. You want to have a birthday party at a coffee shop. You want to invite some classmates. How do you invite them?

[ ] Written [ ] Oral Content:

[ ] Authentic [ ] Non-authentic

Scenario 5: It's your sister's wedding and she asks you to invite some of your friends. How do you invite them?

[ ] Written [ ] Oral Content:

[ ] Authentic [ ] Non-authentic

Scenario 6a: At a party, you meet an interesting new friend of the same gender and want to know more about him/her. You invite him/her to have some coffee after the party. What do you say?

[ ] Authentic [ ] Non-authentic

Scenario 6b: Also at a party, you meet someone of the opposite gender whom you would like to meet again. Will you ask him/her out directly?

____ Yes _______ No

If yes, what do you say?

If no, will you invite him/her indirectly?

____ Yes _______ No

If yes, how would you invite the person indirectly for a cup of coffee?

[ ] Authentic [ ] Non-authentic

Part B

Please put a check next to your choice in answering to the following questions. For example:

[ ] Yes [+] No

Please read the questions carefully.

1. When you invite someone, do you usually tell him/her who else is also invited?
   [ ] Yes [ ] No
2. When you invite someone, do you usually remind them not to forget to come?
   [ ] Yes [ ] No
3. When you invite someone, do you usually insist that they come on time?
   [ ] Yes [ ] No
4. After finishing your invitation, before saying goodbye to the person(s) invited, do you usually repeat the time and place of invitation?
   [ ] Yes [ ] No

Thank you very much!

Appendix C: Printed Vietnamese birthday invitation sample

Nhân dịp sinh nhật Chi[16]
occasion birthday Chi
On the occasion of Chi's birthday

Thân[17] mời Ý Nhi
closely invite Y Nhi
Y Nhi is cordially invited

Đến dự: Tiệc ngọt[18]
come attend party sweet
To attend a sweet party

Vào lúc: 2 giờ chiều ngày 3 tháng 2 năm 1995
at time 2 hour afternoon day 3 month 2 year1995
At: 2 p.m. on the third of February, 1995

Tại: Số 10, Nguyễn Huệ, Huế
at number 10 Nguyen Hue street Hue
At: 10, Nguyen Hue, Hue

Sự hiện diện của Nhi là niềm vinh hạnh cho Chi.
presence of Nhi be honor for Chi
Nhi's presence will be an honor for Chi.

Thân[19] mời.
closely invite
Cordially,

Chi

Appendix D: Printed Vietnamese wedding invitation sample

```
Trân trọng    kính mời anh chị[20]
respectfully invite   older brother and sister
Respectfully inviting you

Vui lòng đến  dự      buổi tiệc rượu
please   come attend party     wine
To please attend a reception

chung vui cùng gia đình chúng tôi
share joy with family    us
to share the joy of our family

Tại: Số 10, Nguyễn Huệ,                Huế
at   number 10, Nguyen Hue Street, Hue
At: 10, Nguyen Hue, Hue

Vào lúc: 6 giờ  chiều,      ngày 15 tháng 8, năm 1995
at time  6 hour afternoon, day  15 month 8  year 1995
At: 6 p.m., on the 15th of August, 1995

nhằm ngày 20 tháng 7, năm  1995 âm    lịch
aim  day  20 month 7  year 1995 lunar calendar
Which falls on the 20th of the 7th month of the lunar calendar

Sự hiện diện của anh chị
presence     of  older brother older sister
Your presence

là niềm vinh hạnh cho gia đình chúng tôi.
be  honor  for  family  us
will be a great honor to our family.

Trân trọng kính mời
respect    invite
Respectfully,
```

Appendix E: Printed English wedding invitation sample

We request the honor of your presence at our wedding reception at ..... on ......

Your presence will be a great honor to our families.

RSVP.

6 Listener Responses in Vietnamese Conversations

Quỳnh Thị Ngọc Nguyễn
Vietnam National University, Hanoi

Introduction

Observations of listener responses were published as early as the 1950s (Heinz, 2003). Beginning with the works by Kendon in 1967, more researchers in linguistics, psychology, sociology, and communication studies also began examining listener responses in the 1970s (Heinz, 2003), with several examples of the studies done by Dittman and Llewellyn (1968), Dittman (1972), Duncan (1972), and Yngve (1970). In fact, the term *backchannel,* widely used to refer to listener behavior, was first coined during this time (Yngve, 1970). Since then, several studies have focused on the listener, such as those by Schegloff (1982), Jefferson (1984, 2002), Heritage (1984), Goodwin (1986), Tao and Thompson (1991), Drummond and Hopper (1993), Clancy, Thompson, and Suzuki (1996), Gardner (2001, 2007), Bavelas, Coates, and Johnson (2000, 2002), Heinz (2003), Xudong (2008), and Bavelas and Gerwing (2011). These studies show that listener response forms "appear to be one of the most language- and culture-specific interactional devices with respect to the kinds of epistemic, affective, and interactional meanings they display" (Sorjonen, 2002, p. 166). Heinz (2003) demonstrates that although the phenomenon of *backchannelling* itself appears universal, specific listener behavior is particular to language and culture. Similarly, Jefferson (2002) also claimed

Pragmatics of Vietnamese as a native and target language, pp. 213–241
Carsten Roever & Hạnh thị Nguyễn (Eds.), 2013
Honolulu, HI: University of Hawai'i, National Foreign Language Resource Center

that the frequency and placement of listener responses are culturally and linguistically dependent and should thus be included in discussions of varying communicative practices.

In fact, listener responses have been investigated in a wide range of languages such as American English (e.g., Drummond & Hopper, 1993; Yngve, 1970), Australian English (Astbury, 1994; Thwaite, 1993), Chinese (e.g., Tao & Thompson, 1991), Japanese (e.g., Maynard, 1989; White, 1989), Finnish (Sorjonen, 2002), and Swedish (Beach & Lindstrom, 1992). Also, contrastive studies have examined the use of backchannels in Mandarin versus Japanese versus American English (Clancy et al., 1996), Japanese versus American English (Maynard, 1986; White, 1989), Native American culture versus mainstream American culture (Phillips, 1983), Swedish versus American English (Beach & Lindstrom, 1992), Mandarin versus American English (Tao & Thompson, 1991), Khmer-Australian English versus mainstream Australian English (Astbury, 1994), German versus American English (Heinz, 2003), and Mandarin Chinese versus Australian English (Xudong, 2008). The above research has shown that (a) all participants engage in some form of listener responses; (b) both verbal and nonverbal responses are used; and (c) the frequency, distribution, and function of these responses differ from language to language and culture to culture.

The study reported in this chapter, a part of a larger project, investigates listener responses in an under-researched language, Vietnamese. It aims to contribute to the existing bodies of research on listener behaviors in world languages and on Vietnamese social interaction.

The most thorough account of listener responses has been obtained in research informed by Conversation Analysis (CA; Gardner, 2001). Over more than two decades, these CA studies have tackled the highly indexical meanings displayed by different response forms (Sorjonen, 2002), and focused on the meaning and use of these forms in different languages and cultures (for example, Drummond & Hopper, 1993; Heinz, 2003; Heritage, 1984; Jefferson, 1984, 2002; and Schegloff, 1982). These studies are informed by an understanding of talk as action-in-interaction. It has been found that response forms are produced and understood with respect to not only the features of prior talk such as its grammatical structure and prosodic cues, but also, and more importantly, with respect to the types of action that prior talk accomplishes through construction and placement within the ongoing sequence of actions and activity (Sorjonen, 2002). Therefore, the action that the response form is responding to should be treated as a part of its semantics in listener-response analysis (Sorjonen, 2002). Moreover, Heritage (1984) stressed that actions accomplished by response forms, like all actions, are reflective in that they either maintain or alter the line and sense of the activity in which they occur. The current study aligns with this viewpoint.

Listener responses

To begin with, there exist different opinions in the literature not only on the identification of listener actions, but also on how they are termed (Gardner, 2001). These items have been conceptualized as *accompaniment behavior* (Kendon, 1967), *acknowledgement tokens* (Jefferson, 1984), *backchannel behavior* (first named by Yngve, 1970), *backchannel communication* or *backchannel responses* (Duncan, 1972), *backchannel items* (Orestrom, 1983), *verbal listener responses* (Dittman & Llewellyn, 1968), *nonprimary turns* (Schegloff, 1982), *reactive tokens* (Clancy et al., 1996), *receipt objects* (Heritage, 1984), *reinforcers* (Wiemann & Knapp, 1975), and *receipt tokens* (Atkinson, 1992). Clancy et al. (1996) note that during the last three decades, there has been a "profusion of terminology" in regards to turns of the listener (p. 356). The term selection in each of the above studies, as Heinz (2003) claims, reflects the specific methodological approach to the phenomenon studied (i.e., the listener responses).

Researchers have agreed that interlocutors reach a point where one speaker will take the floor, while the other focuses on listening and signals to the speaker that she or he wants this alignment to continue for the time being (Heinz, 2003). The listener does not just *listen* passively, but simultaneously performs actions, either through nonverbal signals such as head nods or eye gaze, or verbal items of various forms and length (Bavelas et al., 2000, 2002; Bavelas & Gerwing, 2011; Dittman & Llewellyn, 1968).

Although there seems to be a consensus that *backchannel responses* (Yngve, 1970) are not to challenge the primary speakership (Brunner, 1979; Clancy et al., 1996; Maynard, 1986; Schegloff, 1982; Tao & Thompson, 1991, among others), there has been a persistent uncertainty in conceptualizing them. This may mainly be due to the fact that researchers are still split on whether to consider listener responses as turns, nonprimary turns, or nonturns (Heinz, 2003). They therefore have not agreed on whether to include such extended responses as long comments or brief questions among listener responses. Several researchers advocating the nonturn stance exclude them and only see minimal tokens as backchannels (Ward, 1996). Others, such as Bilmes (1997), do not adopt this view, as they see that while these short questions still match the criterion of not challenging the speaker's speakership because they specifically offer the floor back to the primary speaker, they are unlike traditional backchannels because they seem to seek to change the course of the other's talk. In fact, many researchers now consider them separate turns and acknowledge that listener responses do not seem to have any specific length requirements (Gardner, 2001; Heinz, 2003; and others), and that there exist listener responses as long as several sentences (Heinz, 2003).

In this study, I will use the CA term *listener responses* to refer to actions by the recipient of the primary speaker that do not challenge the primary speakership. Thus, I excluded listener responses that are the second pair parts of adjacency pairs such as acceptance of a request or an invitation (as shown in [1]) or an answer to the other speaker's information-seeking question (as shown in [2]; transcript conventions can be found in the Appendix):

(1) Response to an Invitation [Lan – Mai]

```
136  Lan: đi cùng với gia   đình   nhé:=
          go together with family AlignM:=
          let's go with my family

137  Mai: =vâng
          =yes
          okay

138       (.)
```

(2) Answer to a Question [Tuan – Nam]

```
47  Tuan: =↑thế bá:c đã    đến    đây  >↑chưa ạ<
          =↑so  yo:u Perf. arrive here >↑yet  PolM<
          so have you been here yet?

48  Nam:  tôi cũng đế:n ơ: (.)  <một vài lần  ↓rồi>
          I   EmM  been e:r (.) <one few times ↓already>
          Yes I have been here er several times already
```

The most significant and comprehensive CA-based research on listener responses by far has been the study by Gardner (2001). He provided a comprehensive account of listener minimal tokens such as *mm, mm hmm,* and *yeah* that are "semantically weak, if not empty" (p. 57), and clearly showed that these tokens are rich in meaning if seen from the action(s) they *do* in the talk. The most important contribution of Gardner's work is perhaps the evidence that CA's powerful theoretical and methodological framework can enable the researcher to tackle the meanings, categories, and regularities in these seemingly meaningless linguistic items.

Gardner introduced the following taxonomy of listener responses:

Continuers, which function to hand the floor back to the immediately prior speaker (e.g., *mm hm, uh huh*)

Acknowledgements, which claim agreement or understanding of the prior turn (e.g., *mm, yeah*)

Newsmarkers and *newsmarkerlike objects*, which mark the prior speaker's turn as newsworthy in some way (e.g., *Really?*, the change-of-state token *Oh*, the idea connector *Right)*

Assessments, which evaluate the talk of the prior speakers (e.g., *Great, How intriguing, What a load of rubbish*)

Brief questions for clarification or other types of *repair*, which seek to clarify mis-hearings or misunderstandings (e.g., *Who?, Which book do you mean?*, or the very generalized *Huh?*)

Collaborative completions, whereby one speaker finishes a prior speaker's utterance (e.g., A: *So, he's moved into...* B: *...commercial interests*)

Change-of-activity tokens, which mark a transition to a new activity or a new topic in the talk (e.g., *okay, alright*)

Many nonverbal vocalizations and kinetic actions (e.g., sighs, laughter, nods, head shakes)

As shown above, the categories of listener responses reflect the *actions* or *activities* done in the talk. The present study adopts Gardner's approach and draws on his taxonomy to understand listener responses in Vietnamese. Given the data-driven approach of this study, this taxonomy will be taken as a starting point and may be modified or extended.

Methodology

Participants

The participants of this study were six Vietnamese speakers. They were selected for this study because they (a) were born in Vietnam, (b) had been residents of Vietnam since birth, (c) were monolingual (participants may not be fluent in any other language and Vietnamese must be their first language), and (d) had had no significant travel or residency in any other country. There was one male and one female over 50 and two males and two females between 18 and 35. The variation of age and gender aimed to achieve a somewhat more representative sample of data. It is important to note that the participants were acquaintances rather than strangers. This was to minimize the effects of initial interactions (see White, 1989). All the participants were volunteers recruited by the researcher. They were told that the study was going to investigate conversational behaviors of Vietnamese, but they were not informed that the focus of the study was on listener responses. This was to reduce the observer's effect on the participants' language use.

Data collection

To increase diversity in the data, the pairs of conversation partners were arranged as follows:

middle-aged woman (Lan) – young woman (Mai)
middle-aged man (Nam) – young man (Tuan)
young woman (Chi) – young man (Minh)

The participants were asked to have two conversations with another person on a given topic. The conversations, all audio-recorded, could last as long as the participants wished. In the first conversation, one participant was asked to tell the other about a favorite memory of a trip (traveling, camping, or picnicking). In the second conversation, this participant would listen to the conversational partner telling his or her experience. For each conversation, the listener was asked to listen to the partner carefully in order to summarize what she or he had just heard to the researcher at the end. According to Norrick (2000), the design of one person's telling an anecdote, in this case of a travel experience, to the other is suitable for research of turns and backchannels (or listener responses). This is because in this kind of conversation, one speaker may have extended turns while the other acts primarily as a listener. The researcher may then investigate how the listener listened and contributed to the conversation. The summary task after each conversation was designed for the purpose of motivating this person to attentively listen to the other's story and be more engaged in the conversation. Whether the participants associated this task with their use of listener responses in the conversations was an unanswered question. However, this design means that the data collected should not be considered naturally occurring, as used in most CA research.

Analytical procedure

This study is informed by the CA approach in its analytical procedure. CA has proven to be one of the most powerful theoretical and methodological frameworks for research on listener responses. First, the decisive feature, according to Drew and Heritage (1992), which distinguishes the CA treatment of interaction and language use from other current approaches, is its *activity focus*, or in other words, its focus on particular actions that are done by the interactants in context. In the case of listener responses, which may include minimal tokens such as *mm* or *uh huh*, CA can show that they 'do' some significant action, and this action can only be understood when considered in context (Gardner, 1994). CA further requires a focus on units that are larger than the individual sentence or utterance. These units are *sequences of activity,* and their component unit turns are turns within sequences.

Additionally, CA is particularly helpful for the current project in its notion of context in interaction. Within the framework of CA, utterances (such as *mhm, yeah*) and the social actions they embody are treated as "doubly contextual" (Drew and Heritage, 1992, p. 18). First, utterances and actions are *context shaped*. This means that their contributions to an ongoing sequence of actions cannot be adequately understood except by reference to the context in which they occur. This context-bound feature of CA is, obviously, not far from that of other discourse analysis approaches such as sociolinguistics and the ethnography of communication. However, where it departs from other context-sensitive approaches to discourse analysis is in its theoretical-analytical stance that actions and utterances are *context renewing*: Every current utterance will itself form the immediate context for some next action in a sequence, and it then inevitably contributes to the contextual framework, in terms of which, the next action will be understood (Drew & Heritage, 1992).

Typically, CA works on naturally occurring interactions. However, researchers have used CA as a methodological approach in various research domains (see Antaki, 2011 for a discussion of CA-inspired linguistics). Some studies have even used CA analytical methods to investigate experimental conversations (see Xudong, 2008 for an example). In these cases, the interactions are audio-taped or video-taped and then transcribed, keeping as much detail (such as overlap talking, pauses, breathiness, or word and syllable stress) in the transcription as possible (Jenks, 2011; ten Have, 1999). Another key point is that CA applies no a priori categories, concepts, or theories at the outset. That is, CA will "articulate a category only if the interactants themselves in some way display an orientation to that category" (Holtgraves, 2002, p. 92). In this study, Gardner's (2001) categories are referenced in the analysis because they themselves are data generated. Further, they will be used as guidance for the analysis but not as a coding system.

In short, CA's approach can be very fruitful for the study of listener responses, an elusive type of behavior that can only be interpreted functionally, sequentially, contextually, and emically.

Analysis

All of the listener response types identified by Gardner (2001), except kinetic actions due to the lack of video data, were found in the study. Examples of these listener response categories are given below.

Continuers

The data showed a great number of minimal tokens that match Gardner's classification of *continuers*. Some of these minimal tokens had minimal semantic meanings such as *vâng, ừ, ờ,* (which are formal and informal forms of *mhm*). Below is an example.

(3) Continuer 1, [Lan – Mai]

```
1    Lan: =từ    Hà Nội (.) đi đế:n ờ  Đồ Sơn (.) đi::
          =from Ha Noi (.) go to:  er Do Son (.) go::
          from Hanoi, we went to er Do Son we went

2         qua  cầu    Phả Lại=
          over bridge Pha Lai=
          over Pha Lai bridge

3 →Mai:   =vâng=
          yes-PolM
          mhm

4    Lan: =rồi  đi:: (.) đế::n (.)    qua  chỗ   Hòn Ga:i=
          =then go:: (.) arrive:: (.) past place Hon Ga:i=
          then we went past Hon Gai
```

The token "*vâng*" at line 3 above has the characteristics of a classic continuer that shows a display of passive recipiency (Schegloff, 1982) and relinquishes rights to the floor, permitting the current speaker to continue talking (Jefferson, 1984). Of note, this token is at the same time a politeness marker, indexing the asymmetric relationship between the participants (Lan is Mai's senior).

In addition, I found many continuer tokens which are vocal sounds that do not have any semantic meanings such as *ồ /ô(hh)* [*oh*] and *à* [*ah*]. The token at line 92 in (4) is an example.

(4) Continuer 2, [Mai – Lan]

```
89    Mai: xưa  đấy (.) vâng< (.)    ví dụ       như là vua
           long EmM (.) yes-PolM< (.) for example like   king
           long time ago, yeah, for example King

90         (.) Đinh Tiên Hoàng là    ngày xưa  xuất thân
           (.) Ding Tien Hoang TopM long ago  originated
           Dinh Tien Hoang long ago he originated

91         từ   một ờ  cái    cá:i     ờ người [chỉ]=
           from one er Class. Cla:ss. er man  [only]=
           from a type type of men who only

92 →Lan:                                      [à   ]
                                               ah
                                               ah

93    Mai: =chăn trâu      thôi thế vậy  mà
           =tend buffaloes only so  then EmM
            tended buffaloes and yet
```

Besides the different vocalized tokens that are similar to what have been found in previous studies on continuers, another type of continuer token was found in the data: a politeness marker *dạ*, sometimes followed by the formal version of *dạ vâng*. An example is seen in (5), line 21.

(5) Continuer 3, [Nam – Tuan]

```
20     Nam:  chúng tôi đi ô TÔ: (.)
             we        go coA:CH (.)
             we went by coach

21→    Tuan: dạ:=
             PolM:=
             mhm

22     Nam:  =xong    đó    trèo    NÚ:i
             =finish  that climb   MOU:Ntain
             then we climbed a mountain
```

Like *vâng, ừ, ờ* (different realizations of *mhm*), the politeness marker *dạ* does not have denotational meaning, but only connotational meaning. However, like the other continuers discussed above, the tokens of this new type pass the floor back immediately to the primary speaker (as defined by Gardner 2001 to be continuers). As will be discussed further below, it is this action that distinguishes them from other listener responses of the same forms (for example *vâng, ừ, ờ*) but as acknowledgements or newsmarkers.

One common feature of the above continuers is that they are minimal responses including only one or two tokens (such as *hừ [uh huh], à [ah], ờ [yeah])*. These are similar to the continuers found in the literature (e.g., Gardner, 2001; Schegloff, 1993). Besides, the data also show that the sound items by the listener doing the action as continuers may be longer than just a couple of words as such. Consider Example 6 below.

(6) Continuer 4, [Chi – Minh]

```
28     Chi: tớ tưởng chỉ có bọn    tớ mới được đi chơi
            I  think only   PluM    we EmM PosM go play
            I thought only us were allowed to go

29          vui vẻ      chứ (0.2)  thế: thế [là   ]
            cheerfully StaM (0.2) so:  so   [then]
            have fun                so so then

30→   Minh:                                       [thế ] rồi
                                                  [so   ] then
                                                   so then

31          thế nào?
            what?
            what happened?
```

```
32    Chi: ừ:: (.)   thế: thế là (.) ừ::    có   một cậu
           yeah::(.) so:  so  be (.) yeah:: have one man
           yeah so so then, yeah, this guy

33         bảo  là   (.) thử lên City View ngồi xem
           tell that (.) try up  City View sit  see
           told us to try going up to City View

34         (.) ở  trên đó    cũng có:   đồ    ăn
           (.) at up   there also ha:ve stuff food
           they also serve food up there

35         ((ho))
           ((coughs))
           ((coughs))

36  →Minh: thế xong   rồi  sao?
           so  finish then how?
           so then what happened next?

37     Chi: thế: thế là   bọn  tớ (.) thế nhưng mà ở trong
            so:  so  then PluM we (.) so  but        inside
            so so then we, but then in

36          hội   bọn  tớ lại có   một (.)
            group PluM we EmM have one (.)
            our group there was this

37          đứa nó bị   ho:
            kid it NegM cou:gh
            girl who was coughing

38    Minh: úi giời=
            oh sky=
            oh god

39     Chi: =nó  cũ::ng bị   ho      nhiều
            =she EmM::  NegM coughed lot
            she was coughing quite a lot actually
```

In lines 30–31, Minh asks a brief question to Chi to get her to move the talk on to what happened next. This reaction comes after Chi shows some signs that she is having problems keeping the talk going: Her pause of 0.2 seconds and repeated use of *thế thế là* [*so so then*] (line 29). The listener's question in this case does not challenge Chi's primary speakership, but invites Minh to go on. In this regard, this question matches all the features of a classic continuer presented above, but differs in that it is longer than just one or two tokens and occurs as a complete question, albeit very brief.

Similarly, at line 36, Minh makes another brief question to prompt Chi to move on, after she had to pause due to coughing. Again, it can be argued that this question does an action of a typical continuer to relinquish the floor immediately back to the primary speaker. Similar to the question at line 30, this question is also very brief.

In another similar episode, provided in Excerpt 7 below, Minh also shows that he wants to maintain the current speakership alignment by asking a question (line 48) after Chi pauses to cough.

(7) Continuer 5, [Chi-Minh]

```
44     Chi: ừ    cảnh đẹ:p       lắm  (.) thế nhưng
            yeah view beau:tiful very (.) so  but
            yeah the view was beautiful, but

45          chỉ mỗ::i  tội   là   cả:nh nó cũng đẹp
            only o::ne fault that vie:w it EmM  beautiful
            the only problem was that the view was beautiful

46          nhưng mà gió:  nó cũng nhiề:u (.) thế:: (.)
            but      wi:nd it also mu:ch (.)  so:: (.)
            but there was also strong wind

47          thế nhưng mà   rồi cuối cùng thì ((coughs))
            so  but    then at  last      then ((coughs))
            so but then at last then ((coughs))

48→Minh: thì  sa:o:?
            then h:o:w?
            so then what happened?

49     Chi: cuối cùng thì  cũng qu:y:ế:t định lên City View
            at   last then EmM  d:e:ci:de     up  City View
            so finally we decidde to go up to City View anyway

50          [bởi vì] khô::ng còn       chỗ   nào   nữ:a
            [because] no::   remaining place what  mo:re
            because there was no other places to go

51     Minh: [à::     ]
             [a::h    ]
              ah
```

The examples above show that the listener's responses can serve as a continuer even when they are longer than just a couple of words and can be complete (but again, brief) questions, thus obviously richer in semantic meaning than what continuers have often been thought of.

Acknowledgements

Like continuers, acknowledgements were also frequently produced by the listeners in the Vietnamese data. The most common acknowledgements are *vâng, ừ, ờ* (various forms of *mhm*) which have the semantic meanings of agreement, comprehension, or reception. This is exemplified in (8) below.

(8) Acknowledgement 1, [Lan – Mai]

```
23     Lan: sau đó      là   bọn  cô     lại   tiếp tục (.)
            after that TopM PluM auntie again continue (.)
            after that we continued
```

24 đi:: ra: (.) chợ: (0.4) đi ra cái
go:: out: (.) mar:ket (0.4) go to Class.
going to the market, going to that

25 chợ Móng Cái đấy=
market Mong Cai EmM=
Mong Cai market you know

26 →Mai: =[vâng]
=[*yes-PolM*]
mhm

27 Lan: [à: x]in lỗi cái chợ ấy là chợ::
[*ah sor*]*ry Class. market that be mar::ket*
oh sorry that market it was

28 để cô <nghĩ: lạ:i> xem nào (.) cái ch:ợ:
let I <thi:nk agai:n> see how (.) Class. mar:k:et
let me think again, the market

29 chỗ ấ:y: (.) thì nó là chợ Hòn Ga::i:=
place th:a:t (.) then it be market Hon Ga::i=
at that place it was Hon Gai market

30→ Mai: =vâng=
=*yes-PolM=*
mhm

31 Lan: =ừ đúng rồi chợ Hòn Gai (.)
=*yes correct EmM market Hon Gai (.)*
=*yes that's right, Hon Gai market*

đồ Trung Quốc rất là nhiều=
stuff Chinese very EmM numerous=
a ton of Chinese stuff

32 → Mai: =vâng=
=*yes-PolM*
mhm

In the excerpt above, the listener responses at lines 26, 30, and 32 are acknowledgements in which Mai claims her understanding of Lan's prior turn (Gardner, 2001) and maintains the current speakership alignment.

Like continuers, acknowledgements have traditionally been identified as minimal tokens only. However, in this study, some more extended responses by the listeners are also found to do this action (Example 9).

(9) Acknowledgement 2, [Nam – Tuan]

```
8     Nam: ừ::   (.) tuần trước  tôi vừa  đi   chơi
           ye::s (.) week before I   just go   play
           yeah last week I just went sightseeing

9          ở Chí Linh=
           in Chi Linh=
           in Chi Linh

10→Tuan: =à Chí Linh  [ạ:     ]
         =ah Chi Linh [PolM:  ]
          oh Chi Linh

11  Nam:                 [thă::m]  a::  (.) đền
                         [visi::t] a::h (.) temple
                         visited   ah the temple of

12        ông Chu Văn An
          Sir Chu Van An
          Sir Chu Van An
```

Again, at line 10 above, the repetition abides by all the requirements of a listener response: (a) It responds directly to the topic of Nam's previous utterance, as it is indeed a part of it; (b) it does not require acknowledgement by the primary speaker, as Nam continues his talking at line 10 without showing any acknowledgement of the repetition; and (c) apparently, it does not challenge the primary speakership. However, in addition to repeating the place name "Chí Linh," which is the final noun in Nam's preceding utterance, Tuan's turn includes a change-of-state token *à* [oh] at the beginning, which marks the turn as an acknowledgement of what Nam just said.

Similarly, in (10) below, the listener also produced a partial repetition of the previous utterance to provide an acknowledgement.

(10) Acknowledgement 3, [Mai – Lan]

83 Mai: =người ta: <giảng giải> cho mình về
=people: <explain> for self about
they explained to us about

84 những cái:: ư:: à:: có nghĩa là về (.h)
PluM thi::ng uh a::h have meaning that about (.h)
those uh ah I mean about

85 những công lao của những vị vua vị::
PluM contributions of PluM Class. king Class::
the contributions of the kings and those honorable

86 ngày xưa [đã có công như thế nào đấy]
day old [Past have contribution how AffM]
how they made their merits in the old days

87→Lan: [ư (.) à: (.) vua chúa]
[uh (.) a:h (.) king lord]
uh ah kings and lords

88 ngày xưa hả=
days ancient QuesM=
of the old days, right?

In this excerpt, the primary speaker, Mai, is talking about the ancient kings but she seems to have problems finding the second part in the collocation *vua chúa* [kings lords] as she speaks its first part *vua* [king] and then stretching her sound in *vị::* (an honorific classifier) perhaps to search for the second part. She seems to fail to find this part and therefore moves on with *ngày xưa* [in the old days]. Lan acknowledges that she understands what is being said by using the token *à* [ah] and then provides a reformulation to this collocation (lines 87–88). In this regard, the acknowledgement has the following nuanced features: First, it is an extended utterance including a full sentence with seven words, rather than just a one- or two-word token like traditional acknowledgements; second, it partially repeats the previous utterance by the primary speaker, like in (9) above; and finally, the listener in fact contributes her knowledge to the talk by providing the reformulation as explained above. This cooperation of the listener makes this reaction, to some extent, similar to a *collaborative completion*, in Gardner's terms, which will be discussed further below.

Newsmarkers and newsmarkerlike objects

Although not as common as continuers and acknowledgements, newsmarker listener responses were also found in the data. An example is given in Extract 11.

(11) Newsmarker 1, [Minh – Chi]

2 Minh: đợ:t ờ vừa rồ:i: thì: bọn tớ có đi
pe:riod er just p:a:st the:n PluM we AffM go
recently we just went to

3 ơ: Sa:pa: (.) bọn tớ: có hội
e:r Sa:pa: (.) PluM we: have group
er Sapa. we were in a group

4 là:: (.) bố:n ngư:ờ:i
be:: (.) fou:r p:eo:ple
of four people

5 Chi: ừ:=
ye:s=
mhm

6 Minh: =có mình tớ là con giai [ờ]]
=have only me be Class. male [er]
I was the only guy

7 → Chi: [thế:] à::.
[rea:l]ly::.
really

8 Minh: ừ (.) ừ::: (.) thế là đi với cả: (.)
yeah (.) yea:::h (.) then be go with all: (.)
yeah (.) yeah (.) then I went together with

9 ba: cô bạn gái nữ:a=
three: Class. friend girl mo:re=
three other female friends

10 Chi: =[ừ::]
=[yea::h]
mhm

At line 7, Chi produces a listener response to mark that the piece of information that Minh has just provided is newsworthy and interesting. By stretching her reaction *'ừ'* [yeah], Chi shows her interest in the talk without challenging Minh's speakership. As will be discussed further, this listener response differs from a brief question *thế à?* [really?] in its low pitch (rather than a high-rising pitch as in the cases of questions).

Assessments

Unlike the above three types of listener responses, the data showed a more open range in terms of the form or realization of assessments. They include both the formulaic minimal tokens such as *tốt* [good] and other longer comments, as shown in (12), line 15.

(12) Assessment, [Lan – Mai]

```
13      Lan: qua   khách sạn nghỉ lại   một đê:m (.) đến
             over hotel     stay again one night (.)arrive
             we stayed at the hotel one night then

14           ngày hôm sau (.) là:: (.) <lênh đênh trên biển>=
             day  next    (.) TopM (.) <floating  on    sea>=
             the next day, we were sailing away on the sea

15→    Mai: =ôi  thích      [thế  cô]  nhỉ
             oh   enjoyable [so   aunt] AlignM
             oh so fun, wasn't it, auntie?

16      Lan:                 [bằ::ng ] (.) tàu    thuỷ=
                             [by::   ] (.) Class. ship=
                              by ship
```

The assessments found in the Vietnamese data are presented in Table 1.

Table 1. Vietnamese assessments by nonprimary speakers

Vietnamese expressions	English translations
tốt /ừ tốt	good /yeah good
tuyệt đấy	that's excellent

đẹp thật	so beautiful
hay thế /thú thật /thật là thú đấy	(that's) so interesting/cool
hay quá nhỉ /thú thật đấy nhỉ	that sounds so interesting/cool
ôi thích thế cô nhỉ	oh that was so fun, wasn't it?
may quá	so lucky
to quá nhờ	that's really big, isn't it?
sướng thế còn gì	you're so lucky
yếu nhỉ	isn't she weak?
ngon thế	that sounds delicious
thích nhỉ	I'd like that

Brief questions for clarification or other types of repair:

Only one example of brief question repair was found in the Vietnamese data. As defined by Gardner (2001), this question sought to clarify mis-hearings or misunderstandings of the prior turn.

(13) Repair, [Minh – Chi]

```
82      Minh: =khô:ng ạ (.)    thế thì ốm        lăn quay ra
              =no:    PolM (.) so then sickness tumble   out
              no way, that would make me fall flat sick,

              chứ  còn  đi chơi làm sao được nữ:a:=
              StaM StaM go play how any PosM m:o:re=
              no way I could have gone on any more

83      Chi:  =thế nhưng mà có ốm khô:ng=
              =then but     yes sick no:=
              but then did you get sick

84 →     Minh: =hả::
              =hu::h
               huh

85      Chi:  có ố:m khô::ng
              yes si::ck no:
              were you sick

86     Minh:  ừ   thì   cũ:ng ờ:: (.)  về     nhà
              yes well  EmM   e::r (.) return home
              yes well, when I came home,

              thì cũ::ng (.) khật khừ:
              then EmM:: (.) exhausted
              I was indeed wiped out
```

In this example, *hả* [huh?] at line 84 is a brief repair by which Minh asked Chi to repeat her question.[1]

Collaborative completions

Collaborative completions are what Jefferson (1973) observed to be "a display of independent knowledge of what is about to be said that can be achieved by starting to talk just as the same object comes due in an ongoing utterance" (p. 8). Gardner simply defined a collaborative completion as a response that one speaker produces to finish a prior speaker's utterance. There are several cases of this type of listener response in the Vietnamese data. One example is in line 28 in the following excerpt.

(14) Collaborative completion 1, [Tuan – Nam]

```
25    Tuan: thì lớp    chá:u: thì có::    (.) kiểu đi
            so  class me::    so  have:: (.) type go
            well my class had this way of travelling

26          cùng     đ' >cùng     Lớp<   (.)
            together t' >together CLAss< (.)
            together traveling as a whole class

27          nên là:: (.)   là:: (.)
            so  be:: (.)   be:: (.)
            so it was it was

28→ Nam:   [vui]
            [fun]
            fun

29    Tuan: [mọi] người  rất  là v:u:i (.)
            [all] people very be h:a:ppy (.)
            everyone was very happy

30          bọ'   ch' [đi  h:a:i] ngà:y   ạ
            PluM' w'  [go two    ] d:a:y  PolM

            we went for two days
```

In line 28, Nam displays his understanding of what is being said by anticipating and completing the primary speaker's talk without challenging the primary speakership.

Change-of-activity tokens

In the Vietnamese data, only one change-of-activity token was found, which was near the end of a conversation, as seen below.

(15) Change of activity, [Tuan – Nam]

```
58     Tuan: dạ    vâ:ng      (.) cháu nghĩ  như  thế (.) là
             polM ye:s-PolM (.) I     think like so   (.) be
             yes I think that was

59           rất  ha::y (.)  rất  bổ ích (.) nó giúp
             very goo::d (.) very useful (.) it help
             very good very useful it helped

60           m:ì:nh coi      như là::
             u:s:   consider as  be::
             us consider

61           >có   một cái   gì<   đó:: (.)   cần  phải
             >have one thing what< so::me (.) need must
             what we must do

62           sống sao cho nó xứng ĐÁ:ng với  cả=
             live somehow it wo:rTHy    with EmM=
             in our lives to be worthy of

63     Nam:  =ờ=
             =yeah=
             mhm

64     Tuan: =thầy giáo ơ  >Chu Văn An hơn<=
             =teacher   er >Chu Van An more<=
             Teacher er Chu Van An more

65→    Nam:  =NÊN    như  vậy=
             =SHOULD like that=
             should be like that

66     Tuan: =VÂ:ng
             =YE:s-PolM
             yeah

67     Nam:  THẾ:=
             SO:=
             so

68     Tuan: =dạ vâ:ng
             =PolM ye:s-PolM
             yeah
```

Nam's listener response at line 65 suggests a closing of the current sequence. The primary speaker aligns with this closing (lines 66, 68). This listener response marks a transition to a new state in the talk (an end of the current topic), which fits Gardner's classification of a change-of-activity token. Previous research indicates that in English, these tokens are normally spoken with distinctive prosodic features, such as significantly high pitch, loud voice, lengthened vowel(s), or followed by a significant pause. These features are also found in this case of Vietnamese, as Nam produced this token (line 67) with a louder volume and lengthened vowels.

In sum, all seven categories of listener responses identified by Gardner (2001) were found in the collected Vietnamese data. In general, these categories of listener responses account for the majority of the utterances made by the listeners in the data. However, I also found some listener responses that did not seem to fit any of Gardner's categories. In what follows, I propose a new category of response, *cooperative expansions*. These are preliminary findings limited to my data, and they serve as a starting point for further empirical research.

Cooperative expansions

The data analysis shows that the listener, in some cases, makes either a comment or an *expansion* to the primary speaker's utterance without any indication that he or she will be taking the floor further than the expansion. An example can be seen in line 93 in the extract below.

(16) Cooperative expansion, 1 [Lan – Mai]

```
91     Lan: tập trung      hàng hoá nhiều lắ:m (.)  mà
            concentration goods    many  ve:ry (.) but
            there was a great concentration of goods but

92          >toàn là bọn  lậu        thôi<=
            >all  be gang smugglers only<=
            there were just gangs of smugglers

93→   Mai: =>đúng  rồi     [bởi vì  có   khách du lịch ]<
            =>right already [because have guest tourist]<
            that's right, because there were tourists

94     Lan:                 [cho nên  rẻ::             ]
                            [therefore chea::p         ]
                             so they were cheap

95          (0.5) <rất  rẻ>=
            (0.5) <very cheap>=
                  very cheap
```

The listener in this case, Mai, agrees with the primary speaker *(đúng rồi* [that's right]) and adds an explanation for a detail in Lan's story, which does not seem to challenge the speakership alignment (line 93). In fact, she maintains her loyalty to it by not speaking further than line 93. The primary speaker, Lan, also aligns with this speakership and continues to take the next turn in line 94. What is interesting about Lan's turn here is that syntactically it builds on her own turn back in line 92 *as well as* Mai's turn in line 93. In so doing, Lan is treating Mai's turn as a smooth insertion into her turn or an extension of it, but not as a turn that she needs to respond to.

Again, it is believed that this utterance, although longer in form than traditional listener responses, is indeed a listener response because it meets the three criteria defined by the study. The response directly comments on what is being said, but does not cause any change to the speakership alignment. The comment is similar to an assessment as it shows what the listener thinks about the content/topic the primary speaker is talking about. Excerpt 17 shows another example (the participants were talking about monkeys).

(17) Cooperative expansion 2, [Lan – Mai]

```
36   Lan: ô:ng í:    (.) gõ     đế:n     (.) ông í
          ma:n tha:t (.) strike to:ward (.) man that
          the man stroke to, the man

37        mới gõ     cái    kẻng (.) thế là   tấ:t cả
          new strike Class. gong (.) so  then a:ll
          just stroke the gong and all of them

38        xếp     hàng  đâ::u  vào  đấy=
          arrange line  a::ll  in   place=
          made a line all at once


39→Mai:   =à  kỷ luật=
          =ah  discipline=
          oh discipline

40  Lan:   =đấ::y  (.) đến    lúc  ông  ấy   ra:
          =the::re (.) toward when man  that ou:t
          then when that man came out

41        ông  ấy  cắt chuố:i:
          man that cut bana:na:s
          he cut the bananas

42  Mai:   vâng=
          yes-PolM
          mhm

43  Lan:   =ông ấy   lệ::nh  một cái    tất cả nó
          =man that or::der one Class. all    it
          he gave a signal and all of them

44        xông   vào nó cướ:p=
          jumped in  it sto:le =
          jumped in to grab the bananas

45  Mai:   =((laughs))
```

Mai's comments in line 39 on what Lan is telling of the monkey does not challenge the speakership, which is evidenced by Lan's continuing to tell the story in the next turn. Again, this listener response is also similar to an assessment as it is commentary. However, I would argue that it differs from assessment in Gardner's terms in that it does not directly comment on the content of the previous talk (i.e., such as *good* or *interesting* as Gardner specified), but rather provides an interpretation of the content, in this case, of what the monkey's queuing up means (i.e., having discipline). In this regard, Mai elaborates on Lan's talk and aligns with Lan.

In addition, the data also show some cases in which the listener's response adds on to what is being said as in the following.

(18) Cooperative expansion 3, [Mai – Lan]

```
91   Mai:  chăn trâu    cắt cỏ     mà
           tend buffalo cut grass StaM
           just tending buffaloes and cutting grass yet

92         đứng  lên để tập hợ:p binh sĩ::  mà:  à::=
           stand up  to gathe:r  soldie::rs bu:t a::h=
           they rose up to organize an army and uh

93 → Lan: =cờ   [lau  hả: ]
           =flag  [reed ha:h]
            reed flags huh

94   Mai:          [dẹp       loạn ]  mười hai sứ quân đấy=
                   [put away chaos ] twelve    lords    StanM=
                    defeat the twelve lords
```

In this example, Lan's response is not only related to what was being told, but adds to it by referring to a metaphorical image of grassroots uprisings in Vietnamese history, when the rebels created flags from reeds. Mai also treats Lan's turn as not challenging her current speakership and continues her storytelling in line 94. Thus, the listener contributes to the ongoing story and uses her own knowledge to expand on it.

Both the comments and expansion in these excerpts seem to imply to the primary speaker that "yes, I am with you now, and this is my knowledge of it, too," while they do not mean to take the floor beyond the expansion turns. For this reason, I propose that these listener responses be combined into one category, *cooperative expansions*.

As shown above, these expansions are all rather short, albeit much longer than traditional listener responses. This could be because they are not designed to challenge the primary speakership. In particular, when an insertion occurs right after a Transition Relevance Place (TRP; Jefferson, 1984) as in (16), it is successfully incorporated into the primary speaker's next turn without any overlap. In contrast, in (18), when the listener response occurs at a non-TRP, an overlap occurs with the initial part of the next primary speaker's utterance.

These cooperative expansions are not included in Gardner's (2001) taxonomy of listener responses. However, they are not new. In studies on storytelling, researchers have also found that speakers can spontaneously collaborate on the story (for example, Coates, 1996, 2001, 2005; Leung, 2009; among others). However, there has not been sufficient knowledge of these linguistic phenomena in talk with speakership alignment (as in this study) when the listeners produce these collaborative expansions to co-construct the talk but not to challenge the other's speakership. Further research is needed to shed more light on this type of listener response, particularly in talk with speakership alignment.

Concluding comments

This study contributes further empirical evidence from the Vietnamese language that the sound items made by the listener may be much richer in meaning and activity than their surface forms show. In research on listener responses, there has been a persistent uncertainty regarding how to treat longer responses and whether they are listener responses of any kind. Although some researchers at times refer to them or use occurrences in their examples as previously discussed, there seems a common avoidance of dealing with these longer and more extended items.

Using a CA methodological approach, this study proposes a firm view that an item, no matter of minimal or longer length, *is* a listener response as long as it (a) responds to the content or topic of an utterance or a series of utterances of the primary speaker who is taking the floor and maintaining this alignment at the time; (b) does not require acknowledgement by the primary speaker, although acknowledgement is optional and possible; and (c) does not challenge the primary speakership or in other words, does not change the role of the primary speaker into the nonprimary one and vice versa. In this regard, this study provides a methodological framework for dealing with longer and more extended listener responses, and helps to resolve the issue of length.

All the listener response categories identified by Gardner (2001), except for kinetic ones, were found in the data. What is interesting is that the nuanced features of these categories are different between English (Gardner's data) and Vietnamese (this study). Particularly, the use of politeness markers in the responses by a junior participant toward a senior participant may be language specific. Future research may investigate whether listener responses are more frequent in dyads with asymmetric age and power relationship than in equal dyads. Further, this study showed that the listener can expand and elaborate on the primary speaker's narrative without challenging speakership. Whether these collaborative expansions are more common in

Vietnamese than in other languages and cultures remains a question for future research. Finally, this study is limited to audio data although listener responses can be multimodal. Future research should employ video data in order to examine the embodied actions that listeners may make in response to a primary speaker.

Note

1 Note that although Chi is the listener throughout most of the narrative, when she asks the question at line 83, she is claiming the floor and thus is no longer a listener.

References

Antaki, C. (Ed.). (2011). *Applied conversation analysis: Intervention and change in institutional talk.* Basingstoke: Palgrave Macmillan.

Astbury, V.E. (1994). The use of turn-taking resources in a Khmer-Australian English conversation. *Australian Review of Applied Linguistics Series S11,* 173–184.

Atkinson, J.M. (1992). Displaying neutrality: Formal aspects of informal court proceedings. In P. Drew & J. Heritage (Eds.), *Talk at work: Interaction in institutional settings* (pp. 199–211). Cambridge: Cambridge University Press.

Bavelas, J.B., Coates, L., & Johnson, T. (2000). Listeners as co-narrators. *Journal of Personality and Social Psychology, 79,* 941–952.

Bavelas, J.B., Coates, L., & Johnson, T. (2002). Listener responses as a collaborative process: The role of gaze. *Journal of Communication, 52,* 566–580.

Bavelas, J.B., & Gerwing, J. (2011). The listener as addressee in face-to-face dialogue. *International Journal of Listening, 25*(3), 178–198.

Beach, W.A., & Lindstrom, A.K. (1992). Conversational universals and comparative theory: Turning to Swedish and American acknowledgement tokens in interaction. *Communication Theory, 2*(1), 24–49.

Bilmes, J. (1997). Being interrupted. *Language in Society, 26*(4), 507–531.

Brunner, L. (1979). Smiles can be back channels. *Journal of Personality and Social Psychology, 37*(5), 728–734.

Clancy, P.M., Thompson, S.A., Suzuki, R., & Tao, H. (1996). The conversational use of reactive tokens in English, Japanese, and Mandarin. *Journal of Pragmatics, 26,* 355–387.

Coates, J. (1996). *Women talk: Conversations between women friends.* Oxford: Blackwell.

Coates, J. (2001). "My mind is with you": Story sequences in the talk of male friends. *Narrative Inquiry, 11*(1), 81–101.

Coates, J. (2005). Masculinity, collaborative narration and the heterosexual couple. In J. Thornborrow & J. Coates (Eds.), *The sociolinguistics of narrative* (pp. 89–106). Amsterdam: Benjamins.

Dittman, A.T., & Llewellyn, L.G. (1968). Relationship between vocalizations and head nods as listener responses. *Journal of Personality and Social Psychology, 9*(1), 79–84.

Dittman, A.T. (1972). Developmental factors in conversational behavior. *Journal of Communication, 22,* 404–423.

Drew, P., & Heritage, J. (1992). Analyzing talk at work: An introduction. In P. Drew & J. Heritage (Eds.), *Talk at work: Interaction in institutional settings* (pp. 3–65). Cambridge: Cambridge University Press.

Drummond, K., & Hopper, R. (1993). Back channels revisited: Acknowledgement tokens and speakership incipiency. *Research on Language and Social Interaction, 26*(2), 157–177.

Duncan, J.S. (1972). Some signals and rules for taking speaking turns in conversations. *Journal of Personality and Social Psychology, 23,* 283–292.

Gardner, R. (1994). Conversation analysis: Some thoughts on its applicability to applied linguistics. *Australian Review of Applied Linguistics Series S11,* 97–118.

Gardner, R. (2001). *When listeners talk: Response tokens and listener stance.* Philadelphia, PA: Benjamins.

Garfinkel, H. (1967). *Studies in ethnomethodology.* Upper Saddle River, NJ: Prentice Hall.

Goodwin, C. (1986). Between and within: Alternative sequential treatments of continuers and assessments. *Human Studies, 9,* 205–217.

ten Have, P. (1999). *Doing conversation analysis: A practical guide.* London: Sage.

Heinz, B. (2003). Backchannel response as strategic responses in bilingual speakers' conversations. *Journal of Pragmatics, 35,* 1113–1142.

Heritage, J. (1984). A change-of-state token and aspects of its sequential placement. In M. Atkinson & J. Heritage (Eds.), *Structures of social action* (pp. 299–345). Cambridge: Cambridge University Press.

Holtgraves, T.M. (2001). *Language as social action: Social psychology and language use.* Mahwah, NJ: Erlbaum.

Hutchby, I., & Wooffitt, R. (1998). *Conversation analysis.* Cambridge: Polity Press.

Hymes, D. (1962). The ethnography of speaking. In T. Gladwin & W. Sturtevant (Eds.), *Anthropology and human behavior* (pp. 15–53). Washington, DC: Anthropological Society of Washington.

Jefferson, G. (1973). A case of precision timing in ordinary conversation: Overlapped tag-positioned address terms in closing sequences. *Semiotica, 9,* 47–96.

Jefferson, G. (1984). Notes on systematic deployment of the acknowledgement tokens "Yeah" and "Mm hm". *Papers in Linguistics, 17,* 197–216.

Jefferson, G. (1983). Two explorations of the organization of overlapping talk in conversation. *Tilburg Papers in Language and Literature, 28.* Tilburg: Tilburg University.

Jefferson, G. (2002). Is 'no' an acknowledgement token? Comparing American and British uses of (+)/(–) tokens. *Journal of Pragmatics, 34,* 1345–1383.

Jenks, C.J. (2011). *Transcribing talk and interaction: Issues in the representation of communication data.* Amsterdam: Benjamins

Koiso, H., Horiuchi, Y., Tutiya, S., & Ichikawa, A. (1995). The acoustic properties of 'sub-utterance units' and their relevance to the corresponding follow-up interjections in Japanese. *AI Symposium '95 (SIG-J-9051–2),* 9–16.

Kubota, M. (1991). The use of backchannel behaviors by Japanese and American bilingual persons (Unpublished doctoral dissertation). Indiana University, Bloomington, IN.

Labov, W. (1972). *Sociolinguistic patterns.* Philadelphia, PA: University of Pennsylvania Press.

Lerner, G. (1996). On the 'semi-permeable' character of grammatical units in conversation: Conditional entry into the turn space of another speaker. In E. Ochs, E. Schegloff, & S. Thompson (Eds.), *Interaction and Grammar* (pp. 238–276). Cambridge: Cambridge University Press.

Leung, C.B. (2009). Collaborative narration in preadolescent girl talk: A Saturday luncheon conversation among three friends. *Journal of Pragmatics, 41*(7), 1341–1357.

Levinson, S.C. (1983). *Pragmatics.* Cambridge: Cambridge University Press.

Markee, N. (2000). *Conversation analysis.* Mahwah, NJ: Erlbaum.

Maynard, S.K. (1986). On back-channel behavior in Japanese and English casual conversations. *Linguistics, 24,* 1079–1108.

Maynard, S.K. (1989). *Japanese conversation: Self-contextualization through structure and interactional management.* Norwood, NJ: Ablex.

Maynard, S.K. (1990). Conversation management in contrast: Listener response in Japanese and American English. *Journal of Pragmatics, 14*(3), 397–412.

McClave, E.Z. (2000). Linguistic functions of head movements in the context of speech. *Journal of Pragmatics, 32,* 855–878.

Mehrabian, A. (1972). *Non-verbal communication.* Chicago, IL: Aldine-Atherton.

Mizutani, N. (1982). The listener's responses in Japanese conversation. *Sociolinguistics Newsletter, 13*(1), 33–38.

Norrick, N.R. (2000). *Conversational narrative: Storytelling in everyday talk.* Amsterdam: Benjamins.

Oreström, B. (1983). *Turn-taking in English conversation* (Lund Studies in English, 66). Lund: CWK Gleerup.

Paltridge, B. (2000). *Making sense of discourse analysis.* Queensland: Gerd Stabler.

Phillips, S.U. (1983). *The invisible culture: Communication in classroom and community on the Warm Springs Indian Reservation.* New York, NY: Longman.

Talbot, M. (1992). 'I wish you'd stop interrupting me!': Interruptions and asymmetries in speaker-rights in equal encounters. *Journal of Pragmatics, 18,* 451–466.

Sacks, H. (1992). *Lectures on conversation* (Vol. 2). Oxford: Blackwell.

Schegloff, E.A. (1982). Discourse as an international achievement: Some users of 'uh huh' and other things that come between sentences. In D. Tannen (Ed.), *Analyzing discourse: Text and talk.* (Georgetown University Round Table on Languages and Linguistics, pp. 71–93). Washington, DC: Georgetown University Press.

Schegloff, E.A. (1992). On talk and its institutional occasions. In P. Drew & J. Heritage (Eds.), *Talk at work: Interaction in institutional settings* (pp. 101–136). Cambridge: Cambridge University Press.

Silverman, D. (1998). *Harvey Sacks: Social science and conversation analysis.* New York, NY: Oxford University Press.

Sorjonen, M.L. (2002). Recipient activities: The particle no as a go-ahead response in Finish conversations. In C.E. Ford, B.A. Fox, & S.A. Thompson (Eds.), *The language of turn and sequence* (pp. 165–195). Oxford: Oxford University Press.

Tao, H., & Thompson, S.A. (1991). English backchannels in Mandarin conversations: A case study of superstratum pragmatic 'interference.' *Journal of Pragmatics, 16,* 209 -233.

Thwaite, A. (1993). Gender differences in spoken interaction in same-sex dyadic conversations in Australian English. *Australian Review of Applied Linguistics Series S10,* 147–179.

Trần Vũ Mai Yên (2010). Vietnamese expressions of politeness. *Griffith Working Papers in Pragmatics and Intercultural Communication, 3*(1), 12–21.

Ward, N. (1996, October). *Using prosodic clues to decide when to produce back-channel utterances.* Paper presented at the 4th International Conference on Spoken Language Processing, Philadelphia, PA.

White, S. (1989). Backchannels across cultures: A study of Americans and Japanese. *Language in Society, 18,* 59–76.

Wiemann, J.M., & Knapp, M.L. (1975). Turn-taking in conversations. *Journal of Communication, 25,* 75–92.

Xudong, D. (2008). The use of listener responses in Mandarin Chinese and Australian English conversations. *Pragmatics, 18*(2), 303–328.

Yngve, V.H. (1970). On getting a word in edgewise. *Papers from the Sixth Regional Meeting of the Chicago Linguistics Society,* 567–578. Chicago, IL: Chicago Linguistics Society.

Zimmerman, D.H., & C. West. (1975). Sex roles, interruptions and silences in conversation. In B. Thorne & N. Henley (Eds.), *Language and sex: Difference and dominance* (pp. 105–129). Rowley, MA: Newbury House.

Appendix: Transcription conventions (cf. ten Have, 1999)

Sequencing

[A *single left bracket* indicates the point of overlap onset.

] A *single right bracket* indicates the point at which an utterance or utterance-part terminates vis-à-vis another.

= *Equal signs*, one at the end of one line and one at the beginning of a next, indicate no 'gap' between the two lines. This is often called *latching*.

Timed intervals

(0.0) *Numbers in parentheses* indicate elapsed time in silence by tenth of seconds, so (7.1) is a pause of 7 seconds and one tenth of a second.

(.) *A dot in parentheses* indicates a tiny 'gap' within or between utterances.

Characteristics of speech production

word *Underscoring* indicates some form of stress, via pitch and/or amplitude; an alternative method is to print the stressed part in *italic*.

:: *Colons* indicate prolongation of the immediately prior sound. Multiple colons indicate a more prolonged sound.

\- *A dash* indicates a cut-off.

. *A period* indicates a continuing intonation, like reading items from a list.

? *A question mark* indicates a rising intonation.

The absence of an utterance-final marker indicates some sort of indeterminate contour.

↑↓ *Arrows* indicate marked shifts into higher or lower pitch in the utterance-part immediately following the arrow.

WORD *Upper case* indicates especially loud sounds relative to the surrounding talk.

° Utterances or utterance parts bracketed by *degree signs* are relatively quieter than the surrounding talk.

< > *Right/left carats* bracketing an utterance or utterance-part indicate speeding up.

.hhh A *dot-prefixed row of* hs indicates an inbreath. Without the dot, the *hs* indicate an outbreath.

w(h)ord A parenthesized *h*, or a *row of* hs *within a word,* indicates breathiness, as in laughter, crying, etc.

Transcriber's doubts and comments

( ) *Empty parentheses* indicate the transcriber's inability to hear what was said. The length of the parenthesized space indicates the length of the untranscribed talk. In the speaker designation column, the empty parentheses indicate inability to identify a speaker.

(word) *Parenthesized words* are especially dubious hearings or speaker identifications.

(( )) *Double parentheses* contain transcriber's descriptions rather than, or in addition to, transcriptions.

Index

D

E

F

G

H

I

K

L

M

R

S

T

Pragmatics & Interaction

Gabriele Kasper, series editor

Pragmatics & Interaction ("P&I"), a refereed series sponsored by the University of Hawai'i National Foreign Language Resource Center, publishes research on topics in pragmatics and discourse as social interaction from a wide variety of theoretical and methodological perspectives. P&I welcomes particularly studies on languages spoken in the Asia-Pacific region.

PRAGMATICS OF VIETNAMESE AS NATIVE AND TARGET LANGUAGE

Carsten Roever & Hanh thi Nguyen (Editors), 2013

The volume offers a wealth of new information about the forms of several speech acts and their social distribution in Vietnamese as L1 and L2, complemented by a chapter on address forms and listener responses. As the first of its kind, the book makes a valuable contribution to the research literature on pragmatics, sociolinguistics, and language and social interaction in an under-researched and less commonly taught Asian language.

282pp., ISBN 978–0–9835816–2–8 $30.

L2 LEARNING AS SOCIAL PRACTICE: CONVERSATION-ANALYTIC PERSPECTIVES

Gabriele Pallotti & Johannes Wagner (Editors), 2011

This volume collects empirical studies applying Conversation Analysis to situations where second, third, and other additional languages are used. A number of different aspects are considered, including how linguistic systems develop over time through social interaction, how participants 'do' language learning and teaching in classroom and everyday settings, how they select languages and manage identities in multilingual contexts, and how the linguistic-interactional divide can be bridged with studies combining Conversation Analysis and Functional Linguistics. This variety of issues and approaches clearly shows the fruitfulness of a socio-interactional perspective on second language learning.

380pp., ISBN 978–0–9800459–7–0 $30.

TALK-IN-INTERACTION: MULTILINGUAL PERSPECTIVES

HANH THI NGUYEN & GABRIELE KASPER (EDITORS), 2009

This volume offers original studies of interaction in a range of languages and language varieties, including Chinese, English, Japanese, Korean, Spanish, Swahili, Thai, and Vietnamese; monolingual and bilingual interactions; and activities designed for second or foreign language learning. Conducted from the perspectives of conversation analysis and membership categorization analysis, the chapters examine ordinary conversation and institutional activities in face-to-face, telephone, and computer-mediated environments.

430pp., ISBN 978–0–8248–3137–0 $30.

Pragmatics & Language Learning

Gabriele Kasper, series editor

Pragmatics & Language Learning ("PLL"), a refereed series sponsored by the National Foreign Language Resource Center, publishes selected papers from the biannual International Pragmatics & Language Learning conference under the editorship of the conference hosts and the series editor. Check the NFLRC website for upcoming PLL conferences and PLL volumes.

PRAGMATICS AND LANGUAGE LEARNING VOLUME 13

TIM GREER, DONNA TATSUKI, & CARSTEN ROEVER (EDITORS), 2013

Pragmatics & Language Learning Volume 13 examines the organization of second language and multilingual speakers' talk and pragmatic knowledge across a range of naturalistic and experimental activities. Based on data collected among ESL and EFL learners from a variety of backgrounds, the contributions explore the nexus of pragmatic knowledge, interaction, and L2 learning outside and inside of educational settings.

292pp., ISBN 978–0–9835816–4–2 $30.

PRAGMATICS AND LANGUAGE LEARNING VOLUME 12

GABRIELE KASPER, HANH THI NGUYEN, DINA R. YOSHIMI, & JIM K. YOSHIOKA (EDITORS), 2010

This volume examines the organization of second language and multilingual speakers' talk and pragmatic knowledge across a range of naturalistic and experimental activities. Based on data collected on Danish, English, Hawai'i Creole, Indonesian, and Japanese as target languages, the contributions explore the nexus of pragmatic knowledge, interaction, and L2 learning outside and inside of educational settings.

364pp., ISBN 978–09800459–6–3 $30.

PRAGMATICS AND LANGUAGE LEARNING VOLUME 11

Kathleen Bardovi-Harlig, César Félix-Brasdefer, & Alwiya S. Omar (Editors), 2006

This volume features cutting-edge theoretical and empirical research on pragmatics and language learning among a wide variety of learners in diverse learning contexts from a variety of language backgrounds and target languages (English, German, Japanese, Kiswahili, Persian, and Spanish). This collection of papers from researchers around the world includes critical appraisals on the role of formulas in interlanguage pragmatics, and speech-act research from a conversation analytic perspective. Empirical studies examine learner data using innovative methods of analysis and investigate issues in pragmatic development and the instruction of pragmatics.

430pp., ISBN 978–0–8248–3137–0 $30.

NFLRC Monographs

Richard Schmidt, series editor

Monographs of the National Foreign Language Resource Center present the findings of recent work in applied linguistics that is of relevance to language teaching and learning (with a focus on the less commonly taught languages of Asia and the Pacific) and are of particular interest to foreign language educators, applied linguists, and researchers. Prior to 2006, these monographs were published as "SLTCC Technical Reports."

NEW PERSPECTIVES ON JAPANESE LANGUAGE LEARNING, LINGUISTICS, AND CULTURE

Kimi Kondo-Brown, Yoshiko Saito-Abbott, Shingo Satsutani, Michio Tsutsui, & Ann Wehmeyer (Editors), 2013

This volume is a collection of selected refereed papers presented at the Association of Teachers of Japanese Annual Spring Conference held at the University of Hawai'i at Mānoa in March of 2011. It not only covers several important topics on teaching and learning spoken and written Japanese and culture in and beyond classroom settings but also includes research investigating certain linguistics items from new perspectives.

208pp., ISBN 978–0–9835816–3–5 $20

DEVELOPING, USING, AND ANALYZING RUBRICS IN LANGUAGE ASSESSMENT WITH CASE STUDIES IN ASIAN AND PACIFIC LANGUAGES

JAMES DEAN BROWN (EDITOR), 2012

Rubrics are essential tools for all language teachers in this age of communicative and task-based teaching and assessment—tools that allow us to efficiently communicate to our students what we are looking for in the productive language abilities of speaking and writing and then effectively assess those abilities when the time comes for grading students, giving them feedback, placing them into new courses, and so forth. This book provides a wide array of ideas, suggestions, and examples (mostly from Māori, Hawaiian, and Japanese language assessment projects) to help language educators effectively develop, use, revise, analyze, and report on rubric-based assessments.

212pp., ISBN 978–0–9835816–1–1 $20.

RESEARCH AMONG LEARNERS OF CHINESE AS A FOREIGN LANGUAGE

MICHAEL E. EVERSON & HELEN H. SHEN (EDITORS), 2010

Cutting-edge in its approach and international in its authorship, this fourth monograph in a series sponsored by the Chinese Language Teachers Association features eight research studies that explore a variety of themes, topics, and perspectives important to a variety of stakeholders in the Chinese language learning community. Employing a wide range of research methodologies, the volume provides data from actual Chinese language learners and will be of value to both theoreticians and practitioners alike. *[in English & Chinese]*

180pp., ISBN 978–0–9800459–4–9 $20.

MANCHU: A TEXTBOOK FOR READING DOCUMENTS (SECOND EDITION)

GERTRAUDE ROTH LI, 2010

This book offers students a tool to gain a basic grounding in the Manchu language. The reading selections provided in this volume represent various types of documents, ranging from examples of the very earliest Manchu writing (17th century) to samples of contemporary Sibe (Xibo), a language that may be considered a modern version of Manchu. Since Manchu courses are only rarely taught at universities anywhere, this second edition includes audio recordings to assist students with the pronunciation of the texts.

418pp., ISBN 978–0–9800459–5–6 $36.

TOWARD USEFUL PROGRAM EVALUATION IN COLLEGE FOREIGN LANGUAGE EDUCATION

John M. Norris, John McE. Davis, Castle Sinicrope, & Yukiko Watanabe (Editors), 2009

This volume reports on innovative, useful evaluation work conducted within U.S. college foreign language programs. An introductory chapter scopes out the territory, reporting key findings from research into the concerns, impetuses, and uses for evaluation that FL educators identify. Seven chapters then highlight examples of evaluations conducted in diverse language programs and institutional contexts. Each case is reported by program-internal educators, who walk readers through critical steps, from identifying evaluation uses, users, and questions, to designing methods, interpreting findings, and taking actions. A concluding chapter reflects on the emerging roles for FL program evaluation and articulates an agenda for integrating evaluation into language education practice.

240pp., ISBN 978–0–9800459–3–2 $30.

SECOND LANGUAGE TEACHING AND LEARNING IN THE NET GENERATION

Raquel Oxford & Jeffrey Oxford (Editors), 2009

Today's young people—the Net Generation—have grown up with technology all around them. However, teachers cannot assume that students' familiarity with technology in general transfers successfully to pedagogical settings. This volume examines various technologies and offers concrete advice on how each can be successfully implemented in the second language curriculum.

240pp., ISBN 978–0–9800459–2–5 $30.

CASE STUDIES IN FOREIGN LANGUAGE PLACEMENT: PRACTICES AND POSSIBILITIES

Thom Hudson & Martyn Clark (Editors), 2008

Although most language programs make placement decisions on the basis of placement tests, there is surprisingly little published about different contexts and systems of placement testing. The present volume contains case studies of placement programs in foreign language programs at the tertiary level across the United States. The different programs span the spectrum from large programs servicing hundreds of students annually to small language programs with very few students. The contributions to this volume address such issues as how the size of the program, presence or absence of heritage learners, and population changes affect language placement decisions.

201pp., ISBN 0–9800459–0–8 $20.

CHINESE AS A HERITAGE LANGUAGE: FOSTERING ROOTED WORLD CITIZENRY

Agnes Weiyun He & Yun Xiao (Editors), 2008

Thirty-two scholars examine the sociocultural, cognitive-linguistic, and educational-institutional trajectories along which Chinese as a Heritage Language may be acquired, maintained, and developed. They draw upon developmental psychology, functional linguistics, linguistic and cultural anthropology, discourse analysis, orthography analysis, reading research, second language acquisition, and bilingualism. This volume aims to lay a foundation for theories, models, and master scripts to be discussed, debated, and developed, and to stimulate research and enhance teaching both within and beyond Chinese language education.

280pp., ISBN 978–0–8248–3286–5 $20.

PERSPECTIVES ON TEACHING CONNECTED SPEECH TO SECOND LANGUAGE SPEAKERS

James Dean Brown & Kimi Kondo-Brown (Editors), 2006

This book is a collection of fourteen articles on connected speech of interest to teachers, researchers, and materials developers in both ESL/EFL (ten chapters focus on connected speech in English) and Japanese (four chapters focus on Japanese connected speech). The fourteen chapters are divided up into five sections:

- What do we know so far about teaching connected speech?
- Does connected speech instruction work?
- How should connected speech be taught in English?
- How should connected speech be taught in Japanese?
- How should connected speech be tested?

290pp., ISBN 978–0–8248–3136–3 $20.

CORPUS LINGUISTICS FOR KOREAN LANGUAGE LEARNING AND TEACHING

Robert Bley-Vroman & Hyunsook Ko (Editors), 2006

Dramatic advances in personal-computer technology have given language teachers access to vast quantities of machine-readable text, which can be analyzed with a view toward improving the basis of language instruction. Corpus linguistics provides analytic techniques and practical tools for studying language in use. This volume provides both an introductory framework for the use of corpus linguistics for language teaching and examples of its application for Korean teaching and learning. The collected papers cover topics in Korean syntax, lexicon, and discourse, and second language acquisition research, always with a focus on application in the classroom. An overview of Korean corpus linguistics tools and available Korean corpora are also included.

265pp., ISBN 0–8248–3062–8 $25.

NEW TECHNOLOGIES AND LANGUAGE LEARNING: CASES IN THE LESS COMMONLY TAUGHT LANGUAGES

Carol Anne Spreen (Editor), 2002

In recent years, the National Security Education Program (NSEP) has supported an increasing number of programs for teaching languages using different technological media. This compilation of case study initiatives funded through the NSEP Institutional Grants Program presents a range of technology-based options for language programming that will help universities make more informed decisions about teaching less commonly taught languages. The eight chapters describe how different types of technologies are used to support language programs (i.e., Web, ITV, and audio- or video-based materials), discuss identifiable trends in e-language learning, and explore how technology addresses issues of equity, diversity, and opportunity. This book offers many lessons learned and decisions made as technology changes and learning needs become more complex.

188pp., ISBN 0–8248–2634–5 $25.

AN INVESTIGATION OF SECOND LANGUAGE TASK-BASED PERFORMANCE ASSESSMENTS

James Dean Brown, Thom Hudson, John M. Norris, & William Bonk, 2002

This volume describes the creation of performance assessment instruments and their validation (based on work started in a previous monograph). It begins by explaining the test and rating scale development processes and the administration of the resulting three seven-task tests to 90 university-level EFL and ESL students. The results are examined in terms of (a) the effects of test revision; (b) comparisons among the task-dependent, task-independent, and self-rating scales; and (c) reliability and validity issues.

240pp., ISBN 0–8248–2633–7 $25.

MOTIVATION AND SECOND LANGUAGE ACQUISITION

Zoltán Dörnyei & Richard Schmidt (Editors), 2001

This volume—the second in this series concerned with motivation and foreign language learning—includes papers presented in a state-of-the-art colloquium on L2 motivation at the American Association for Applied Linguistics (Vancouver, 2000) and a number of specially commissioned studies. The 20 chapters, written by some of the best known researchers in the field, cover a wide range of theoretical and research methodological issues, and also offer empirical results (both qualitative and quantitative) concerning the learning of many different languages (Arabic, Chinese, English, Filipino, French, German, Hindi, Italian, Japanese, Russian, and Spanish) in a broad range of learning contexts (Bahrain, Brazil, Canada, Egypt, Finland, Hungary, Ireland, Israel, Japan, Spain, and the U.S.).

520pp., ISBN 0–8248–2458–X $30.

A FOCUS ON LANGUAGE TEST DEVELOPMENT: EXPANDING THE LANGUAGE PROFICIENCY CONSTRUCT ACROSS A VARIETY OF TESTS

Thom Hudson & James Dean Brown (Editors), 2001

This volume presents eight research studies that introduce a variety of novel, nontraditional forms of second and foreign language assessment. To the extent possible, the studies also show the entire test development process, warts and all. These language testing projects not only demonstrate many of the types of problems that test developers run into in the real world but also afford the reader unique insights into the language test development process.

230pp., ISBN 0–8248–2351–6 $20.

STUDIES ON KOREAN IN COMMUNITY SCHOOLS

Dong-Jae Lee, Sookeun Cho, Miseon Lee, Minsun Song, & William O'Grady (Editors), 2000

The papers in this volume focus on language teaching and learning in Korean community schools. Drawing on innovative experimental work and research in linguistics, education, and psychology, the contributors address issues of importance to teachers, administrators, and parents. Topics covered include childhood bilingualism, Korean grammar, language acquisition, children's literature, and language teaching methodology. [in Korean]

256pp., ISBN 0–8248–2352–4 $20.

A COMMUNICATIVE FRAMEWORK FOR INTRODUCTORY JAPANESE LANGUAGE CURRICULA

Washington State Japanese Language Curriculum Guidelines Committee, 2000

In recent years, the number of schools offering Japanese nationwide has increased dramatically. Because of the tremendous popularity of the Japanese language and the shortage of teachers, quite a few untrained, nonnative and native teachers are in the classrooms and are expected to teach several levels of Japanese. These guidelines are intended to assist individual teachers and professional associations throughout the United States in designing Japanese language curricula. They are meant to serve as a framework from which language teaching can be expanded and are intended to allow teachers to enhance and strengthen the quality of Japanese language instruction.

168pp., ISBN 0–8248–2350–8 $20.

FOREIGN LANGUAGE TEACHING AND MINORITY LANGUAGE EDUCATION

Kathryn A. Davis (Editor), 1999

This volume seeks to examine the potential for building relationships among foreign language, bilingual, and ESL programs towards fostering bilingualism. Part I of the volume examines the sociopolitical contexts for language partnerships, including:

- obstacles to developing bilingualism;
- implications of acculturation, identity, and language issues for linguistic minorities; and
- the potential for developing partnerships across primary, secondary, and tertiary institutions.

Part II of the volume provides research findings on the Foreign Language Partnership Project, designed to capitalize on the resources of immigrant students to enhance foreign language learning.

152pp., ISBN 0–8248–2067–3 $20.

DESIGNING SECOND LANGUAGE PERFORMANCE ASSESSMENTS

John M. Norris, James Dean Brown, Thom Hudson, & Jim Yoshioka, 1998, 2000

This technical report focuses on the decision-making potential provided by second language performance assessments. The authors first situate performance assessment within a broader discussion of alternatives in language assessment and in educational assessment in general. They then discuss issues in performance assessment design, implementation, reliability, and validity. Finally, they present a prototype framework for second language performance assessment based on the integration of theoretical underpinnings and research findings from the task-based language teaching literature, the language testing literature, and the educational measurement literature. The authors outline test and item specifications, and they present numerous examples of prototypical language tasks. They also propose a research agenda focusing on the operationalization of second language performance assessments.

248pp., ISBN 0–8248–2109–2 $20.

SECOND LANGUAGE DEVELOPMENT IN WRITING: MEASURES OF FLUENCY, ACCURACY, AND COMPLEXITY

Kate Wolfe-Quintero, Shunji Inagaki, & Hae-Young Kim, 1998, 2002

In this book, the authors analyze and compare the ways that fluency, accuracy, grammatical complexity, and lexical complexity have been measured in studies of language development in second language writing. More than 100 developmental measures are examined, with detailed comparisons of the results across the studies that have used each measure. The authors discuss the theoretical foundations for each type of developmental measure, and they consider the relationship between developmental measures and various types of proficiency measures. They also examine criteria for determining which developmental measures are the most successful and suggest which measures are the most promising for continuing work on language development.

208pp., ISBN 0–8248–2069–X $20.

THE DEVELOPMENT OF A LEXICAL TONE PHONOLOGY IN AMERICAN ADULT LEARNERS OF STANDARD MANDARIN CHINESE

Sylvia Henel Sun, 1998

The study reported is based on an assessment of three decades of research on the SLA of Mandarin tone. It investigates whether differences in learners' tone perception and production are related to differences in the effects of certain linguistic, task, and learner factors. The learners of focus are American students of Mandarin in Beijing, China. Their performances on two perception and three production tasks are analyzed through a host of variables and methods of quantification.

328pp., ISBN 0–8248–2068–1 $20.

NEW TRENDS AND ISSUES IN TEACHING JAPANESE LANGUAGE AND CULTURE

Haruko M. Cook, Kyoko Hijirida, & Mildred Tahara (Editors), 1997

In recent years, Japanese has become the fourth most commonly taught foreign language at the college level in the United States. As the number of students who study Japanese has increased, the teaching of Japanese as a foreign language has been established as an important academic field of study. This technical report includes nine contributions to the advancement of this field, encompassing the following five important issues:

- Literature and literature teaching
- Technology in the language classroom
- Orthography
- Testing
- Grammatical versus pragmatic approaches to language teaching

164pp., ISBN 0–8248–2067–3 $20.

SIX MEASURES OF JSL PRAGMATICS

Sayoko Okada Yamashita, 1996

This book investigates differences among tests that can be used to measure the cross-cultural pragmatic ability of English-speaking learners of Japanese. Building on the work of Hudson, Detmer, and Brown (Technical Reports #2 and #7 in this series), the author modified six test types that she used to gather data from North American learners of Japanese. She found numerous problems with the multiple-choice discourse completion test but reported that the other five tests all proved highly reliable and reasonably valid. Practical issues involved in creating and using such language tests are discussed from a variety of perspectives.

213pp., ISBN 0–8248–1914–4 $15.

LANGUAGE LEARNING STRATEGIES AROUND THE WORLD: CROSS-CULTURAL PERSPECTIVES

Rebecca L. Oxford (Editor), 1996, 1997, 2002

Language learning strategies are the specific steps students take to improve their progress in learning a second or foreign language. Optimizing learning strategies improves language performance. This groundbreaking book presents new information about cultural influences on the use of language learning strategies. It also shows innovative ways to assess students' strategy use and remarkable techniques for helping students improve their choice of strategies, with the goal of peak language learning.

166pp., ISBN 0–8248–1910–1 $20.

TELECOLLABORATION IN FOREIGN LANGUAGE LEARNING: PROCEEDINGS OF THE HAWAI'I SYMPOSIUM

Mark Warschauer (Editor), 1996

The Symposium on Local & Global Electronic Networking in Foreign Language Learning & Research, part of the National Foreign Language Resource Center's 1995 Summer Institute on Technology & the Human Factor in Foreign Language Education, included presentations of papers and hands-on workshops conducted by Symposium participants to facilitate the sharing of resources, ideas, and information about all aspects of electronic networking for foreign language teaching and research, including electronic discussion and conferencing, international cultural exchanges, real-time communication and simulations, research and resource retrieval via the Internet, and research using networks. This collection presents a sampling of those presentations.

252pp., ISBN 0–8248–1867–9 $20.

LANGUAGE LEARNING MOTIVATION: PATHWAYS TO THE NEW CENTURY

Rebecca L. Oxford (Editor), 1996

This volume chronicles a revolution in our thinking about what makes students want to learn languages and what causes them to persist in that difficult and rewarding adventure. Topics in this book include the internal structures of and external connections with foreign language motivation; exploring adult language learning motivation, self-efficacy, and anxiety; comparing the motivations and learning strategies of students of Japanese and Spanish; and enhancing the theory of language learning motivation from many psychological and social perspectives.

218pp., ISBN 0–8248–1849–0 $20.

LINGUISTICS & LANGUAGE TEACHING: PROCEEDINGS OF THE SIXTH JOINT LSH-HATESL CONFERENCE

Cynthia Reves, Caroline Steele, & Cathy S. P. Wong (Editors), 1996

Technical Report #10 contains 18 articles revolving around the following three topics:

- Linguistic issues—These six papers discuss various linguistic issues: ideophones, syllabic nasals, linguistic areas, computation, tonal melody classification, and wh-words.
- Sociolinguistics—Sociolinguistic phenomena in Swahili, signing, Hawaiian, and Japanese are discussed in four of the papers.
- Language teaching and learning—These eight papers cover prosodic modification, note taking, planning in oral production, oral testing,

language policy, L2 essay organization, access to dative alternation rules, and child noun phrase structure development.

364pp., ISBN 0–8248–1851–2 $20.

ATTENTION & AWARENESS IN FOREIGN LANGUAGE LEARNING

Richard Schmidt (Editor), 1996

Issues related to the role of attention and awareness in learning lie at the heart of many theoretical and practical controversies in the foreign language field. This collection of papers presents research into the learning of Spanish, Japanese, Finnish, Hawaiian, and English as a second language (with additional comments and examples from French, German, and miniature artificial languages) that bear on these crucial questions for foreign language pedagogy.

394pp., ISBN 0–8248–1794–X $20.

VIRTUAL CONNECTIONS: ONLINE ACTIVITIES AND PROJECTS FOR NETWORKING LANGUAGE LEARNERS

Mark Warschauer (Editor), 1995, 1996

Computer networking has created dramatic new possibilities for connecting language learners in a single classroom or across the globe. This collection of activities and projects makes use of email, the internet, computer conferencing, and other forms of computer-mediated communication for the foreign and second language classroom at any level of instruction. Teachers from around the world submitted the activities compiled in this volume—activities that they have used successfully in their own classrooms.

417pp., ISBN 0–8248–1793–1 $30.

DEVELOPING PROTOTYPIC MEASURES OF CROSS-CULTURAL PRAGMATICS

Thom Hudson, Emily Detmer, & J. D. Brown, 1995

Although the study of cross-cultural pragmatics has gained importance in applied linguistics, there are no standard forms of assessment that might make research comparable across studies and languages. The present volume describes the process through which six forms of cross-cultural assessment were developed for second language learners of English. The models may be used for second language learners of other languages. The six forms of assessment involve two forms each of indirect discourse completion tests, oral language production, and self-assessment. The procedures involve the assessment of requests, apologies, and refusals.

198pp., ISBN 0–8248–1763–X $15.

THE ROLE OF PHONOLOGICAL CODING IN READING KANJI

Sachiko Matsunaga, 1995

In this technical report, the author reports the results of a study that she conducted on phonological coding in reading kanji using an eye-movement monitor, and draws some pedagogical implications. In addition, she reviews current literature on the different schools of thought regarding instruction in reading kanji and its role in the teaching of nonalphabetic written languages like Japanese.

64pp., ISBN 0–8248–1734–6 $10.

PRAGMATICS OF CHINESE AS NATIVE AND TARGET LANGUAGE

GABRIELE KASPER (EDITOR), 1995

This technical report includes six contributions to the study of the pragmatics of Mandarin Chinese:

- A report of an interview study conducted with nonnative speakers of Chinese; and
- Five data-based studies on the performance of different speech acts by native speakers of Mandarin—requesting, refusing, complaining, giving bad news, disagreeing, and complimenting.

312pp., ISBN 0–8248–1733–8 $20.

A BIBLIOGRAPHY OF PEDAGOGY AND RESEARCH IN INTERPRETATION AND TRANSLATION

ETILVIA ARJONA, 1993

This technical report includes four types of bibliographic information on translation and interpretation studies:

- Research efforts across disciplinary boundaries—cognitive psychology, neurolinguistics, psycholinguistics, sociolinguistics, computational linguistics, measurement, aptitude testing, language policy, decision-making, theses, and dissertations;
- Training information covering program design, curriculum studies, instruction, and school administration;
- Instructional information detailing course syllabi, methodology, models, available textbooks; and
- Testing information about aptitude, selection, and diagnostic tests.

115pp., ISBN 0–8248–1572–6 $10.

PRAGMATICS OF JAPANESE AS NATIVE AND TARGET LANGUAGE

GABRIELE KASPER (EDITOR), 1992, 1996

This technical report includes three contributions to the study of the pragmatics of Japanese:

- A bibliography on speech-act performance, discourse management, and other pragmatic and sociolinguistic features of Japanese;
- A study on introspective methods in examining Japanese learners' performance of refusals; and

- A longitudinal investigation of the acquisition of the particle *ne* by nonnative speakers of Japanese.

125pp., ISBN 0–8248–1462–2 $10.

A FRAMEWORK FOR TESTING CROSS-CULTURAL PRAGMATICS

THOM HUDSON, EMILY DETMER, & J. D. BROWN, 1992

This technical report presents a framework for developing methods that assess cross-cultural pragmatic ability. Although the framework has been designed for Japanese and American cross-cultural contrasts, it can serve as a generic approach that can be applied to other language contrasts. The focus is on the variables of social distance, relative power, and the degree of imposition within the speech acts of requests, refusals, and apologies. Evaluation of performance is based on recognition of the speech act, amount of speech, forms or formulae used, directness, formality, and politeness.

51pp., ISBN 0–8248–1463–0 $10.

RESEARCH METHODS IN INTERLANGUAGE PRAGMATICS

GABRIELE KASPER & MERETE DAHL, 1991

This technical report reviews the methods of data collection employed in 39 studies of interlanguage pragmatics, defined narrowly as the investigation of nonnative speakers' comprehension and production of speech acts, and the acquisition of L2-related speech-act knowledge. Data collection instruments are distinguished according to the degree to which they constrain informants' responses, and whether they tap speech-act perception/comprehension or production. A main focus of discussion is the validity of different types of data, in particular their adequacy to approximate authentic performance of linguistic action.

51pp., ISBN 0–8248–1419–3 $10.

www.ingramcontent.com/pod-product-compliance
Lightning Source LLC
LaVergne TN
LVHW010607100826
845148LV00014B/2878

9780983581628